A LIFE FOR DEER

A LIFE FOR DEER

A DEER VET TELLS
HIS STORY AND THEIRS

John Fletcher

with vignettes by Maggy Lenert

VICTOR GOLLANCZ
in association with
PETER CRAWLEY

First published in Great Britain 2000
by Victor Gollancz
in association with Peter Crawley
An imprint of Orion Books Ltd,
Orion House, 5 Upper St Martin's Lane,
London WC2H 9EA

A CIP catalogue record for this book is
available from the British Library

ISBN 0 575 07090 0

Typeset by Selwood Systems, Midsomer Norton

Printed and bound in Great Britain by
Butler & Tanner Ltd, Frome and London

CONTENTS

vi ~ *Contents*

ILLUSTRATIONS

(Unless otherwise noted, all photographs are by the author)

Propose to any Englishman any principle ... however admirable, and you will observe that the whole effort of the English mind is directed to find a difficulty, a defect, or an impossibility in it. If you speak to him of a machine for peeling a potato, he will pronounce it impossible. If you peel a potato with it before his eyes, he will declare it useless, because it will not slice a pineapple.

Charles Babbage (1792–1871)
often credited with the invention of the computer

To Nickie

INTRODUCTION

Beneath our clothes we are all hunter-gatherers. The species to which we belong, *Homo sapiens*, with brains and bodies almost identical to our own, evolved in Africa about 130,000 years ago. Thus during some five thousand generations as *Homo sapiens*, to say nothing of the three hundred thousand generations before that, our bodies became exquisitely adapted to eating and metabolising a diet of wild food: plants provided fruits, berries and nuts as well as roots, but animal protein, often fish, was also crucial.

Then, about ten thousand years ago, humans in several parts of the world began to cultivate certain plants and animals. The animals provided dung for the plants as well as a means of drawing ploughs and carts, and with careful selection they came to yield more and more milk and wool as well as a valuable carcase. From the huge array of animals available only a very few were selected; so that today, for example, of the hundred or so grazing species worldwide, only sheep, goats, cows and pigs are domesticated as food animals on any scale. In ten millennia there have been virtually no additions to that short list of domesticants, although each of the species domesticated has changed significantly.

One of the most remarkable changes has been the development of fatter and fatter carcases. Our grandparents wanted fat to sustain their physically demanding lifestyle as well as to help them keep warm. But in particular they needed tallow, to provide candles with which they could penetrate the darkness and shorten the long nights. Now, of course, we have electricity. Despite strenuous efforts to breed leaner carcases we find that existing domestic animals have a carcase composition which is damaging our health. Our bodies over those many thousands of generations evolved to cope well with game meat, but cannot yet perfectly metabolise the products of domesticated animals, to which we have only been exposed in volume for ten or twelve generations. The answer seemed clear to me when I started to work with deer thirty years ago, but I had underestimated the modern tabus that were to face us.

During the mediaeval period there are thought to have been nearly two thousand deer parks in England and Wales. Those parks were for meat production. Venison was a vital commodity for those who could afford meat, and until the industrial revolution deer were evidently an important part of our life in Europe. Not surprisingly there is a wealth of myth ascribing strange attributes to deer. They even appear in the symbolic pavement in Westminster Abbey on which British monarchs are anointed.

Almost universally, as human populations grow and before rural depopulation intervenes, game animals become threatened. Deer were close to extinction in many parts of Britain in the eighteenth and nineteenth centuries. It was this that deflected the attention of the stag hunts to the inedible fox.

Now, however, the numbers of deer are increasing dramatically throughout the developed world. Britain has over one million, more than at any time since at least Roman times. We cannot ignore them. In many areas they prevent the regeneration of woodland; in England they have destroyed habitats vital for nightingales and orchids, in Sweden they are the major cause of motor accidents, and, fairly or otherwise, they are incriminated in the spread of Lyme disease. The perception of deer as rare and precious creatures to be glimpsed at dawn and dusk is, sadly, under threat.

Yet deer are deservedly objects of wonder: their antlers, for example, can grow two or three centimetres in a day to hold the record as the fastest-growing mammalian tissue, and the spectacular way in which the antlers are annually renewed could hold the key to our under-standing of wound healing and regeneration. We need to know more about these animals that are becoming so numerous. This book is an effort to encourage a realisation of the growing part that deer will play in industrialised and urbanised societies and the potential value of that role.

ACKNOWLEDGEMENTS

In carrying out the work that is the basis for this story I have accumulated many debts of gratitude and I welcome the opportunity to acknowledge some of these.

First of all I wish to thank my mother and my late father who always encouraged me to write, and especially my mother who has endlessly but invaluably badgered me to finish the job.

I am writing in a small cottage above Elgol on Skye, and as I do so I can see through the window the Isle of Rum floating in the mist. This is very fitting because it was on that island that my story really began. I was very privileged to work there with Roger Short, Fiona Guinness, Gerald Lincoln and Tim Clutton-Brock who each in their own way inspired me. So, a few years later, did the late Sir Kenneth Blaxter who never failed to provide encouragement.

After that came the farm at Auchtermuchty, to which enterprise a great many have contributed help over the years. In particular Alfie Barnard, the son and husband of vets, arrived early on and shared our ups and downs before ill health forced him to leave us. The young Richard Pirie was a committed and enthusiastic colleague who, had he lived, would still have been with us at Reediehill. Heather and Magnus Doull have been great friends for many years, and now Magnus, with patient common sense, trims my most extravagant flights of fancy while helping me to realise those that are possible. Gillian Winterborn likewise has been an invaluable confidante and adviser for many years; she typed the early chapters of this book and encouraged me to believe it had worth. Barry Burns has been a loyal friend and skilled butcher.

We have been very fortunate in our neighbours, especially Clare du Boulay, who have among other things had to put up with traffic to the farm shop and occasional wandering deer.

In Sussex Carl Wheeler has been a wonderful and generous friend whilst Janice and Adrian Gumbley have never failed to provide friendly help. Amongst vets, those at the Moredun Research Institute and the members of the Veterinary Deer Society have been especially good friends, whilst within the deer-stalking fraternity Sandy Masson and Donald Ewan Darroch are particularly supportive.

I wish to thank Damaris Fletcher who read an early draft and was perceptive and generous, Susie Lendrum and Paul Broda who provided bolt-holes, Anthony Turner for his interest and diplomacy in editing, and especially Peter Crawley who radiated enthusiasm about the book from the very beginning.

A particular debt of gratitude is due to my dear friend Maggy Lenert for her entertaining and inspired embellishments in the form of vignettes at every chapter head.

Fiona Guinness has allowed me to use several photographs of deer on the Isle of Rum; these pictures are the distillation of a lifetime's photographic work and for her to give me free access to those is a touching act of great generosity. Rex Forrester kindly allowed me to use his photograph of deer being lifted by helicopter. If I have used any photographs without attributing the source, I can only apologise most sincerely; it is simply because I do not know whence they came.

I wish to thank Luath Press in Edinburgh for their generous permission to use material from *Rum: Nature's Island* by Magnus Magnusson.

Most of all there are Nickie, Stella and Martha who have always been encouraging, and without too much opposition from me have often suggested that the occasional extra day trucking through France was permissible if it yielded another few thousand words.

Over the years deer farming has brought me many friends in Britain and overseas, too many to name, but the subject attracts individualists and all of them in their own way have helped to make my life, and Nickie's, entertaining, exciting, occasionally exasperating, but always fun. I am grateful to them all.

Finally the deer must be thanked for all the pleasure they have given me.

1 HIJACKED ON THE ROAD TO THE ISLES

Late and dark, pitch black and rain sluicing down. Also I am hungry and drive the ageing little lorry round Tarbert harbour twice, looking for somewhere to eat. But no hostelry quite lives up to the anticipation. Tired, restless and indecisive, I roll on towards the ferry pier at Kennacraig. On into the country again another few miles, until, under trees, the rain seems less and a widening of the road lets me pull in for the night.

Grabbing my bag I jump down from the cab and climb through one of the side doors into the back. I light a candle, spread a bale of straw, arrange a pillow, set an alarm clock for 5 a.m., take all my clothes off and slip into the old down sleeping bag. Liberated feathers float in candlelight but are extinguished with one breath. Now it's really crow black.

Contentment spreads through my stiff muscles and I actually savour the hard bed and the loud twangs of rain on the metal roof. Like millions of campers in Scotland I ponder why raindrops from trees seem bigger than raindrops from the sky.

It was 1980 and relaxation under such circumstances was easier then.

Hailed, with justification or not, as the pioneer of British deer farming, I was caught up in a movement which was already threatening to revolutionise agriculture in the Scottish Highlands and had the potential to transform livestock farming worldwide. We were creating perhaps the first new domesticated animal for five thousand years. History was in the making. There was the sudden realisation that red deer were the ideal animal for converting grass into a magnificent almost fat-free meat to which man was uniquely adapted. No problems stood in our way. The present difficulty in locating breeding stock was just a stepping stone on the road to an established 'industry'.

Successive politicians had assured us that subsidies for sheep, and indeed all sectors of farming, had the skids under them. A host of agricultural journalists had passed the message on loud and clear. That was just what we wanted; we were doing the right thing.

With a warm glow I think of how the deer I hope to catch next day on the island of Jura will, after a period of acclimatisation, soon be speeding to Denmark where, I know, they thrive as they never could on the impoverished grazings of our Scottish hills. Many wild Highland deer never make it through the winter, perishing in the spring.

The survivors remain, stunted, not calving until three or four years old, whereas on the farm, their sleek relatives usually calve at two years, and the cosseted youngsters which they produce reach the weight of an adult wild deer at eighteen months, and grow for another year still. Wild Scottish hinds, if they're lucky enough to reach maturity, may produce in their lifetime seven or eight calves, of which perhaps only four or five may reach breeding age. Satisfied, I lie back and contrast this with my farmed red deer. Of those, more than nine out of ten will themselves come to motherhood, and can be expected to achieve families of fourteen in their average sixteen years of life. And all of that without once becoming thin.

I relish being able to supply an alternative and superior venison to that from the Highland estates and the game dealers. Wild venison is always a by-product of the sporting business, its quality varying from the very best to a fifteen-year-old stag that would tax the teeth of a lion. Though the properties of wealthy men, Highland estates are invariably loss-making now and if they continue to suffer losses I fear for their employees, several of whom I am proud to call friends. The supply of wild hinds for breeding stock to deer farmers is already proving a valuable new source of income to those estates.

Ironic that it was Danes in their longships a thousand years ago who had called Jura 'the Island of Deer'. Perhaps they too had taken Jura deer back to Jutland.

My heart warms at the prospect of these stout wee animals which, I have found, when accustomed to life on the farm, once lifted from the rain- and wind-lashed romantic isle to the lush grasslands of Jutland, are temperamentally ideal for farming. Only a few weeks previously on a trip to Denmark I had seen Jura deer transformed in twelve months to docile contented beings with their calves, conceived in Scotland, already enormously larger than their stay-at-home contemporaries, and almost as big as their authentic Scots mothers.

Transplanting often seems to have this effect – so many people from the same Highlands and Islands, uprooted 150 years ago, had, within one or two generations, surpassed in material wealth the wildest dreams of their ancestors. Now, visiting Scotland, the descendants of those émigrés, hunting out their roots, were usually of a markedly rounder physique, testifying to a change of diet from oats, potatoes and occasional herring to hamburgers and French fries.

> A single violet transplant,
> The strength, the colour, and the size,
> (All which before was poore, and scant,)
> Redoubles still, and multiplies.

A strange irony that here am I lying in the Highlands dreaming of the English poet, John Donne, who had worked in London under the Scots King James. That same James VI had transplanted himself and his court to England leaving the creation of fine Scots culture rudderless in the absence of a court. Perhaps, I drowsily muse, Donne's reference to the benefits of transplanting was intended to flatter his new patron?

Anyway, like John Donne's violets overcrowded in their bed, the benign effects of transplanting deer are clear. But how had the Scottish deer come to their present predicament? Was it really overcrowding, stretching a limited supply of food? Or an environment so bleak that it could never yield a population of deer as well fed and productive as my farm animals?

It is common knowledge that the present Highland red deer herd, from near-extinction in the late eighteenth and early nineteenth centuries, has grown to a number not previously known in Scotland since the last glaciation, if even then. From only a few thousand in the 1790s, red deer have thrived on the depopulated pastures. The human clearances that came with the collapse of the clan system were made in the name of sheep but the rise of Australasian flocks with their superior wool, coupled later on with the advent of refrigeration and the arrival of New Zealand lamb, had soon turned those large 'sheep walks' into treeless deer forests. Ironic that those faraway flocks and their masters had so often grown from livestock and shepherds transported from Scotland.

The thoughts flow round me like ripples in still water which continue even after the boat which caused them has ceased to move.

Then with Balmoral, and Albert's Teutonic love of hunting red deer, came royal patronage of the sport of deer stalking; and the sort of obsequious adulation that allowed Landseer to paint *The Monarch of the Glen* as a commission for the House of Lords Refreshment Room.

Thus began 150 years of protection from poaching and, throughout that time, arguably never quite sufficient deer were killed by the sportsmen. Even as recently as the early 1970s the Red Deer Commission assessed deer numbers at less than 200,000, and by 1990 they had risen to around 300,000. Was the diminutive size of the Scottish red deer due to this rapid build-up of numbers? The grazing pressure was also exacerbated by rising sheep numbers: Malthus' 'perpetual struggle for room and food'? Or was it the absence of woodland shelter from predators and the wind? No doubt my erstwhile colleague Tim Clutton-Brock with his team working on the Isle of Rum and elsewhere would answer these questions in his indefatigably energetic way.

Trees have been in a decline ever since the advent of man with his slash-and-burn tactics, and later his more sophisticated needs for shipbuilding and for charcoal for smelting iron ore, and all the time his livestock nibbling at the seedling trees.

Undoubtedly those modern deer that successfully sneak into the commercial woodlands, when the fences are covered in snow or flattened by fallen trees, are astonishingly more productive than their luckless colleagues excluded from shelter. And then those shut out may have lost their best grazing to trees. In winter, belts of fenced woodlands can prevent access to the shelter of the glens. The size and prolificacy of those woodland wild deer are often comparable with the best farmed deer. There are even rumours of calves conceiving at four months of age in the very best woodlands.

And that is the last coherent thought dredged up. The very prospect of Tim's enthusiastic delvings must have been too much for I am asleep and know no more.

Zzzzzzzzzzzzzzzzzzzzzzzz.

Suddenly I am galvanised into activity. Someone is starting the engine. Visions of being driven south to Glasgow incarcerated in my own beloved vehicle are enough. Like a Greek god, with winged heels, I leap naked from my sleeping bag, out of the rear of the truck, a few yards down the road, and hurl myself into the cab through the passenger door even as we begin to move. Desperation refreshes my jaded muscles. Taking advantage of what I hope is my new-found chauffeur's terror, in one smooth movement I lean over, grab the steering wheel, open the driver's door and push him out, simultaneously wrestling the vehicle to a standstill. Immediately the mood of action leaves me. I wind down the window and look back. A drunken West Highlander is resignedly walking along after me.

'So where were you going anyway?' I shout.

'Och and wasn't I only looking for a lift tae the bloody ferry.'

Either that soft West Coast accent softens me or my Christian education triumphs and a deeply instilled reflex to reconcile and forgive at all costs takes over, for I find myself saying, 'Well just get in, that's where I'm going too.' So my would-be villain hoists himself up, into the passenger's seat this time. Conscious of an enviable odour of alcohol, and of my nudity uncomfortably illuminated by the glow from the panel lights, I drive silently the last mile or so to the hideous yellow mercury-vapour illuminations, reflected in the wet road, that mark the ferry terminal ahead.

2   INITIATION

In the late 1970s and early 1980s those late-night drives north to catch early ferries were welcome interludes in an increasingly frenetic pursuit of breeding stock for the steady growth of deer farms in Britain and overseas.

For several years I was responsible for capturing and rehabilitating some thousand hinds per annum and probably, all told, the rest of the deer-farming industry was taking another thousand. Feeding hungry deer into a deer-fenced enclosure in the bottom of a Highland glen is not too difficult. The owners of the deer, the lairds of the sporting estates, who had their stalkers catch these deer for sale to myself and other deer farmers, found this a welcome new source of income to sustain those financially precarious tracts of hill. The only other way to prevent deer starving to death is to shoot them, and the price we paid for those hinds we took away live was much greater than would have been realised from the sale of venison to the game dealer.

How had I come to this? How had I found myself so embroiled in this new agricultural project?

So far as I can remember, my interest in deer began very young when I was ill in bed and my mother read me *The Story of a Red Deer* by

Fortescue. But that was sentimental; I wanted to get closer to these animals, beneath their skin and *know* them, not just remain a distant admirer. When I joined with three young friends and, as a twelve-year-old, cycled round the Isle of Arran, my principal objective had been to see the wild red deer. I browbeat my best friend, Sam, to come with me on a day of lashing rain. We two climbed from the youth hostel at Lochranza up and south, through the rain into thick mist, until we knew that Glen Iorsa was somewhere below us. Dispirited we sat down with our backs to a peat bank and had something to eat whilst we planned our next move.

In the literary world such moments are known as epiphanies: the mist rolled back and Sam and I were surrounded by more deer than I could have dreamt of. We lay quite still and they came around us. We could hear them grazing, the calves squeaking and the hinds' low bleats back. Then at once they left us and the clouds descended again. I was satisfied. I knew what I wanted. I needed to find out more about these animals. How did such large wild animals survive in such a hostile environment?

It wasn't good enough just sentimentally to admire their graceful movements and beauty. Even then I knew that the deer did not have an easy ride in the Scottish Highlands. Sam and I had seen enough corpses on our walk to make me understand that.

Deer, unknowing, are constantly burdened with the epithet of nobility. I came to understand that whatever fine names we give them you can be sure they would rather have shelter and good food. Deer are flesh and blood, unlikely to be impressed by the admiration of sportsmen and naturalists who revere them as 'noble'. They would, I believe, exchange it all for a life of good grass. This is what I have spent my life trying to give them.

I completed my veterinary course at Glasgow University in 1970. I have no especially strong memories of the course. From the seclusion of a home in the country and a boarding school, the excitements of Glasgow came very welcome. Though I do remember some problems with buses. I remember queuing on Great Western Road and getting on. Was it going to Bearsden I asked the conductor. 'No,' it was not. 'Y'd better ger off.' I did, but by then the bus was going at about thirty miles an hour. I hung on to the shiny steel pole on the back for a while, feet flying and body horizontal. Then I let go and slid along the road for a few yards before limping back to the shocked queue and wondering whether I should go to the end or rejoin the front. My clothes were torn and I was bleeding.

Later there were rounds of boozy parties, generally revolving around Glasgow University Mountaineering Club, the 'Gum Club'; initiations into heart-breaking young love, and ... in the manner of Tristram Shandy, there is a digression which I should like to make that concerns my student days but has nothing whatsoever to do with my general tale.

There was a quiet and retiring Singhalese student on the veterinary course called Candiah. He lived at the Catholic Centre. I became quite friendly with Candiah. One day he came into lectures looking rather nervous and confided in me the following. (Did I dream all this or was it reality?) Candiah said: 'I am living this last few days by myself at the Catholic Centre because the priest who normally resides there is away for a few days. Yesterday I was working at home when there was a knock at the door. I opened it and there was a man, quite well dressed, who said: "I have come from the Metropolitan Museum in New York. I am trying to trace a plaster model which we believe Michelangelo used as a study for his marble *pietà* that is now in St Peter's in Rome. We believe it is here. Can we come and look?" I didn't know what to do but he seemed sincere and I let him in. We walked around the building and sure enough, on the window of the staircase, was a plaster sculpture of a *pietà*. So this man says: "Yes undoubtedly that is it. You should look after it very carefully. I have done my work and will make a report." And then he left.'

I was staggered by Candiah's story. I had read *The Agony and the Ecstasy* so I was an authority. 'What did you do, Candiah?' 'I was terrified,' he said. 'I hid it under the bed and that is where it is now. I do not know whether I dare come to lectures today. You must come and see it this evening.' And so I did. Candiah pulled out a white plaster model about two feet tall which looked for all the world like the *pietà* in St Peter's. I turned it over and there in the unfinished plaster of the base were fingerprints. Were they Michelangelo's? The priest came back in a few days and Candiah was able to hand it over and sleep more soundly. We never saw the *pietà* again. The establishment had taken its own.

But above all I remember and have cause to be thankful for the days I spent on the rocks and hills with the Gum Club. They nurtured in me a fascination for the red deer which eke out their existence in that inhospitable terrain. There remain memories of descending from the tops in the gloaming, eyes still dazzled by the snow, and all around the bleached, parched brown vegetation, its colour, after the whiteness, unnaturally vivid. And there would be the deer in groups steadily grazing away on this impoverished herbage. Whilst we went into the shelter of a bothy for the night they would remain outside, in their element.

One pivotal day I remember well. I had conceived a bold solo expedition that was to draw me still closer to the red deer. I planned to use skins tied to the bottom of skis. These cunning devices are nowadays synthetic, but were originally made from real sealskin and, by virtue of their pile, slide easily forward but only reluctantly backwards, so that skiing uphill becomes possible. Eager to try them, I took advantage of a spell of Arctic cold and sunshine. Catching a train one afternoon from Glasgow to Corrour railway station, inaccessible by road, I skied off the end of the platform. My plan was to go the ten or so miles to Ben Alder cottage, an unmanned bothy offering shelter to all, and then ski back. Progress was simple until, about half-way there, the binding of one of my skins broke.

Time was of the essence and dusk was looming. And, since the snow was in good condition, I decided to make myself an igloo. Construction proceeded apace until I realised I had made a fundamental error. I couldn't reach to put the top block on and was too lacking in confidence in my building skills to risk climbing up the outside. So I lay there in my sleeping bag relishing the views of the constellations but not able to recapture the true Inuit atmosphere. I slept adequately but in the morning felt quite pleased to have an excuse – the broken skin – to abandon the project and head back to

Corrour. If I had skied down to the bothy at Ben Alder that would have been fine, but the climb back up with only one skin would have been tricky. The weather was wonderful then but it wouldn't last for ever. I chose discretion.

Not having so long a journey for the next day and that mostly downhill, I was in no hurry, and when I saw a freshly dead stag thought it would be interesting, in a spirit of veterinary investigation, to skin him and open him up as an autopsy.

I still have the slides I took of that stag with his skin on first, and then half skinned, and I still use them when I lecture to vet students. It is an impressive testimony to the suffering of our wild deer. He was only a young stag of two or three years and I don't suppose he had many more warbles than his living colleagues, but it came as a shock to me in my ignorance. There must have been two to three hundred half-inch-long warble maggots waiting under the skin to emerge in the early spring.

For those who don't know this horrid parasite, its maggots drop from the back of living deer in March and April, immediately turning into pupae that rapidly develop into bee-like flies and take to the air in the Highland spring, when the nights hardly become dark, to search out red deer on which to lay their eggs. Even newly born calves are fair game. The eggs hatch and the minute larvae penetrate the hide and move through the deer to develop under the skin of the back during the winter before they again bore their way out to leave a running sore as they fall to the ground to complete their sordid cycle. They do not seem to me worthy of their godly name, *Hypoderma diana* (illustration 2b).

Similar parasites used to be commonplace in cattle but it is one of the less publicised, yet most humanitarian, successes of the veterinary profession to have eliminated the cattle warble from Britain. It was fortunate for that eradication programme that the deer warble can distinguish deer from cattle and prefers venison.

The poor old red deer has also to carry the burden of nostril bots. If I had split open the head of that dead animal it would have revealed a score or so of three-centimetre-long maggots, well equipped with bristles, at the base of his nostrils.

The dead stag left a deep impression on me. The suffering of wild deer due to warbles, the death of so many from starvation and the attrition of weeks of winter weather, climaxes in the spring when most sportsmen are away. Only a few of those who come to the hills to shoot deer will ever skin one and see the full horror.

As we in the Gum Club participated in mountain rescues and lost our own club members at a shameful rate, comparable to a wartime front line, so grew my admiration for the ability of the deer to resist exposure and still multiply. Voraciously I read Lea McNally's books about deer and then Frank Fraser Darling's *Herd of Red Deer*. Listening to his Reith Lectures and climbing the hills as a student at Glasgow Vet School, I learnt my vocation.

I therefore cast around for an opportunity to work with Scottish red deer and was offered a chance to join a team based at the Cambridge University Veterinary School investigating the deer on the Isle of Rum in the Inner Hebrides. I don't think I realised at the time just how lucky I was.

Roger Short, the vet from Cambridge who supervised me for my Ph.D., was and still is a brilliantly innovative scientist whose forte is an ability to coalesce the research results of other scientists, as well as his own, into the general scheme of things and then communicate them to a wide audience. Would that there were more like him. His interest in unravelling the mysteries of reproductive behaviour in man and beast had led him to red deer as a subject for research. That may seem a rather odd choice but, as I came to realise, the reason is that red deer are extraordinarily seasonal in their breeding pattern. In effect the stag experiences an annual puberty. Why are they so seasonal? The answer was soon to become clear to me. Also, of which more later, their antlers reflect their reproductive condition and indicate hormonal status as unmistakably as litmus paper signifies acidity.

I had to go down to Cambridge for an interview with Roger and was immediately in his, and the department's, thrall. There have been two or three occasions in my academic career when I have been the recipient of good news and each time I have been so completely overwhelmed with astonishment and delight that I have momentarily swooned. When Roger broke his news to me I was sitting on a wooden laboratory stool, and so great was the shock that I had to save myself from falling off.

Roger was keen for me to work with deer in Thetford Forest just north of Newmarket but I was able to persuade him that the red deer on Rum would be more interesting, and he agreed. My predecessor, who had started the work on Rum with the deer, was Gerald Lincoln. A tall, gaunt and brilliant scientist who was starting to write up his Ph.D. thesis as I began research for mine, he still lives near me in Fife and remains a close friend. Gerald has a formidable mind and a natural curiosity about things biological and he was then, all those years ago, a very hard act to follow, exuding tremendous physical vigour and a great sense of fun. He was also highly competitive.

Just before I joined the Cambridge team I was told that Gerald had published an anonymous paper in that most prestigious scientific journal, *Nature*. To publish anonymously in *Nature* is almost unheard of, but the editor understood that he wished to save his colleagues embarrassment. In the correct scientific spirit of measuring everything, Gerald had apparently developed the habit of weighing his electric-razor shavings each morning. This provided a crude measure of fluc-tuations in his levels of testosterone, the male sex hormone. On Rum, in monastic seclusion, he had noticed, no doubt with a certain amount of apprehension, that his beard growth declined but he had been fascinated, and surely equally relieved, to record a repeatable increase in beard growth associated with the infrequent visits of his lady friends.

What was important scientifically was the fact that this occurred in anticipation of the visit: as soon as notice reached Gerald of impending female companionship, his beard would start into rapid growth. This demonstrated that the higher centres of the brain could influence testosterone secretion – something that had not hitherto been appre-ciated. It is perhaps truly all in the mind.

The other person whom I was privileged to join on Rum was Fiona Guinness (illustration 2c). She had arrived to join the team for the first time one year before me. Her stamina and persistence in learning to recognise each animal simply by its face and body, became, over the thirty or so years she was to work on the island, legendary. Many could not believe this skill, and few could emulate it, so that we had to attach ear tags to the deer to prove her right.

After twenty-five years studying the deer on Rum her feet have now worn a path in the peat; but in her first year it was bare feet she wore. By walking the same route every day she was eventually able to touch some of the deer. Fiona was recently awarded an honorary degree by Edinburgh University and must be a contender for the distinction of being the first honorary graduate to wear jeans for the occasion.

It seems astonishing now, but in the late sixties no one even knew the precise length of pregnancy in the red deer hind, let alone such simple matters as when they come into heat, for how long, and so on. Gerald, Roger and Fiona had managed to unravel these basic facts just prior to my arrival and soon published the results; but there was plenty more left to find out.

3 DOMINANCE, PHEROMONES AND HUMILITY ON RUM

Like, I fancy, most visitors to that island, I remember my first arrival on Rum in September 1970 very clearly. The *Loch Arkaig*, the Mac-Brayne's steamer, comes into the shelter of Loch Scresort, suddenly calm after the swell, and there is the red sandstone excrescence of Kinloch Castle at the head of the loch, an Edwardian pile. The ship cannot come alongside on Rum and so a tender is employed. It is early morning, overcast and drizzling, but Fiona is there on the pier head with a Land Rover and drives us the few hundred yards to the castle for porridge which she has specially made for the occasion.

The *Loch Arkaig* was a converted minesweeper that had been designed with a wooden hull so as to avoid detonating magnetic mines, and yet – with what seemed to me a fundamental flaw in marine architecture – she had been given a substantial metal superstructure. Consequently she rolled. She rolled so alarmingly that I would always plot out my escape route ready for a quick dash in case she never did come back up. Another consequence was that I did not eat Fiona's porridge with much conviction. I cannot recall she ever offered them* to me again.

---

* It is customary in Scotland to refer to porridge in the plural, as, I suppose, in oats. They should also be eaten whilst standing or slowly walking, presumably to allow more to be packed in.

That first day was long. Skoots, one of the tame deer kept in the enclosure behind the castle, had managed to enter the disused squash court where we kept the bags of feed and had gorged herself. The ruminant's digestive system is complicated and delicate. Even as an eager, newly qualified vet, keen to be a hero, there was not much I could do. Fiona must have had great hopes awaiting the arrival of this tyro vet but Skoots died late the next night and we were both despondent. Such deaths were extremely unusual in our tame deer on Rum; indeed I believe that was the only one of those hinds that we ever lost. Over the years since, I have come to learn just how susceptible deer are to overeating grain and how difficult it is to save them.

In the afternoon, abandoning the sick Skoots for a few hours, we found time for a hasty visit up to the north of the island, beautiful Kilmory, reached by twelve miles of very rough Land Rover track. The builders of Kinloch Castle, the Bullough family, had used that road to enable their washing to be done well away from the castle. The wooden building, clad with corrugated iron, remains, now in tatters, at Kilmory and is still called the Laundry. And there I saw for the first time the wild deer Fiona was working with. She had already decided to make the hinds her especial study; Gerald had worked with the stags, and so this was logical. It is much more difficult to work with wild deer, of course. Even after Gerald's painstaking efforts to make the stags accessible by enticing them with maize, they were still wild animals, and, at that time, Fiona's hinds could only be approached to a few hundred yards.

It was fortunate, from my point of view, even if less romantic, that it wasn't only the wild deer we worked with. I was lucky in being able to study a group of eleven deer that had been taken from the hill as young calves and bottle-fed by Dick Youngson who later became a stalker for the Red Deer Commission. These hinds had names often taken from their places of discovery such as Cnap an Breaca – a Gaelic name meaning the speckled hill – and Shellesder who had been born in Glen Shellesder; or less beguilingly, Moke because she looked like a donkey, and Sandy for her colour – or was it because she had been found in Sandy Coire? These were to become my future, and not just during the Rum years.

Dick had, aided I think by the Nature Conservancy stalkers, caught these deer during their first few days of life when they lie prone and can be picked up and reared on the bottle. This may seem heartless but one has to remember that a sizeable proportion of the calves born in the wild will die owing to predation from eagles, lack of adequate mothering skills in their dams, or just insufficient milk; or they may drown in a bog, or be born too small to survive their first winter. By taking a calf from a hind at least she is saved the great nutritional stresses of lactation and may yield a more viable calf the next year. Indeed the hind herself may survive a winter that might otherwise have carried her off. Certainly the calf, pampered with a bottle, will stand a better chance of survival than if it were to be left with its mother on the hill.

Homo sapiens and the pygmy chimpanzee or bonobo are probably unique amongst mammals in enjoying copulation at any or all stages of the female cycle. As Roger Short and Malcolm Potts recently explained in their enlightening book *Ever since Adam and Eve*, this is to strengthen family bonds and ensure the prolonged parental care which large-brained animals require. No wonder we need Viagra. In all other species the female will accept, or is attractive to, the male, only at certain times when the chances of conception are at their highest. This period is known as 'oestrus' or 'heat'. Within seasonal limitations, imposed by changing day-length, red deer hinds in Britain will come into heat every eighteen days, starting around 1 October and continuing until February or March in the unlikely event of their not becoming pregnant; they are thus known as seasonally poly-oestrous short-day breeders.

When I first went to Rum no one had accurately reported this; no one knew whether the hinds came into heat more than once, or for how long, or even how long pregnancy lasted. We already had a pretty good idea that roe deer females, or does, needed to be vigorously chased by the bucks in order to induce their ovulation and oestrus, but this didn't seem likely in the red deer hinds. We wanted to find out.

Accordingly Gerald, Roger and Fiona had run Dick Youngson's bottle-fed hinds with a vasectomised stag, Ed, so that we could record his ineffective matings and thus define the hinds' heat periods. We knew these would begin in the autumn but we didn't know whether – or for how long – the periods would recur and the hinds continue to cycle.

Dick's hinds were running in the enclosure at the back of the castle and in the old walled garden. Feeding them every day and recording their interactions it was surprising to me that their 'peck order' or dominance hierarchy was almost completely linear. That is to say that Moke would be dominant to Mini, and Mini to Shellesder, and Shellesder to Kilmory, whilst triangular relationships – for example, had Shellesder been dominant to Moke, or Kilmory to Mini – were very unusual. Of course, this was a highly artificial group, all brought up together and all of the same age, but it was nevertheless interesting.

Each morning Fiona and I would feed the deer from a long line of troughs and sit and watch them for a set period of time. This is a most fascinating exercise and I was very privileged to have the opportunity. I came to see things which I would never, from the elevated stance of a newly qualified vet, have previously believed. First of all it soon became obvious that it is not difficult, given time, to recognise each animal by its face. This soon became so clear that it was simpler to use the face than the individual identification tags for recognition. Much more remarkable were the family resemblances. It was easy to confuse daughters with dams, or sisters with each other; but no other confusion was really possible when you had become familiar with the animals. These resemblances seemed to me more pronounced than those between people and I put this down to the highly mobile faces of humans. The outward appearance of people must come to reflect their temperament, or the facial expressions they use most. I often think that the sensual pouting of the lips of French girls is due to their vowel pronunciation, though my theory does not explain why French men do not have equally seductive lips. But then I am not an objective observer in this matter.

There were other interesting things to be learnt from the chance to become intimate with a group of deer. For example, grooming behaviour, in which one animal spends minutes standing, evidently entranced, whilst another individual uses her teeth to comb the other's coat, was a regular activity, which anthropomorphically we might consider to be subservient activity. But it was only ever carried out by Beauty, who was the most dominant hind. Shades, perhaps, of the Maundy ceremony in which British monarchs symbolically bathe the feet of the poor. In any event I removed Beauty for a month with her daughter and one or two other deer and watched what happened. In the main group there were many times when one hind would approach another and wait expectantly to be groomed but each time they were disappointed: on no occasion did grooming take place. On the day when Beauty was returned to be with her friends again she groomed six other hinds in the first hour.

The stalkers had implausible stories to tell us about the deer and we were, as confident young scientists, highly sceptical. After all, was not the following strange Gaelic proverb discussing the age of the stag believed into the nineteenth century?

> Thrice the age of a dog, the age of a horse;
> Thrice the age of a horse, the age of a man;
> Thrice the age of a man, the age of a deer;
> Thrice the age of a deer, the age of an eagle;
> Thrice the age of an eagle, the age of an oak tree.

I have since learnt that this myth of the long-lived stag exists not only in Celtic folklore but also dates back to the *Precepts of Chiron*, ascribed to the Greek poet Hesiod. It forms the basis for the mediaeval pavement in front of the high altar at Westminster, in the centre of which English monarchs were anointed and crowned.

But back to Rum ... one tale that was often presented to us by the stalkers definitely tested our credulity; were they having us on? We were told that stags with an injury such as a broken leg would 'ae grow a twisted horn', usually on the opposite side. Over the years we came, to our bemusement, to see that this phenomenon is unquestionably real. Deer show an extraordinary capacity for repairing fractures spontaneously, but where the pain of a healing limb – or other wound – was present when the antler was growing, an asymmetrical antler with distorted growth, normally very rare, was the almost inevitable accompaniment. Perhaps, we reasoned, this might have an explanation in common with acupuncture? By stimulating nature's own painkillers, the endorphins, could this affect the nervous outflow from the brain and disturb the growth of the antler? It is the biologist's duty to benefit from these unexplained natural experiments and make deductions; we must be voyeurs seeking deep insights when, for a moment nature lets her dress slip.

Pheromones were very much in the wind, as you might say, at Cambridge in those days. These are scents which animals use to transmit messages, usually sexual. It is, for example, presumed that pheromones are the means by which young women in dormitories are often found to have unconsciously synchronised their menstrual cycles. Roger suggested that I investigate the vaginal odours and secretions from the hinds to see if we could identify the scents which the stag uses to detect heat. While Roger had thought that we might train a dog to do this, Fiona and I decided to start off using our own noses. We found it difficult enough to get close to the rear end of the hinds ourselves, and we felt that the deer would take a very long time to become accustomed to being sniffed by dogs. So it was, that for many months, each morning would find us notebook in hand, sniffing the backsides of the deer as they took their daily feed; an unlikely sight and one which found its way into the pages of *The Scotsman*.

Actually, the scent of hinds on heat had already been described by Henry Evans, the great nineteenth-century deer researcher, who wrote of the red deer on the Isle of Jura: 'The beds of bands of hinds through October have a strong odour, quite different from the rut odour of stags.'

I was given special dispensation to work for my doctorate outwith the prescribed normal limit of five miles from the church of St Mary's, Cambridge and commuted every few weeks between flat Cambridge and mountainous Rum. There were four boats a week to the island from the fishing port of Mallaig. It used to take me about eleven hours of hard driving in my Mini Moke. I remember one evening at around 6 p.m., after work in the lab at Cambridge, making a decision, on a whim, to dash up for the 6 a.m. boat. I stopped for a good supper at Wetherby and then blazed on, going well, in winter darkness but with deserted, dry roads and no frost, until at Appleby, then with no bypass, the law caught up with me. They were understanding when I explained that no, there was no fire, but I did have a ferry to catch at Mallaig in five hours' time. They would press no charges, but perhaps I could join them for a chat in their squad car for a while until I had cooled down a little? They talked to me for half an hour, which they judged would just be about enough to remove any possibility of my catching the boat.

They were probably right but my blood was up. Eschewing comfort stops, I tore on north, hurtling through Glasgow in the wee small hours and then beside the black water of Loch Lomond and through the immensity of familiar Glencoe. On the long, tortuous single-track road between Fort William and Mallaig there was a steady stream of articulated trucks carrying herring south to the continent. And by now there was a rising wind and squalls of rain. Each lorry entailed a few moments' frustration and I knew that when I reached the pier it would be neck and neck. I was right. The *Loch Arkaig* was just six feet away from me, separated by a rapidly growing strip of black, oily water. I was so angry that I tore hair out as I sat on the breakwater and watched her diminishing lights.

As she turned south to round Sleat Point I could see her port light glowing red and becoming fainter. And then . . . what was happening . . . surely that was green? And wasn't it growing brighter?

She had decided the weather was too bad and put back into harbour. I was forced to spend two days in Mallaig waiting for the gales to abate. As so often, divine providence seemed to be asking me to revise my philosophy. A young, arrogant scientist with a determined disbelief in things that cannot be proven, I found it hard to believe in a power trying to tell me to slow down. I didn't listen.

4 RED DEER RULED BY SEX

The fruitless copulations of our vasectomised stag, Ed, had shown us that hinds not becoming pregnant will keep on coming into heat from early October until February or March. Naturally the hind on the hill, exposed every few minutes to the violently competitive and turbulent stag in his frenzied checking, is unlikely to pass through an oestrous cycle unnoticed and so will normally conceive early in the season. Nevertheless tales of very late calves are common in Scotland, presumably because the often poor nutrition of the hinds prevents their coming into heat until late. I remember seeing a wild hind on Rum being mated in December. Even as late as that, the stags were vigilant to the slender chances of perpetuating more of their genes and a local, short-lived Yuletide rut resulted.

The intensity of the hind's heat grows with each successive cycle, so that in October the oestrus is almost imperceptible to the human observer but come December she is rampant with the overt urge to be mated and solicits the stag shamelessly. By spring some of her ardour is abating.

Fiona found that the hinds came into oestrus every eighteen days, plus or minus two days, and that on each occasion the stags would mate them once, twice and occasionally, late in the year, three or four times during a heat that might last twenty-four hours. No mean achievement when you consider that a stag on a farm may successfully cover seventy or eighty hinds in a three- or four-week period! No wonder the stag finishes the rut as a thin, haggard vestige of his sleek, late summer self; he has lost maybe a fifth of his body weight and has to feed hard to recover some condition before the winter closes in.

We removed Ed and replaced him with a fertile stag to allow some of Dick Youngson's hinds to conceive in the early spring when the oestrous cycles were declining. It was from this that Fiona, Gerald and Roger were able to establish that the pregnancy of a red deer hind lasts on average 231 days, plus or minus four or five days; that is, about seven and a half months. Later Fiona and others were able to show that the less well-fed hinds on the hill had a very slightly shorter gestation.

The inevitable consequence of this was that we had a number of autumn-born calves which we ended up bottle-rearing, otherwise they would surely have perished. The mothers would have been unlikely to have had sufficient milk in the depths of the winter just when the calves would have been at their hungriest. This meant that we had a nursery of several calves to feed at all hours of day and night. Their beauty was bewitching and strengthened my continuing obsession.

I remember vividly the patter of hard little deer calves' hooves on the brown lino in our kitchen at the back of the castle that winter, and the only slightly softer rattle of deer droppings descending on the same surface. The regular pools of urine were even more silent and inconvenient. One morning Roger awoke to find his slippers, left warming by the Raeburn stove, awash with the yellow liquid. That solved the naming problem for that particular calf and it was curious, years later, to see Slipper, standing huge and black, roaring belligerence on the hill.

One of those late-conceived births was epoch-making. Gerald, Fiona and I had by some wonderful coincidence gathered to watch Sandy give birth. Strangely, although wild hinds will make off into the hills for miles to find solitude for their births, bottle-fed hinds remain apparently oblivious to onlookers, seeming completely absorbed in the business of creating a new life. So we watched, festooned with cameras, and fascinated and privileged to witness that magical process.

Sure enough, on to the autumn leaves, like a fish out of water, flopped a spluttering and sneezing calf. 'It's a bit small,' I ventured.

The others agreed. Sandy was our biggest hind; this was a disappointment. But while we were expecting her to get on with the business of expelling her afterbirth, and then of eating those hormonally valuable tissues, it became clear that she was showing no sign at all of having completed her labour.

The feet of deer calves, like other hoofed species, are encased in bright yellow cartilage; these soft 'golden slippers' protect the mother and allow the embryo to carry out its very necessary muscle-strengthening kicking exercises in the womb without any risk of the feet tearing it. The golden slippers were of interest to us because they wear off in the first day or two of life as the calf makes its first ungainly gambols on the abrasive heather and we didn't often have a chance to examine them. Gerald as usual was the first to notice anything unusual. 'She's having another,' he whispered excitedly and at the same time we could all see the two golden slippers of a second calf being forcefully squeezed out. The enthusiasm was understandable; twins carried to full term in red deer were at that time unrecorded, at least in Scottish deer (illustration 6b).

Sandy, doing what was probably the most sensible thing for a Scottish hind, abandoned those calves. It was too close to winter, they would certainly not have survived, and her job was to get back into condition so that she could stand the best chance of conceiving and rearing a calf at the right time next year. So we had to raise those two on a bottle, and Bonnie and Clyde became quite celebrated. The late Lea McNally, deerstalker and chronicler of Highland natural history, was so surprised – and perhaps a little sceptical – that he came over to Rum especially to see what was happening and wrote it all up in an enthusiastic article.

It is pretty clear now that if given adequate feeding, as on a deer farm, about one in a hundred hinds will give birth to twins. In the wild on the Scottish hills the figure is about one in a thousand, reflecting their straitened circumstances.

All this, while fascinating, and indeed thrilling for me, was secondary to the main object of our interest. Red deer, like all herbivores in a temperate climate, are intensely seasonal, for their survival depends on the birth of the calves coinciding with the flush of spring vegetation. I had noted in my mountaineering expeditions with the Gum Club just how desperate was their struggle to survive the miserable Highland winter. All those deer which may look so relaxed and well fed in the late summer are actually on a knife-edge. Unconsciously their whole life, every pattern of behaviour and every movement, is directed towards their own survival, and ultimately to bringing as many as possible of their progeny to breeding condition.

Perhaps there is a parallel in educated man when, for example, we see the determined sacrifice of career prospects made by British politicians to find what they perceive to be the best possible schooling for their family, even when it may be contrary to their avowed political policy and so, presumably, what they judge to be the common good! Extrapolation of points of animal behaviour to humans is unwise and rightly frowned on by scientists. Nevertheless this is far from being a scientific treatise, and it is fascinating to think how we all strive so energetically 'to do the best' for our families. It is only during the last few decades in our own affluent society that material prosperity has come to be dissociated from our ability to rear large families. Does our collective subconscious still tell us that a 'good start' will increase the chances of our progeny rearing a family and perpetuating our genes?

For the stag, anyway, all efforts are directed into maximising his success in the rut, the mating season. His weight, his vigour in fighting other males, in remaining vigilant against other stags encroaching on his harem, his ability to deter other stags by roaring strongly and frequently, perhaps the strength of his rutting odour, the thickness of his neck, the length of his neck mane, the depth of his colour achieved by wallowing in peat hags, as well as the size of his antlers and no doubt many more subtle features will determine his success. And underlying all that is the size of his energy store, the fat deposits which he has achieved during the summer to enable him to conduct a successful rut and still survive the rigours of the winter, so that he can live to fight again the next year and sire yet more progeny.

Gerald had written of the importance of all this in the stag and shown much of the way in which the sex hormone, testosterone, is the chemical messenger responsible for these life-and-death affairs. But who sends the messenger?

We wanted to find out more about the ways in which the seasonal cue, which we knew was day-length, acts on the animal and is translated into the hormonal changes which bring about the rise in testosterone in the male and of other hormones in the female. For the crucial point is that the stag ruts so dramatically each autumn in order not to miss the short hours during which the female will accept the male, as well as to stimulate her to come into heat. The period is brief because in our very seasonal climate it is of vital importance that the young are born at such a time as to allow the hind to lactate during the short season when the pasture is at its best. Farmers, and mothers themselves, know just how much of a strain is lactation. Many, usually men, comment on the enormous strain on the stag's metabolism of growing antlers; this is insignificant compared to the resources demanded of the lactating female. How often do breast-feeding ladies start to lose their hair? Even with abundant good feeding lactation is a burden. Accurate synchronisation of birth, and consequently lactation, is fundamental to the survival of any grazing species in our temperate climate. The few weeks of good grass are crucial to the chances of a deer calf making it through its first winter. The only way in which this accuracy can be achieved is by using the changes of day-length as a cue.

The lactation of the hind, when she may daily yield up to two kilogrammes (nearly five pounds) of very concentrated milk, is a huge nutritional demand and she will certainly lose weight for a period. This is especially important in Scotland where the rain and wind of winter are so extreme, and the quality of winter feed so poor, and the summer so short, that the number of calves succumbing in their first year is terribly high. Between February and April an average of one in four calves will die and in some particularly harsh winters on the most exposed deer forests the figure is much higher. And the wild deer calves most likely to die are those born either early or late in the calving season, especially the latter. Over the years the successful deer is the one who synchronises his mating in such a way as to ensure that his progeny are born in mid-season.

This principle is of the utmost importance also to the farmer, of course. During the northern European summer the grass is only at its best during a brief few weeks between awakening from the winter cold and reaching the flowering stage, because once flowered, most of the protein in the herbage is lost. In our Scottish spring the day-length is very long, so that the light-dependent growth of the vegetation is impressive for just those few weeks before flowering. Cattle and sheep, originating far from our temperate climate, will, left to their own devices, drop their young at times inappropriate to our spring grass flush in the Scottish hills.

On Rum I watched with horrified fascination the feral goats whose ancestors nibbled the sparse vegetation of the arid desert edge, as now they dropped their kids in February on the storm-lashed sea cliffs. For the first time, I thought how much more natural to farm deer.

As a young vet I soon found that although my all-round education in the way mammals work was the best possible, I had much to learn about the survival strategy of the wild animals. It is easy enough to comprehend the principles of Darwin's theory of evolution but only by observing wild animals, and the intensity of their struggle, does its relevance become really clear. Unless an individual leaves at least one offspring which in its turn successfully procreates, then in biological terms that individual might as well have never lived. Every facet of an animal's behaviour has been honed by natural selection to achieve that end with ruthless efficiency.

To accomplish this all-important spring calving it is clear that, since the duration of pregnancy is a near-constant, synchrony of mating is pivotal. To watch the simultaneous efforts of hundreds of red deer stags each striving to secure as large a group of hinds as he can immediately prior to their coming into heat is spectacular. In their life-and-death struggle to mate as many hinds as possible, they create what is probably the most impressive wildlife phenomenon in Europe. Because of the severity of the conditions and the high level of mortality among the calves, there is a dreadful urgency for the deer; they must impregnate all hinds they can in that narrow window of time to allow the fruits of their couplings the best chance of surviving until they too in their turn can mate. Red deer are the largest European land mammal – saving the few surviving bears and the moose – and when stags cease eating to devote all their resources of fat, painstakingly accumulated in the lazy days of summer, into a pent-up orgy of courtship and mating, it is awe-inspiring.

Turbervile, in his book *The Noble Art of Venerie*, written in 1576 but owing much to earlier French authors, gives a good account of the rut in a chapter entitled 'The Vault of Hartes':

> Harts do beginne to Vault about the middlest of September, and their Rut doth continue about two monethes, and the older that they be, the hottere they are, and the better beloved of the Hyndes. The old harts go sooner to vault than the yong, and they are so fierce and so proude, that until they have accomplyshed their lust, the yong harts dare not come neare them, for if they do, they beate them and dryve them away. The yong Deere have a marvellous craft and malice, for when they perceive that the olde Hartes are wearie of the Rut and weakened in force, they runne uppon them, and eyther hurt or kill them, causing them to abandon the Rut and they remayne maisters in their places.
>
> Hartes do much sooner kyll each other when there is scarcitie of Hyndes, for if there be Hyndes plentie, then they separate themselves in one place or other. It is a pleasure, to beholde them when they goe to Rutte and make their vaulte. For when they smell the Hynde, they rayse their nose up into the ayre, and look aloft as thou they gave thankes to nature which gave them so great delight.

That argues for a good deal of time spent watching the deer, since mating, especially amongst woodland red deer, is not often witnessed. The raising of their noses in the air is the act of 'flehmen' by which we believe the stags are testing the urine of the hinds to check whether they are on heat.

From time to time during the rut we would come across stags so exhausted as to lie asleep, eyes closed. I remember being able to walk up to one such sated wild monarch, normally unapproachable, and touch him before he leapt up and away. Cameron in his *Wild Red Deer of Scotland* notes this too, of the rutting stag: 'his slumbers are deep, for twice in a single season did the Grand Duke Sergius Michaelovitch surprise sleeping stags which never woke.' Hardly sporting, I should have thought.

It is not just the effort of the rut that makes rutting stags sleep, I think. It is well known that ruminants do not sleep in the normal way but stay awake with glazed eyes chewing their cud. Analysis of their brain's electrical activity at that time shows a great resemblance to the sleep patterns seen in other animals during conventional sleep. Yet in the rut stags do not eat. Over those few days they lose perhaps a fifth of their body weight. Could the absence of periods of cudding compel them to take naps just as do those animals that do not ruminate?

In the larger open glens of Rum, such as Guiridil or Glen Shellesder; or on the flat top of Fionchra, as elsewhere in the Highlands, each autumn one can watch stags roaring from the steep sides of the hills; weighing up their opponents: who can roar largest and loudest and most often? Who looks biggest and blackest? Who smells strongest? Who carries the largest antlers and who the heaviest body? And then perhaps, at the end of a long day of challenging, two mighty stags may come to combat. A slow, stiff-legged approach leads into the famous parallel walk. The two combatants march side by side, only a few metres apart, in a highly ritualised display, stopping frequently to roar, thrash the peat with their antlers and jerk their penises and spray urine. (And perhaps even sperm. Gerald, ever the scientist, had found spermatozoa on vegetation doused by a stag at the climax of his ecstasy. 'Was he masturbating?' asked Gerald. If so, what could be the evolutionary value of that?) From a few seconds to half an hour or more the appraisal continues with two possible outcomes. One stag's nerve may break and he runs for his life or else the fight is really on. Then with frightening speed antlers are locked and, flattening themselves to maximise pushing power, the stags struggle. On the steep hillsides the uppermost has the advantage.

And while the battles rage there is often a lone wandering dis-possessed stag eyeing up his chances before sneaking quietly in on a hind.

These contests exact a price. On Rum, broken antlers are almost the norm, as are broken ribs, whilst lost eyes and fractures of the limbs are often seen. Gerald one autumn saw our revered Kilmory patriarch,

Aristotle, thrown by an opponent clean off his feet and rolled twice, head to tail, right over on the steep slopes of the Bloodstone Hill.

Watching such duels with even a glimmer of understanding of the reason behind their actions, it is difficult not to extrapolate to man and, like Jung, search for reasons for his tribal, religious and nationalist struggles. Animals have more excuse; we should be able to understand the value of co-operative effort. Our evolution is now, one hopes, on a psychosocial level and our progress intellectual, capable of being passed from generation to generation by book and example. Could that be the basis of our urge to 'make a name for ourselves' or 'to be remembered after our time'? Yet how frequently apparently educated societies are pulled down not only to the animal level of courtship rivalry, but beyond, even into the mire of 'ethnic cleansing'. We have to believe that man will progress beyond that mindless aggression otherwise it is difficult not to despair.

Of course, the rut is not just about roaring, though that is what the word rut means, or even fighting; it is about siring calves. A stag expends much of his energy at this time in trying to herd his hinds together into a tight harem and then in chasing them to see if at last they will stand and accept his advances. This very chasing, and the roaring and the stink of the stags, must all serve to bring hinds into heat. Eventually, late in the rut, the hinds will stand, and after some nervous clumsy attempts the stag will rapidly come to ejaculation, and presumably orgasm, and with one colossal thrust lift all his four legs off the ground and push the hind forwards. As Turbervile put it: he 'will begin to vault, and to bellow, casting him selfe with a full leape upon the Hynde to cover hir, and that quickly'.

I worked on and off Rum for four years, overlapping at the end with Tim Clutton-Brock who built up a team of behaviourists at Cambridge and who was able to work with Fiona to monitor the life histories of the wild deer at Kilmory to good effect. Tim was a very highly motivated evolutionary behaviourist. We had shared a house together in Cambridge and I came to know him very well. To Gerald and myself, red-blooded physiologists, interested in the mechanisms, what made animals tick etc., the study of behaviour always seemed perhaps a little effete, rather nebulous. Nevertheless Tim's work was pursued with ferocious intensity, but, more importantly, with highly professional analysis, at a time when evolutionary behaviour was just becoming fashionable. Desmond Morris's *The Naked Ape* had appeared, and Robert Ardrey's *Territorial Imperative*, but *The Selfish Gene* and *The Blind Watchmaker* by Richard Dawkins only became bestsellers years later. Tim, capitalising on Fiona's ability to recognise the deer as individuals, was able to examine just how successful each one of a significant number of individual deer had been in achieving progeny during their lives. Such longitudinal studies of large mammals are, for good reason, very rare. With wild red deer stags living as long as twelve years and hinds up to fifteen or more, vertical studies of this species ideally need to last about twenty years.

An interest in what Tim was trying to do was borne in on me when he asked in his bantering way why I thought it was that hinds bark and stags don't. What he was referring to is the alarm bark that one of a group of hinds will often make when she is being approached and she becomes suspicious. It is a noise that is the bane of stalkers, or even of field biologists, trying to approach a group of hinds without disturbing them. Stags on the other hand rarely make this noise. The question was why not?

Of course I hadn't thought about it very much and hadn't a clue, although the answer provided by Tim seems very clear to me now, and like all good theories makes you wonder why you hadn't thought of it sooner. Hinds generally spend their lives with close relatives: a mature hind is normally accompanied by her daughters of successive years and by her sisters. (In fact Roger and Fiona had shown that stags castrated as calves will associate even more closely with their dams than do the hinds.) Stags on the other hand tend to disperse quite widely as one- and two-year-olds, and so are much less likely to associate with close relatives. Now, as readers of *The Selfish Gene* know only too well, an animal has a strong interest in doing everything it can to protect and procreate its own genes, whilst the more distantly related another animal is, the less advantage there is in assisting its chances of survival. Indeed quite the reverse; this distant relative represents competition and there may be advantage in hindering its chances of reproducing.

Thus will a lion taking up with a new lioness often kill the cubs she has borne to his predecessor and the Hanuman langur, an Indian monkey, makes infanticide of his spouse's babies a way of life. By killing the suckling baby he causes lactation to halt abruptly and oestrus and ovulation to resume, making an early fertile copulation possible. More disquietingly, Potts and Short point out that human stepfathers are up to sixty times more likely than the biological father to kill a baby. But back to the deer: obviously then the hind barking will, by alarming her family, improve their chances of survival even at some small risk to herself, whereas the stag, surrounded by much less closely related individuals, does not find the risk worth while and keeps quiet, looking after number one. Tim's explanation as to why hinds give the alarm bark and stags don't seemed plausible to me. At the same time in a complementary way we physiologists could probably explain many other things.

Thus I suggested, contentiously, a reason why hinds often roar like stags in the few days prior to calving but at no other time: during late pregnancy, oestrogen levels rise but we know that until a few days before giving birth the hormone of pregnancy, progesterone, is also present at high levels and that this hormone seems to neutralise the effects of oestrogens on the brain. When progesterone levels fall in those last few days of gestation then the brain is exposed to the full behavioural effects of oestrogen and, as I had been able to demonstrate in the work I had done for my Ph.D., oestrogen mimics the male hormone testosterone in acting to stimulate roaring in either sex. So, probably, if my conjecture was correct, the occasional roar prior to calving had no significant survival value one way or the other. If it had then it would either have disappeared or become more common. The hind's roar was, I argued, merely a hormonal accident.

Tim, by careful statistical analysis of all the data collected by himself, his students and especially Fiona, was able to unravel all sorts of fascinating points. One of the most interesting was his identification of the fact that the hinds most dominant in competing with other hinds had a more than average chance of producing a male offspring. This is real grist to the mill of the evolutionary biologist, who may argue that because stag calves are likely to be larger and drink more milk than hind calves they are more 'expensive' to produce but that equally, if they survive, they may have better prospects of promulgating their genes.

Not quite biological determinism, but perhaps enough to make you question your own motives and always look for the mechanistic solution.

5 THE HISTORY OF A SCOTTISH ISLAND – HOW STRANGE A CYCLE

From the first day, together with the incessant rain, the island's past soaked in. Fiona and I were lodged in Kinloch Castle, albeit in the servants' quarters, and we worked every morning in the remains of the walled garden behind the castle. Sometimes our stags rutted and hinds calved within ruined glasshouses where once, in living memory, turtles and humming-birds had revelled in heated luxury. What a monument to the vanity and impermanence of material achievement.

Conversely during much of the day, and especially in the evenings, we were walking through the remains of the abandoned village at Kilmory with the graveyard beside it, raised high over several centuries by the accumulation of mortal remains. The only legible gravestone there told of the shepherd, Murdo Mathieson, losing five of his family in three days to diphtheria in 1873 (illustration 3). That had been enough for him, poor man, he had upped sticks and transplanted himself to New Zealand where his family, like John Donne's violet, prospered: his son gave his name to Lake Mathieson.

I suppose most folk who have come to spend some of their lives on the Isle of Rum become haunted by the history of the place. Like the landscape, its story is very stark and I soon became immersed in the subject, researching and eventually writing some of it into my thesis. Although my particular interest was, of course, the deer, it would not be possible to remain unmoved by the vicissitudes of the human population on such a largely inhospitable piece of land.

I want to describe the history of Rum, its people and its deer in a little detail now. My task has been made easier by *Rum: Nature's Island*, written by Magnus Magnusson and published in 1998 by Luath Press to aid Scottish Natural Heritage in their work on the island now in their care.

The story of the islanders and the deer seems to me a perfect microcosm of man's struggle to develop in disparate environments worldwide, and his influence on the environment and on game, and so may reveal some universal patterns applicable elsewhere in the world. More modestly, it is undeniable that many parts of the west and north of Scotland have a very similar story to tell, and I believe that man's interactions with deer on Rum represent, at the very least, a pattern for our involvement with grazing and browsing wild animals, certainly in the temperate regions populated by deer.

As on Rum, so elsewhere, it appears that from its beginnings the rural human population grows, slowly at first and then all too quickly, and as it does so, it eliminates or reduces the large wild game whilst usually removing most of the woodlands. These two go together, since in all societies, with the advent of food production, that is farming, there is a need to destroy forest, and this tends to expose animals to hunting pressures which also increase with the density of the human population.

During the next phase, urbanisation, there is a progressive depopulation of the countryside associated with the move into cities and towns, and game numbers rebound. Throughout the developed world, deer populations, for example, are with few exceptions now increasing very rapidly, and efforts to control them are not always proving successful. In Scotland between 1970 and 1992 deer numbers, despite pressure from the Deer Commission on the sporting estates to kill more, increased from around 190,000 to over 300,000, although strenuous efforts to increase the cull have now perhaps recently stabilised numbers. In France the roe deer population is thought to be doubling every twenty years, and in England the muntjac population is increasing by 10 per cent per annum. But it is in the United States that deer numbers are most impressive. Thus the American white-tailed deer numbered less than half a million at the beginning of the twentieth century, but around twenty million by the 1980s. The deer hunters of the United States were, in 1976, killing some two and a half million deer per annum and spending as an industry 2,600 million dollars in doing it. Now they are killing over six million deer per annum.

In Sweden, Linnaeus, the eighteenth-century biologist, is thought never to have seen a moose, yet now there are more than 300,000 in his country, of which 100,000 are shot annually. Moose in Sweden also represent the major cause of car accidents.

On Rum the relationship between man and deer showed the same cycle and it is remarkably well documented. We know, for instance, that the island was visited very early in Scotland's history since recent excavations have shown, in a field behind Kinloch Castle, the earliest known evidence of human habitation in Scotland, dating back almost nine thousand years. Unfortunately these sites have not yet revealed much of what was being eaten except for some hazelnut shells and, much more recent, about five thousand years old, a brew identified (from pollen analysis of material found attached to a piece of pot) as oats and barley flavoured with meadowsweet, heather honey and bog myrtle. This sounds to me suspiciously like the Athole brose well known in nineteenth-century Scotland.

Deer bones do appear elsewhere, in the midden of a cave site which may date to the Mesolithic, and it seems likely that deer were present in large numbers on Rum from soon after the last ice age. It is logical to assume that those early visitors found the deer on Rum a valuable addition to their diet as well as a source of antler and leather.

There are quite abundant early references to Rum, reflecting the relative ease of movement by water as against land transport, and consequently the value of islands. Yet as islands go it was always a particularly inhospitable, infertile place – for example, in 1549 when Donald Monro, Dean of the Isles, wrote one of the first descriptions of Rum, a permanent human population had still probably not been established or was at least very small. Monro wrote: '. . . ane forrest of heigh mountains, and abundance of little deir in it, which deir will never be slain downwith, but the principal settis must be in the height of the hills, because the deer will be called upwards always by the tinchel, or without the tinchel they will pass up . . . also many wild nests upon the plaine mure as men pleasis to gadder, and yet by reason the fowls has few to start them except deire'.

The 'settis' or setts to which Dean Monro refers would be traps or funnels, often known as 'elricks', designed to allow a large body of people – a 'tainchell' or 'tinchell' – to drive a number of deer through a narrow defile in which they could be slaughtered by waiting armed men.

In 1796 the Old Statistical Account of Scotland describes how these were thought to have functioned on Rum: 'Before the use of firearms, their method of killing deer was as follows: on each side of a glen, formed by two mountains, stone dykes were begun pretty high in the mountains, and carried to the lower part of the valley, always drawing nearer, till within three or four feet of each other. From this narrow pass, a circular space was inclosed by a stone wall, of a height sufficient to confine the deer; to this place they were pursued and destroyed. The vestige of one of these inclosures is still to be seen in Rum.'

Such setts or elricks on Rum can still be just about made out and two have been described high up on the south slopes of Orval by John Love, while in 1995 Historic Scotland reported a further three possible setts on Rum.

Shortly after Dean Monro's account, in about 1580, the king commissioned a description of the islands which reported that Rum could only be relied on to muster six or seven fighting men compared to sixty from Eigg. The same report described Rum as 'an ile of small profit . . . the hills and waist glennis are commodious only for the hunting of deir'.

In 1703 Martin Martin published his *Description of the Western Isles*, a volume that was taken with them and much used by Boswell and Johnson on their tour of the Hebrides seventy years later. Martin describes some hundreds of deer on Rum at the time of his writing and he also, interestingly, recounts a tradition among the resident Macleans of not shooting at them in one specific area, the slopes of Fionchra, for to do so 'they say proves fatal to the posterity of Lachlin, a cadet of Maclean of Coll's family'. Yet despite this early and far-sighted piece of nature conservation, reinforced by superstition, deer numbers continued to fall. In his *Report of the Hebrides* of 1764 and 1771, Walker wrote, 'although the wood is now gone, a herd of red deer still remains'. At that time the human population was, he said, 304 in fifty-seven families; hardly surprising that so many people on such an inhospitable island, together with their livestock, should have eliminated the trees.

Boswell and Johnson were blown past Rum in 1773 in a storm and although Boswell 'became very sick' he was able to report that there were still deer in the hills of Rum. When next year Thomas Pennant managed to land he was told there were just eighty deer left. The setts, aided latterly by firearms, had almost finished their work.

Finally the Old Statistical Account of 1796 reported not only the loss of the trees but also the end of the deer: 'In Rum there were formerly great numbers of deer; there was also a copse of wood, that afforded cover to their fawns from birds of prey, particularly from the eagle: while the wood throve, the deer also throve; now that the wood is totally destroyed, the deer are extirpated.'

Thus it is pretty clear that by about 1790 the deer had gone and it is hard not to believe that the human population was as important a predator of the deer as the eagles. By then they had access to firearms. Is it too fanciful to imagine that the collapse of the clan system, due to the ravages of the Duke of Cumberland's forces after Culloden and other economic factors, meant that such pieces of clan lore and restraint as that of the Macleans described by Martin had fallen into decay? Might this have just saved the deer from extinction?

It seems unlikely. All the accounts suggest a very small human population on Rum until the mid-seventeenth or early eighteenth century. But from 1728, when a census carried out by the Society for the Propagation of Christian Knowledge recorded 152 persons over the age of five years, to around 1770 when Walker's census revealed 304 inhabitants, and to the figure of 443 in 1796 when the Old

Statistical Account was compiled, it is very clear that population growth was massive. A consequent growing demand for firewood would be likely to reduce any woodland and that, together with the obvious requirement for food, must have put tremendous pressure on the deer. Their extinction was inevitable, and reflected a similar pattern throughout the Highlands and Islands where deer numbers had become very low by the end of the eighteenth century. In southern Britain comparable reasons led to the decline of stag hunting to be followed by the new fad for chasing the 'uneatable' fox, though the use of carted deer allowed many through the eighteenth century and later to go on hunting deer in areas where they had become rare or extinct.

The astonishing rise in the human population is typical of much of Scotland in that period and its causes remain conjectural: possibly the introduction of the potato, improved systems of cultivation of grain, smallpox vaccination, or just a more stable life following the disruption of the clan system; or a combination of all three factors.

After his first and last military victory at Culloden in 1746, the fat Duke of Cumberland, his reputation preserved by Handel who commemorated his achievement by writing 'See the Conquering Hero Comes', had behaved with terrible brutality, encouraging his soldiers to kill and mutilate the wounded. And thereafter he had his men lay waste much of the Highlands, killing men, women and children alike.

The clan system, already fatally damaged, then broke down quickly as chieftains began to exact their dues in cash instead of fealty, to provide for, among other things, their education in Paris at the Sorbonne as well as elsewhere in Europe. Nevertheless, as the old order collapsed there came a new period of calm which may have contributed to the population build-up.

There was also a rapid change from a grain-based diet to one dangerously dependent on the potato. In fact, there is evidence that few of the islanders on Rum were even making cultivations for grain production until the early eighteenth century. John Walker in 1764 reports the recent death of an inhabitant of Rum aged one hundred and three. This man was described as having been fifty years old before having ever tasted bread: 'I was even told, that this old man used frequently to remind the younger People, of the simple and hardy Fare of former times, used to upbraid them with their Indulgence in the Article of Bread, and judged it unmanly in them to toil like Slaves with their Spades, for the production of such an unnecessary Piece of Luxury.' This account must be typical of legions of comments made over many millennia wherever food-production systems overtook those of the hunter-gatherer.

The potato came much later than grain, of course. It hadn't made its appearance in the islands before the early to mid-eighteenth century. Did this vegetable allow such an improved diet that the fertility of the people could improve? In fact it would seem that, on Rum at least, the expansion of the human population preceded the arrival of the potato. Nevertheless, dependence on the potato exposed people to risks of crop failure due to blight, and the resulting potato famines and associated cholera epidemics which visited Scotland and Ireland between 1846 and 1856.

A more important consideration was the introduction of smallpox vaccination. In 1764 John Walker had noted of Rum: 'the island was then accounted populous, as it had not been visited by the Small Pox for 29 years; for by this Disease upon former Occasions, it had been almost depopulate.' And Samuel Johnson describes the laird of the Isle of Muck arranging vaccination of his islanders when he visited in 1773.

Whatever the answer the conclusion was inevitable. Pennant had described 'famine in the aspect' of the Rum islanders as early as 1772, and in 1812 and again in 1817 Maclean of Coll had been forced to provide grain shipments for his starving clansmen. But by 1825 personal economic pressures compelled him to take drastic action and he leased Rum to Dr Lachlan Maclean of Gallanach on Coll, a kinsman by marriage. At Whitsun 1825 the islanders were all given twelve months to quit in order to make way for eight thousand blackface sheep.

On 11 July 1826, three hundred islanders of all ages were cleared into two ships, the *Dove of Harmony* and the *Highland Lad* bound for Port Hawkesbury in Nova Scotia. Fifty years later the scene was recalled by John McMaister, a shepherd on Rum at the time, as 'of such stressful description that he would never be able to forget it till his dying day ... the wild outcries of the men and the heart-breaking wails of the women and their children filled all the air between the mountainous shores of the bay.'

That left only around fifty people on Rum and these were shipped off two years later in the *Saint Lawrence*, together with 150 from the Isle of Muck. Only one family of native islanders remained, eleventh-generation Macleans, though Dr Maclean was then obliged to import a dozen families from Skye and Mull to look after his sheep.

In the event the wool and mutton industry soon collapsed, ironically owing to imports from Australia and New Zealand, destinations for so many emigrants. Throughout the Scottish Highlands and Islands famine ensued, though never reaching the severity of the great Irish hunger.

In 1838 two members of the Statistical Society of Glasgow published a report entitled *Remarks on the Evils at present Affecting the Highlands and Islands of Scotland* in which they referred to Rum as: '... one of the most rugged, bleak and barren of the Hebrides ... so peculiarly liable to violent storms of wind and rain, as, with the exception of a few hundred acres of low lying land, to afford no encouragement to the raising of crops on any part of its surface. It is occupied as a sheep farm by Dr Maclean, who, with his family and shepherds and a few cotiers, forms its only inhabitants.'

Hugh Miller, born in 1802 in Cromarty, a small village on the north-east coast of Scotland, was one of those towering intellects of the nineteenth century whose nonconformist example inspires wonder and humility in those of us who look back from a world full of all advantages. A wild and intractable boy, he left school young and became a stonemason. His experiences with the rocks led him to become an internationally renowned geologist and palaeontologist, corresponding with Darwin and Agassiz. Despite this he remained a creationist and became editor of the Free Church journal, *The Witness*. He wrote prolifically and his writings are highly readable and well worth exploring today. I find his prose compelling and inserted the following stomach-churningly melancholic account from his book *The*

Cruise of the Betsy into my thesis. He is describing Rum as he found it in 1846, that is twenty years after the clearance.

> The armies of the insect world were sporting in the light this evening by millions; a brown stream that runs through the valley yielded an incessant poppling sound; ... along a distant hillside there ran what seemed the ruins of a gray stone fence, erected, says tradition, in a remote age, to facilitate the hunting of the deer; there were fields on which the heath and moss of the surrounding moorlands were fast encroaching, that had borne many a successive harvest; and prostrate cottages, that had been the scenes of christenings, and bridals, and blythe new-year's days; ... but in the entire prospect not a man nor a man's dwelling could the eye command. I do not much like extermination carried out so thoroughly and on a system; ... and I cannot quite see on what principle the ominous increase which is taking place among us in the worse class, is to form our solace or apology for the wholesale expatriation of the better ... It did not seem as if the depopulation of Rum had tended much to any one's advantage. The single sheep farmer had been unfortunate in his speculations, and had left the island, and the proprietor, his landlord, seemed to have been as little fortunate as the tenant, for the island itself was in the market; and a report went current at the time that it was on the eve of being purchased by some wealthy Englishman, who purposed converting it into a deer forest. How strange a cycle!

Indeed, as Hugh Miller indicated, the next phase of the cycle, as for so many other parts of the Highlands and Islands of Scotland, was transformation into a deer forest or sporting estate.

Though materially often destitute, the islanders had been culturally rich and well able to mount a ceilidh in honour of visitors. Thus the geologist John MacCulloch, visiting the very remote glen of Guiridil on the north-west of Rum six years prior to the evictions, wrote: 'There was an old fiddle hanging up in a corner, very crazy in the pegs and in the intestines, but still practicable ... A ball here requires no great preparations. The lassies had no shoes and marvellous little petticoat; but to compensate for these deficiencies they had an abundance of activity and good will. Where shall I go into such a house in England, find such manners and such conversation ... and see such smoky shelves covered not only with the books of the ancients, but of the moderns ... well thumbed and well talked of?'

The material life these people lived was not so very different from that of the Neolithic, yet it is a bizarre fact, typical of so many Highland communities, that no sooner had the indigenous peoples been removed, in a process not unlike ethnic cleansing, than they were replaced by Victorian and Edwardian magnates at the cutting edge of global industrialisation.

Despite their poverty, the strong culture and civility of the Hebridean islanders had also been commented on by Boswell, fifty years earlier. Of his time on the Isle of Raasay in 1773 he wrote: 'More gentleness of manners, or a more pleasing appearance of domestick society, is not found in the most polished countries.'

In the case of Rum the wealthy Englishman alluded to by Hugh Miller was the second Marquis of Salisbury, whose son came to be prime minister. He bought the island in 1845. His object was clearly and simply the creation of a sporting estate and he set about this with a will. In an effort to improve the fishing he employed three hundred workmen for two years cutting a channel through rock and constructing a dam. Unfortunately the dam was built back to front, that is concave instead of convex, and burst two days after completion. This £11,000 folly is still clearly visible and known to all on Rum as 'Salisbury's Dam'.

Of much greater interest to me, however, is Salisbury's role in reintroducing deer to Rum. As well as making an ill-judged attempt to establish the softer fallow deer on the island, he also imported red deer from Scottish estates and English parks and by the time he sold the island in 1860 there are thought to have been about six hundred red deer on the island. The period of their absence must have only been some seventy years.

After one more change of hands the island was purchased by John Bullough, a Lancastrian industrialist, whose improvements to the weaving loom brought him and his family great wealth. His son, Sir George Bullough, was responsible for Kinloch Castle where Fiona, Gerald and I were originally billeted, on the east side of Rum. It took three hundred men from Eigg and Lancashire almost three years to build, and history relates that they were paid a shilling a week extra to wear the new Rum tartan kilts, while smokers received twopence per week extra as an incentive to deter the midges. How strange a cycle, indeed!

The castle at Kinloch was supplied by a hydroelectric system and was only the second place in Scotland to be lit by electricity – the first being Glasgow. The walled garden in which Fiona and I worked with our tame deer was in total decay by 1970, but in its heyday it had been home to six domed palm houses with humming-birds, turtles and alligators.

The castle, it has been argued, remains the most intact example of an Edwardian country house in Britain. It has been much described and always fascinates but it is peripheral to the present story. Suffice it to say that Sir George died in 1939 whilst playing golf in Boulogne-sur-Mer and he now lies in the huge Doric temple of a mausoleum which he had erected for his father at Harris on the south-west coast of Rum. His wife, the celebrated beauty, Lady Monica, sold Rum to the Nature Conservancy in 1957 for the very modest price of £23,000. She lived on, in Newmarket, until 1967 and now too lies beside Sir George.

Before we finally leave the Bulloughs to rest in their mausoleum beside the storm-lashed beach of Harris there are two little coincidences which serve to bring this recent history into perspective.

In 1970 my grandfather, who had spent his life in the Yorkshire textile industry, came to visit me in Kinloch Castle. He was then well into his eighties and was able to recount how he had regularly done business with Howard and Bullough Ltd in Accrington. And secondly, Roger Short had been filling his car with petrol near Cambridge in 1967, prior to making a trip north to Rum, when he fell into conversation with the garage proprietor who also ran a fleet of taxis and hearses. When Roger mentioned he was bound for Scotland the garage keeper remarked that he had only the previous month visited Scotland with a hearse on a most curious mission. He had been accompanying Lady Monica to her last resting place, the final few miles of which they had had to accomplish with the coffin in a Nature Conservancy Land-Rover. No longer were the roads maintained by fourteen full-time roadmen; the journey to Harris had become a bottom-gear job.

Returning now to the broader picture; from the point of view of the deer, what happened on Rum is, as I have pointed out earlier, a microcosm of what occurred elsewhere in the Scottish islands and through the Highlands. Deer numbers were high at the beginning of the historical epoch but as the human population swelled, the deer declined. By the late eighteenth century Scottish deer numbers had become very low. Samuel Johnson describes firearms as being so prevalent at the time of his visit in 1773 that he believed that deer on the islands must soon become extinct. And then, finally, with the clearance of the people there were few mouths left to eat venison and at the same time the deer were protected. Consequently their numbers rose almost without interruption to the present levels which, in con-junction with the hill sheep, have become ecologically damaging and arguably responsible for creating what Frank Fraser Darling called the 'wet desert' which covers much of the Highlands today. Recently I played host to a party of deer farmers from the north of Sweden and even they commented that the Highlands of Scotland seemed a desert.

A rather similar story may be told over much of the world: growth in human populations leads to the diminution, and in some cases extinction, of wild grazing mammals, and a decline in biological diversity. The diet changes from wild foods to the products of farms and a much higher intake of animal fats. There then often follows a period of urbanisation with a resulting decline in the human rural population. Pressure on land use is alleviated as still more specialised crop-production systems are introduced to feed the urban population, and, in many areas those wild grazing animals become once more numerous. There are more deer in Britain now than at any time since at least Roman times. Could this give us hope for the grazing animals of Africa? Rural depopulation tragically accelerated by the AIDS epidemic is already occurring locally, but the rocketing human population of Africa makes the destruction of natural grazing, and especially browsing, systems seem inevitable. Potts and Short have pointed out that 'there were 255 million people in the whole of Africa in 1960. By the year 2000 there will be 780 million and the population will be set to double in another twenty-six years.' It is hard to imagine any ecosystems surviving that pressure. A similar fate awaits many other developing parts of the world.

6 FISHING NETS, ANTLERS AND HORNS, AND TRANQUILLISERS

The days on Rum rushed by for me. Working at such close quarters with the deer continued to be an adventure; something unpredictable was always happening.

Man's thoughtlessness had then, in 1970, and probably still does have, an implication for the stags on Rum and other sea-coast deer forests in a very practical way that no one could have anticipated: surprisingly often, stags entangle themselves in fishing nets which trawlers have discarded to litter the beaches. Thrashing their antlers is a normal activity for stags and if they succeed in decorating themselves with vegetation then, during the rut especially, this is a bonus making them more intimidating to other stags.

One late summer evening shortly after I had arrived on Rum I was scoring down specific behaviour patterns in a group of stags at Kilmory against the amazing backdrop of the Skye Cuillins. Chief amongst those stags was one of Gerald's old stalwarts called Crusader; aged perhaps ten years, he was our most mature and impressive stag. During my half-hour observation session Crusader wandered the few hundred yards to the beach and once I had finished I strolled off in his wake.

When I caught up with him his peaceful economy of movement had changed; he had found the great nylon cod-end of a fishing trawl washed up on the beach and must have playfully worked his newly cleaned antlers into it. Inevitably they had become entangled and now the old stag had panicked. He was thrashing his antlers in earnest and desperately trying to rid himself of the burden.

I realised there was no hope of my catching him and even the sharpest knife would make heavy weather of the thick twisted nylon. I rushed up to the Land-Rover for the tranquilliser darting equipment. By the time I had got back to the beach with the loaded dart, perhaps five minutes later, the scene had changed. Now, following a common panic reaction, Crusader had swum out a few yards into the rocky bay until the net was pulling him under. Red deer are very strong swimmers, normally thinking little of swimming a mile across a loch to sweeter grazing on the other side, but this heavy net was too much for poor old Crusader. I tore off my boots and jumped in, covering the few yards easily, but I was too late. Fiona had arrived and she also ploughed into the freezing water, but it was no good. We dragged Crusader's body ashore.

Once our teeth had stopped chattering and we were in dry clothes again, my enthusiasm for venison overcame my reluctance to eat old friends even in those days. I persuaded Fiona to come with me that evening to help take his corpse back for our freezer. This must seem pretty heartless but I think that a reluctance to see waste, inculcated during my Yorkshire Methodist upbringing, has something to do with it.

Also perhaps, studying and grappling with the mysteries of physiology, respect grows for the beauty and complexity of a living system which makes one reluctant to just let it all rot away. I often wonder if vegetarians have considered the fate of all the animals that would either require killing to protect crops, or which would die as a result of populations of herbivores overgrazing their habitats. I for one would find it very difficult to kill animals and then leave them to rot; that connection between hunting, food preparation and eating seems to have permeated at least my own and I believe other people's subconscious.

Anyway, Crusader was desperately tough eating and for the first time I came to understand the importance of age in the quality of meat! Or perhaps it was the stress of his final moments that had rendered the meat all but uneatable.

Other stags entangled in fishing nets lasted longer. Some were found secured by the nets to rocks where they had eventually starved to death. And, in at least one harrowing instance, a stag dragging a length of net, no doubt fancying his new-found headgear, picked a fight, or perhaps just a friendly spar, with another stag. The result was horribly predictable: the two stags were occasionally seen during the winter, grazing together for weeks or months in unnaturally close proximity until death should intervene or, if they were lucky, eventually one, and then the other, should cast his antlers in the spring. I could not get near enough to try a dart. Even the stalkers, employed by the Nature Conservancy to take the annual cull on the island in an effort to keep the deer population in bounds, tried unsuccessfully to free these stags by shooting through their antlers. Ultimately it was deemed merciful to shoot both dead.

When Roger Short had been asked to come up from Cambridge University Veterinary School to use the new-fangled darting and tranquillising systems to catch and mark the deer on Rum in 1965, that had been real pioneering work. And Roger, ever curious, had taken the opportunity to develop the deer connexion further and investigate their breeding behaviour. As such pronounced seasonal breeders, and with that perennial yet deciduous curiosity, antlers, as well, deer were of great interest to the reproductive physiologist. Roger's worldwide reputation had been made in the study of hormones at a time when the research which culminated in the development of birth-control pills was getting under way. He was able to see how understanding the way in which deer breed might contribute to our knowledge of the role and action of hormones, with the ever-present chance of making advances in human and veterinary areas. Science would have made little progress had it not been for the role of serendipity. As Charles Darwin's grandfather, Erasmus Darwin, wrote: 'a fool ... is a man who never tried an experiment in his life.'

It is hard to realise just how little was known about the life of deer in the 1960s, and just how lowly was rated the study of wild animals in relation to their environment. An Englishman called Henry Evans had devoted many years of his life to an investigation of red deer on the island of Jura, which he published in about 1890 as *Some Account of Jura Red Deer*, a study many years ahead of its time. He had got his stalkers to ear-tag newly born calves and to make systematic counts of dead deer in such a way as to unravel much of the demographics of that population. But it was left to Frank Fraser Darling to describe in detail the behaviour of wild Scottish deer in his *Herd of Red Deer*. This wonderfully readable account, published in 1937, had no follow-up until the work on Rum began in the sixties. Like so many others I had been taught by him to believe in the gravity and inevitability of the ecological crisis. When Fraser Darling died it always seemed to me that the obsequies were inadequate for a Scot of such genius and foresight.

The excitement of the rut and its meaning had stimulated Gerald to investigate the changes in the stag which precede the mating season. For example, the neck muscles of an adult stag, stimulated by the same testosterone that bodybuilders abuse, will double in girth in preparation for the rut and the fighting that will accompany it. With these colossal neck muscles a rutting stag could, I suppose, very easily turn over a small car. And then, of course, there is the yearly antler cycle. Very few people seem to understand this; and, even if they know that the antlers fall off and regrow each year, then many do not understand why.

The fact is that deer are distinguished from grazing species all over the world by, amongst other things, their antlers. Cattle, sheep, antelope, gazelle, goats, all possess *horns* and are called *bovids*; deer on the other hand grow *antlers* and are quite distinct, being called *cervids*. There is thus, you could argue, as close a relationship between, say, cows and goats as there is between, for example, fallow and roe deer; and in any case, it is quite clear that gazelle or antelope are more closely related to sheep or cows than they are to deer. It was for this reason that it came as no surprise to any zoologist that BSE, bovine spongiform encephalopathy, 'Mad Cow Disease', which had originated in cattle fed 'meat and bonemeal' derived from sheep infected with scrapie, also appeared in antelope in zoos but never in the deer.

Incidentally, while we're on that subject, 'meat and bonemeal' has been fed to livestock in Britain since at least the nineteenth century, and scrapie has been a recognised sheep disease for around 250 years. Thus, although we would all, especially journalists, like to allocate blame to greedy 'agribusinessmen' or feckless politicians, it may be a little unfair to pinpoint modern intensive farming practices as the cause of the BSE epidemic. So often we are told how unnatural it is to feed meat and bonemeal to herbivores, yet nothing is ever quite so black and white in biology. Herbivores have developed a strategy of eating vegetation which, especially grass, is highly indigestible, even if usually available in quantity. Cows have therefore only rudimentary skills in hunting other animals for the pot! Yet most grazing animals will, given a chance, chew up dead animals, or even live ones. I have seen deer knock over rabbits diseased with myxomatosis and chew them up, and an interesting paper was published by a scientist on Rum, which described deer waiting on the tops of the mountains for Manx shearwaters to make their nocturnal return to feed their chicks in burrows; the deer killed shearwaters by blows of the foreleg and then ate them. Deer on the impoverished grazings of Rum regularly chew cast antlers and will quite quickly reduce them to a stump – in fact they can sometimes be seen chewing on the antlers of their colleagues while they're still attached to their heads!

Now, I hear you, get back to the point: what is the difference between a horn and an antler? The answer is that the horn is permanent. It does not fall off each year like an antler, but instead is, in the middle, a live, growing thing. The outside is covered by a dead protective layer of keratin, like hooves or fingernails. Because horns grow all through an animal's life but at different rates depending on season and nutrition, the horns of a goat, for instance, have ridges which indicate the seasonal growth surges. In this way you can see the age of a goat by counting the ridges on its horns. The antler, in contrast, falls off each year and is replaced by another antler similar in shape. The antlers of a stag will in successive years tend to become larger, especially in his early years, but after about seven or eight they show little increase and will from about ten years start to become smaller again. It is clear then that stags do not produce a new point each year and there is no truth in the suggestion, dating back to Pliny, that you can age a stag by counting his antler points.

When a stag is growing his antlers, which for the red deer takes place during the summer, they are completely alive with lots of blood coursing through them and grow very rapidly, faster indeed than any other mammalian tissue (illustrations 1a, 5). Thus an adult red deer stag may grow a centimetre a day and its larger relative the Canadian elk up to an inch a day. At this time the antler is covered with fur, has nerves and can feel, as well as having veins and arteries, skin, hair and grease glands, and somehow, the innate ability to regrow in a shape similar to that of previous years. The regeneration of the antler is one of the mysteries of biology which, if we could fully understand it, might even open the door to allowing us to enable amputees to regenerate limbs.

Why do antlers drop off every year? As I have already mentioned, many stags break their antlers in fighting during the rut. On Rum I remember that the stag Cecil broke both his antlers off right at the base one year; but, by being able to make good that damage, the next year he was able to compete, unhandicapped, once more for access to the hinds. Thus a broken antler is not a total disaster for the individual. This means that he can afford to grow much more fancy headgear than the horned animal; for if a horn is broken, the bovid is almost certainly doomed to death and is in any case unlikely to be successful in breeding again. The fracture of an antler is but a temporary inconvenience.

And, while we are at it, why do they have antlers anyway? The answer is plainly and simply that the hard dead antler of deer is present for the rut; it is a weapon and a shield for competing with other stags for the favours of the females. The cleaning of the velvet and the appearance of the hard burnished antler coincides, as Gerald had shown, with the time of rapidly growing male sex hormone levels and it is thus very obviously ready for use in the rut. This comes as no surprise because it is quite clear from watching deer that they grow their antlers as secondary sexual characters. Antlers are deterrents and, since deterrents cannot work if no one dares to test them in earnest, they are also used in fighting off other stags with designs on the same group of hinds. These fights frequently result in injury. Stags may damage their eyes, break bones and, most commonly, their antlers, but usually by the next autumn those wounds have healed and the fight to perpetuate their genes is on again.

Evolutionarily we believe that antlers originated in something rather like the bumps on the heads of giraffes. We can imagine primordial deer fighting with their heads, then developing bony outgrowths which made them more effective in fighting. In a temperate climate only those young born in the spring would survive, so that successful matings could only take place over a short period. Thus the bony knobs would only be needed for a few weeks during which we can imagine them becoming damaged and a scabby growth forming. This scab would bring about healing ready for the next mating season. The larger the resulting bony structure the more intimidating it is and the more likely to be effective in a fight. Evidence for this theory comes from the fact that the velvet antler is seen when examined under the microscope to have much in common with a healing wound. This must all go to strengthen the possibility that a study of velvet antlers could do much to help an understanding of wound healing with possible human and veterinary benefits.

Gerald had gradually enticed a few stags into regular attendance at Kilmory by feeding them outside the Laundry with maize, and eventually this grew into a substantial number. A lot of my time was to be spent capturing these in order to mark them with either ear tags or neck collars. Indeed it had been to catch the deer that Roger had first come to Rum in the early sixties, shortly after the island had been sold to the Nature Conservancy. Sir Frank Fraser Darling had at that time made the memorable remark that Rum should be seen as a 'natural laboratory'. Work on the deer in this natural lab would be seriously impeded if it was not possible to identify them or if they were shot during the annual cull.

Roger, freshly returned from Africa where he had used the revolutionary new drug M99 to capture antelope, was the best man to help the Nature Conservancy. His first efforts involved the use of carrots.

A solution of the highly potent M99 was mixed with DMSO (dimethyl sulphoxide) and sealed into ampoules. DMSO has the fascinating property of being able to 'carry' other drugs through the skin. It used to be a popular trick for students to mix it with oil of peppermint. Dabbing a little on the finger has the remarkable effect of allowing the peppermint to taste in the mouth. The idea with the carrots was that if a phial were concealed in a carrot, a stag would greedily munch up the vegetable and then find himself transported into stupefaction. In practice the idea was not a great success, mostly because the stags had an uncanny facility for picking up a carrot, chewing it and then astonishingly spitting out the fragile ampoules intact.

After this, Roger developed a system using a crossbow, bought at a London toy shop, with metal darts designed by him and made up by the university engineering labs at Cambridge. Pressurised by a spring, the drug was sealed with a plastic tube which broke on impact. Sometimes, if the dart was in the bow for a time before a shot could be made, the plastic would rupture and release a fine spray of the drug. This unpredictable element lent an added dimension to the frisson of excitement as one waited to see if the chosen stag would wander into range.

At the time we were helping the manufacturers to evaluate M99, and had been given a substantial supply of the dry powder which had to be weighed and dissolved for use. This drug was the major breakthrough in the search for a potent tranquilliser for wild animals, as Roger had shown in Africa, where it was now being eagerly taken up for conservation and research work. However, evaluation was still under way and it was not yet available commercially. Before M99 came on to the market the most effective drug had been succinyl choline which had the horrific effect of paralysing the animal rather than rendering it unconscious. It has thankfully been superseded by M99 which seems to act perfectly humanely.

Although much discussion still centres around the means of firing a dart, the real high technology is the drug. It is now, looking back those thirty years, just amazing how effectively M99 and its chemical relatives have stood the test of time. There are still few – if any – drugs as effective. It can be reliably reversed to bring the animal back to consciousness: KO–OK as the manufacturers used to say in their promotional literature. It has allowed scientists to find out much more about large mammals, and one of the first applications was, for example, in the capture and evacuation of rhinos from the area to be flooded by the Kariba dam.

Its one drawback is the susceptibility of man to its effects. We didn't fully appreciate this in the early days, and I remember receiving a substantial dose squirted from a dart into my eye when I was alone and several miles from the nearest possible assistance. I washed it out in a burn and seemed none the worse. But since then some vets have recounted strange sensations from handling the drug and there have even been fatalities.

M99, now marketed as a constituent of the commercially available Immobilon, is also effective in sheep although I have never had occasion to use it for that purpose. A Cambridge research team needing to catch some of the wild Soay sheep on St Kilda once asked me to supply them with the drug, and after taking advice from the Royal College of Veterinary Surgeons, this I agreed to do.

The island of St Kilda is very remote. Its declining population was, sadly but inevitably, and by broad agreement amongst themselves, evacuated in 1930. By the time of their departure the St Kildans and their lifestyle, dependent on the capture of wild seabirds by climbing the huge sea cliffs, had become an anachronism for the amusement of passing tourist ships.

Over one hundred miles off the Scottish mainland, the island has served for years as an army outpost as well as a place for scientists to investigate its unique wild life. The garrison is served by air from Benbecula in the Outer Hebrides about sixty miles away, although there are occasional boat landings as well. By courtesy of the army, regular mail is dropped from aircraft because there is no landing strip. Since the Immobilon was wanted in a hurry it was despatched on the weekly mail drop by air, and because of the dangerous and urgent nature of the package of drugs, it was privileged to be given a mailbag to itself. Along with the other heavier bags, this one was flung out when the aircraft made its low-level pass but, being so light, it was whisked up by the slipstream and became firmly clamped to the tailplane whence it was retrieved after the aircraft had come to a standstill back in Benbecula. Ever helpful, the crew put a brick in the bag, flew back to St Kilda, and this time made an uneventful drop.

7   HUNTING, COOKING
AND WILD FOOD

I came to quite enjoy darting deer with tranquillisers. It had all the excitement of hunting, I suppose, without the *coup de grâce*. Man in those five or six million years before he learnt to domesticate animals must have developed a taste for hunting which was essential to his survival, and became fixed in his genetic make-up. The urge to hunt, now made redundant by farming, is still there, and this compulsion is evidenced by the hordes of modern hunters in North America or Europe and elsewhere, who take to the fields and forest each year, dwarfing even the Allied mobilisation of the Second World War.

The Spanish philosopher Ortega y Gasset wrote: 'Only the hunter, imitating the perpetual alertness of the wild animal, sees everything.' This seems to be the essence of why people enjoy hunting. The poet Ted Hughes was an avid hunter, and of fishing he wrote: 'Any kind of fishing provides that connection with the whole living world. It gives you the opportunity of being totally immersed, turning back into yourself in a good way. A form of meditation, communion with levels of yourself that are deeper then the ordinary self.' And 'hunting and fishing ... reconnect you in a gentle, natural way without going into artificial situations or altered consciousness. You just seem to go into a more natural mode. And people who don't fish and hunt are finding difficulty making that reconnection with the whole cycle.'

The same must be true, I imagine, of gardening. Why else do we have this urge to dabble in the mud every spring? And what about cooking? Upon the practice of these arts to occupy every waking moment depended the survival of our forebears. Isn't it reasonable to suppose that these ingrained survival skills have not left us in the few years since they have been made superfluous by industrial technology? Would you not expect them to have been incorporated into our genetic constitution? They remain the most popular of pastimes even if they are often sublimated in television. Probably more enjoy vicariously the preparation of food on the screen than in the kitchen now. Maybe the sight of others cooking is sufficient to satisfy that inherited urge to cook.

I am not particularly attracted to hunting – perhaps the primeval urge is sated by my work in darting animals – but I do understand the requirement, paradoxically on welfare and environmental grounds, in Scotland at least, both to reduce the deer population and keep it at such a level as to allow trees to regenerate and to prevent huge die-offs in bad winters. We vets are well versed in the practice of euthanasia, 'putting animals to sleep' when they are suffering, and the idea of allowing the wild deer population to increase to starvation point is anathema to most of us, let alone the ensuing environmental damage.

Talking about cooking, we naturally had to cook for ourselves on Rum. This pleased me greatly. Much of my time that should perhaps have been spent on more academic pursuits was spent cooking. Fiona knew about wine, something that Glasgow University had not prepared me for, and, with her knowledgeable participation, we gradually tasted. When she left for a year's overland travels with Gerald in search of the largest surviving reptile, the Komodo dragon, she left behind wine that we had jointly bought and which I shamefully consumed. The guilt remains, and perhaps still adds a certain piquancy to my interest in and enjoyment of wine.

But it was really in an appreciation of food that I passed the long evenings on the island. You might think the scope would have been fairly limited, but the island at that time still possessed a minute dairy herd to supply the inhabitants with fresh milk and cream. And there was a grocery delivery so that telephoned orders would be packed into cardboard boxes for the next day's ferry. And there was always the fish. Most of the daylight hours were sacrosanct – we were just too busy working; but occasionally we would fish for mackerel, and at the right time there were saithe that could be lured on to a hook with the clumsiest of baits – a hooked feather on a piece of twine on a long bamboo. The bay at Kilmory was quite frequently netted by a very respectable poacher in the summer nights, but I never got round to that and the best I achieved was, with Fiona's help, one or two sea-trout on a spinner.

One dark evening, Roger and I were walking back to the bothy. It was high tide and the sea was only a few feet from the post office door. We could not avoid noticing that the water was seething unnaturally. Whitebait were being driven ashore by, we supposed, mackerel. In a trice I had my pullover off and with the sleeves knotted had entangled several suppers' worth. The resulting glut has made me ambivalent to whitebait to this day.

The older folk on the island could recall when herring had been so plentiful that they too were sometimes driven on to the beach so families could fill their buckets, but by the 1970s those days were long gone. Mallaig had become the biggest herring-fishing port in Europe. Decrepit ships, some of which had evidently once depended on sail, were anchored offshore, and loaded herring from the fishing boats to take back to Scandinavia and Russia; they were known as klondikers. With the cured herrings in barrels piled high on their decks they didn't always seem the most seaworthy vessels, and we often found those barrels washed up on the beaches. And there was their modern counterpart, articulated juggernauts loading herring for a dash back to Holland and Germany. As the trucks were being loaded from the boats the herring spilled out on to the quay in great piles and, when in Mallaig, I used to shovel up a few bagfuls for pickling. It was no wonder that herring were less commonly driven ashore on Rum. We were witnessing the death throes of a time-honoured industry.

Once we found piles of labels on the beach at Kilmory. They were in Russian and must have belonged on tins of fish; frugally we used the backs of them for writing notes. Even more exciting was the discovery of an encoded ship's logbook, still clearly legible despite its immersion in the sea. Provocatively I sent a few sample pages up to the Foreign Office in London asking them to name their price for the rest of it; I never expected to hear any more. One evening though, George MacNaughton, the warden of the island and the only survivor of pre-Nature Conservancy days, came and knocked on the door. 'What is it, George?' I asked without the least thought of the logbook. 'Come on in.' George, amongst his many official duties on the small island such as lifeboatman, coastguard, mountain rescuer, etc., was also policeman. He looked unnaturally grave and came uncharacteristically straight to the point. 'Did you find some papers on the beach and send some of them up to London?' There was no denying it. 'They want the rest now and you are legally charged to hand them over.' And off they went, evidently a Russian submarine's log.

For shellfish on Rum we ate crabs and mussels, but the mussels, though extra-delicious, were very small and laborious to prepare. Later, Tim Clutton Brock had a rubber dinghy and lobster pots but it was mostly crabs he caught. I grew some herbs in the garden but the one I remember best was the wild thyme from the hills; perfect with cream and fried mushrooms and puff-balls, gathered on the closely deer-grazed greens above the dunes. I also developed a taste for puddings. Fiona would painstakingly beat egg whites into a meringue with a fork and then we would create queen of puddings, lemon meringue pie and so on.

But above all there was the venison. At that time the culling required to keep the deer population in bounds was carried out by Geordie Stirton, a man from East Scotland. Small in stature but formidable in talent, he was assisted by one or two other stalkers who often tried Geordie's patience. One played the pipes and, encouraged by a little whisky, once waded the Kinloch river in his kilt with pipes in full skirl.

Geordie was an excellent butcher and each household would, in season, receive a weekly venison allowance, magically left on the kitchen table. This was usually from adult deer and as often as not would have a layer of fat around the outside; years later I came to understand that younger deer, up to about two years old, would have no fat. We ate our venison in fairly conservative ways. Braising was a favourite because the rolled and boned shoulder, or whatever it was, could, after a quick browning in the frying pan, be placed in a covered pot with a few onions and put in the Raeburn oven in the morning as we set off to the hill. By the time we returned, often past midnight in the spring, we would be greeted by an exquisite aroma and a magnificent feast. Nothing could be easier; convenience food indeed.

Apart from the slow braising we would sometimes roast a piece of haunch. The Raeburn would be carefully stoked with coal, riddled and have its ash-pit door opened to raise the fire to a good heat, then in with the joint. I learnt that the fat on a mature stag's haunch is almost inedible. It has a very high melting point; certainly it has a distinct and pleasant flavour, but a mouthful taken even quite hot can congeal rapidly in the mouth, especially if inadvertently cooled by a draught of wine, truly rendering the inexperienced venison eater speechless. A similar effect, though less instantaneous, could probably be achieved by chewing candles. Indeed, the use of deer tallow for candles must be almost as old a practice as fire itself. There exist antique serving dishes with a base designed to take hot water so as to keep the meat warm, and these were designed specifically for venison. Now I learnt why.

Geordie, I discovered, took most of the fat off the carcases and turned it into a leather soap for the stalking saddles the ponies wore to carry the carcases down from the hill. And that is one very great advantage of the venison carcase, for the fat is carried, most conveniently for the consumer, around the kidneys and over the haunches; it can be very simply removed to leave the flesh virtually fat-free. Unlike beef and lamb, venison has no fat insidiously lurking in the muscles. That is partly why the meat from the deer is so dark red. This lean meat is, I found, wonderful. I know now that it has less fat even than the skinless flesh of chicken. The market for such a 'designer meat' – one that can be safely recommended for those on low-fat diets and yet which tastes superb and is so tender that it melts in the mouth – had to be assured.

It also crossed my mind that mankind had been eating venison for most of his time and that it was only on the last stroke of midnight, so to speak, that he had resorted to eating 'improved' domestic animals. His system must be better adapted to venison consumption than to the fattier beef and lamb. Later I found that others had pursued this theory in depth, and shown that not only is venison healthier in containing less fat, but that what fats there are, as well as the other constituents such as iron, are present in healthier forms in venison. This meat could, with a willing minister of agriculture, be a valuable weapon in fighting the epidemic of heart disease and obesity.

All my time at veterinary school in Glasgow I had been conscious of the pressure on the meat industry to reduce fat levels, yet here in Scotland, in abundance, was a meat leaner by far than anything that could be produced by cattle, sheep, pigs or even chicken. Like many other students we had eaten wild venison steaks bought at the game dealers in Byres Road; it had been not only good eating then, but also cheap. And, for me, an added attraction was the way in which venison could be obtained so humanely. A quick shot and then oblivion; there was no need for the horrors of the abattoir. An idea began to formulate itself.

I could see the difficulties that even such a perfectionist as Geordie had in achieving really good carcases. Stalking was time-consuming; three or four in a day was good going and required two men. Unless very close to the beast, a head or neck shot was impossible and the chest or heart shot was the objective. That destroyed a lot of the shoulder meat. And then there was the question of age.

Rum is an exception but on all other estates the stags are shot to produce trophies for the paying sportsmen. This means that stag venison is from deer that might be mere 'knobbers' but could be up to ten or even twelve years old. And ageing the hinds, however carefully stalkers try, is never foolproof so that with them too the age at death is very variable. When the hinds are shot it is customary to shoot their calves at foot as well to avoid leaving orphans, so that a proportion of the venison is immature. And after the shot, there is the practical difficulty of retrieving the carcases in good condition from very remote locations. On Rum there are ponies but most estates use 'all-terrain vehicles' of one sort or another.

As a student at Glasgow I had visited a large venison dealer and seen something of the game trade from his side. His difficulties, he had explained, were the very seasonal nature of the business, with something like 60 per cent of the red deer coming into his premises during only a month to six weeks of the year. This meant that the best he could do was freeze everything or hope to get some of it away as quickly as possible to his main market in Germany. He had to arrange collection from remote deer forests, often during the depths of winter, entailing journeys of hundreds of miles for perhaps only two or three carcases. Stalkers, he said, were under great pressure to shoot large numbers of hinds in an effort to control the population and consequently the bullets did not always go where they should, so that there was much damaged meat. Sometimes carcases were left overnight on the hill so that putrefaction developed. In the spring, carcases were often emaciated, whilst in the rut they stank, and in the late summer were too fat. I had already seen the warble damage so I knew that many carcases needed extensive trimming to remove those as well, and the hides were virtually worthless owing to the warble holes.

Ironically, because you could never tell where the deer had been grazing – they might have spent the night on some recently sprayed arable crop, for example – wild venison could not even qualify for organic status.

It became very clear to me that, with the best will in the world, no game dealer could possibly supply venison of the quality that Geordie gave us on Rum, consistently, day in, day out. By the hygiene standards of the beef and lamb trade, game venison would have been almost completely condemned.

Of course that was many years ago and there have been many improvements made, but I could see the intrinsic difficulties then and it encouraged me to ponder the advantages of embarking on a project to produce modern-day park venison from a 'deer farm'. Here quality venison would be the objective and the meat would not be a by-product of the sporting industry.

8 VENISON, THE FOOD OF OUR ANCESTORS

About this time, in 1970 or 1971, word had begun to drift back from the mainland that Kenneth, later to become Sir Kenneth, Blaxter, Director of the Rowett Research Institute, had managed, despite scepticism from an entrenched establishment, to get a scheme off the ground to investigate the feasibility of farming deer. Roger had attended a meeting to discuss the idea in Aberdeen in 1969 and from this had sprung a pilot project.

It says a very great deal for the far-sightedness of Blaxter that he saw this through against heavy odds. His motivation was to provide an alternative for the vast area of marginal land in the Scottish Highlands for which the only choice was then – and is still – hill sheep or trees. This marginal land makes up three-quarters of Scotland and over more than half of this, wild red deer roam.

Blaxter had observed, of hill-sheep farming, how, during the late sixties 'any meagre profit was entirely due to the amount of subsidy support. Indeed it was estimated, on the basis of careful costing, that 130–190 per cent of the net profit of these farms was accounted for by the subsidy payments they received.' The most remarkable thing about this is that the general picture and even the figures remain almost unchanged today, thirty years later: very few hill-sheep farmers, if indeed any, are not wholly dependent on subsidy, even if that subsidy is now passed through the Common Agricultural Policy.

As a result farmers have increasingly reduced their inputs and hill shepherds have become more and more thin on the ground. Yet because the subsidies are paid on a headage basis the flock is undiminished. The sheep are less frequently gathered and have almost become wild animals. Grazing alongside those sheep are the wholly wild red deer which breed so successfully in the Highlands that it is not always easy to keep their population in bounds.

A few preliminary investigations were undertaken at the Rowett Research Institute and proved very encouraging. They showed that deer ate and digested more heather than sheep did on similar grazings, suggesting that they might be dietarily better adapted to the rough hill land. 'Furthermore, the experience gained in handling captive deer ... showed how very tame they could become.'

Blaxter pointed out that venison prices, reflecting demand from Europe, were so strong in the late sixties and early seventies that 'the monetary return from a red deer carcase had ... become about double that from a hill ewe'.

The extensive hill grazing land in the Highlands produces around two to three kilograms of sheep meat per hectare whilst some deer forests achieve over one kilo of venison per hectare. On the face of it this makes the sheep sound more productive than the deer, but it has to be remembered that the sheep are managed to maximise meat production with only a small number of adult males; the overwhelming proportion of the flock is productive ewes and, furthermore, the young stock are removed before winter. The deer herd is, on the contrary, managed with the sole object of yielding more adult males with antler trophies. Consequently a very large proportion of the deer population is made up of unproductive males.

Blaxter continued: 'It seemed possible that meat production from this poor land might well be similar under some type of deer husbandry system to what it was under a subsistence hill farming economy. It also seemed possible that a wild animal, which for many hundreds of years had survived under these poor conditions on the hills, might be better adapted to them than the domesticated sheep.' Blaxter did not say so – perhaps he was too much of a diplomat – but he must also have been thinking that the Middle Eastern origin of sheep hardly encourages us to imagine that they would be at their most efficient in the Scottish Highlands. Developed by man largely for wool production, the fleece of hill sheep now scarcely repays the costs of shearing. The wool of British sheep is ideal for the manufacture of carpets; those woolly pullovers for which Scotland is famous are today often made from wool from Australian sheep and, sadly, are sometimes even manufactured in the Far East.

Eventually Blaxter's ideas led to a meeting, the Rowett Deer Conference of January 1969. When you read the report of that 1969 meeting the sense of dull, entrenched opposition to anything so radical still jumps out of the polite enough text. Almost all the delegates were civil servants or academics and most were very negative.

The eminent Professor Wynne-Edwards, summarising the meeting, stated that: 'Intensive deer farming would, in practice, be fraught with difficulty and almost certainly unprofitable financially.' The Highlands and Islands Development Board representative said: 'Every new development is a process of experimentation which, like marriage, should be entered into with caution and circumspection.' Echoes of the manse there, and Blaxter remarked that it 'appeared that such was the caution and circumspection that the whole concept might never attain a consummation!'

But Blaxter stuck to his guns. He was assisted by the ineluctable fact that venison prices, from animals with non-existent rearing costs, compared very favourably with the price of heavily subsidised lamb. Finally a research project was sanctioned. Funding was offered by the Department of Agriculture, and the Rowett Research Institute and the Hill Farming Research Organisation entered into a joint research programme.

An area of over two hundred hectares mostly lying around one thousand feet above sea level and consisting largely of heather grazings was chosen for the project. The farm is known as Glensaugh and lies above Fettercairn immediately east of the Cairn o' Mount road to

Banchory. It is reached by a long forestry road through pine woods.

The initial breeding stock were collected, as Dick Youngson's had been, by watching hinds to see where they had lain their calves. We used to do the same on Rum in order to ear-tag, weigh and sex wild calves. For the first few days of life a deer calf will rest immobile and can be approached, handled and, for the Glensaugh project, picked up and reared on a bottle. Hinds will leave their calves and travel up to a mile off, returning only two or three times a day to suckle, so this is feasible though testing work. It requires great determination to watch a hind a mile or more away for hours at a time, through a telescope, when midges are feeding. At times even wearing a pair of tights over the head was not enough, and that in any case made using binoculars or a telescope almost impossible.

The calves for Glensaugh were gathered by a dedicated band of enthusiasts and gently loaded into rucksacks for the journey down the hill. Usually within twenty-four hours they were eagerly awaiting their bottle and bidding fair to pull the teat off. The success rate in rearing these calves was good and, of course, it guaranteed friendly breeding stock. Two or three of Dick's Rum deer were contributed to the Glensaugh project as a gesture of goodwill and year by year Kenneth Blaxter's project grew.

Not, it must be said, without opposition. On the first open day Bill Hamilton, the manager, was approached by a titled landowner who confided to him: 'I might as well let you know that I personally hope this project proves completely unsuccessful.' Bill later told me with a twinkle in his eye what he thought of such prejudice. Not all land-owners were like that and Bill was later roped in to present progress reports on the Glensaugh project to the Duke of Edinburgh and other influential Highland landlords.

It was always interesting that the estate deerstalkers, that is to say the men employed as full-time professionals, who guide visiting sportsmen to the stag in the autumn, and then later in the depths of winter shoot hinds, in my experience almost invariably welcomed the deer-farming concept. These stalkers spend their lives working with deer at arm's length, or more accurately rifle's and telescope's length. Yet many do not have the chance to see the deer year round, since the fishing or the grouse may intervene, and in any case the deer are always wild and distant. Avid for real knowledge of their charges, most working stalkers embrace the notion of domesticating the deer with enthusiasm.

These professional stalkers are the ones who know the reality that is the lot of wild red deer: challenged by the weather, often short of feed in the winter and spring, and host to a horrible burden of parasites. Many stalkers have also had direct experience of bottle-feeding orphan calves for one reason or another. With most stalkers, Blaxter's idea of 'farming the red deer' struck a chord: by careful winter feeding and by treatment of the deer to get rid of the warbles and other parasites, they knew the farmed deer would be the lucky ones.

Yet the lairds, often absent endeavouring to earn sufficient to keep their Highland estates, were, like most amateur hunters in Europe and North America, often vigorously and instinctively opposed to the idea of farming deer. Perhaps they felt threatened, or maybe it was their reluctance to lose a dream. They had been brought up in the wonderful tradition of Buchan's John McNab, flavoured with all the Victorian and Edwardian sporting literature of the Scottish Highlands. To these romantics deer are noble and mysterious, leading a life quite independent of man except when prey to the rifle. Any attempt to interfere with their freedom by putting up a fence to contain them, for instance, is an abomination. The fact that each spring several thousand Scottish deer might die of starvation was often overlooked; the laird was not usually about the deer forest then, and the stalker was perhaps not always too keen to let his employer know the scale of deaths on the hill.

Heavy losses of deer and a reluctance to admit to them have perhaps become a thing of the past, largely as a result of the Red Deer Commission (now with responsibility for all deer species and renamed the Deer Commission for Scotland) and the formation of adjoining deer forests into local deer management groups. Over the years many landowners have become sympathetic to deer farming and some have joined our ranks.

It is as well to remember too that the taxpayer actually benefits from the sporting estates which were, until recently at least, compelled to pay rates. The sporting estate may not represent the most popular sector in the public eye, but it is still about the only form of land use in Britain – apart of course from deer farming – that is independent of state handouts. And the incoming sportsmen and women, whether from southern Scotland, England, the Low Countries or the USA, do much to sustain the Highland economy.

Anyway, there was no doubt that the deer at Glensaugh appeared very content. Bottle-fed, they had early come to associate the farmer with the good things in life, and most of those working with deer were delighted how readily even the second generation, that had been suckled naturally by their mothers, were evidently relaxed and approachable. It was those animals themselves that converted some of the sceptics, for who could fail to be charmed by deer that, far from showing any signs of stress, were very obviously more at home in human company than most hill sheep and cattle. I had already been struck by the ease with which the tame deer I had been using for my experimentation on Rum could be managed; the Glensaugh project seemed to me certain to succeed.

And there was another angle to this. As a vet student compelled to rise early to do my dark winter stint at the Glasgow municipal abattoir, the horrors of trucking animals to a massive central killing point had left a forcible impression on me. Slaughter on such a scale is almost inevitably stressful for the livestock and also brutalising for the men paid to do it. My occasional sorties with the deerstalker had seemed less demeaning for man and beast. And if the deer were farmed and approachable to close quarters then their despatch by rifle could be completely instantaneous. A modern deer park or farm, it seemed to me, might be able to provide meat not only of healthier composition but also more humanely than other systems, even if not on a very large scale.

In fact Kenneth Blaxter had understood from the outset that the farmed deer would have to be killed in a slaughtering facility located either on the farm or at a neighbouring abattoir. Years later when I saw those deer passing through a commercial abattoir my worries were largely quieted.

Underwriting the whole concept was my faith in the quality of the meat: demand seemed assured. From the days when as Glasgow students my flatmate Anthony, another embryo vet, and I had vied with each other to produce the most economical and impressive spreads for our girlfriends, the value of good food had been clear to me. Although occasionally, like Ernest Hemingway, I resorted to street pigeons snatched untimely from the claws of our landlords' Burmese cat, Pico, most guests fared rather better. No matter that the girls' ideas of pushing out the boat were limited to spaghetti bolognese; when they came to eat with us it was jugged hare, or, inspired by Elizabeth David, venison cutlets in the Ardennes style. I suppose that I already felt that food, especially flesh, was something sacred which demanded care in its preparation.

Which brings me back to perhaps the most important reason for attempting to farm deer. Kenneth Blaxter's institute, the Rowett, is avowedly concerned with the nutrition of both man and beast and he was anxious to investigate an animal which could not only survive and breed successfully on the impoverished Highlands, when sheep required substantial mollycoddling, but would also yield a carcase with a proportion of prime-grade lean meat that should have been the envy of the cattle and sheep farmers. At that time cattle farmers were still using implants of steroid hormones to make their carcases grow quicker and leaner.

But Sir Kenneth never seems to have made much play of the leanness of venison. Perhaps it was less topical in those days or conceivably he was such a diplomat that he did not want to inflame the cattle and sheep farmers. Instead of the low fat levels of venison, Blaxter and his colleagues concentrated on the conformation of the carcase, pointing out that the proportion of high-value cuts suitable for quick cooking – frying and roasting – was very much higher in deer than in cattle and sheep.

In my eyes it was above all the absence of fat that made the meat, already recognised by me as supremely delicious, also highly marketable. This endowed the deer-farming concept with an ethical basis in that deer farmers would be producing a food that would save lives. We had the basis for a moral crusade.

At that time I didn't know the actual figures or I might have been even more enthusiastic. But I know them now. As the officially accepted figures from the most recent edition of the standard McCance and Widdowson's Composition of Foods show, 100 grams of venison contain only 103 kilocalories compared to beef with 198, lamb with 187, pork with 213, whole chicken 201, or skinned 108. And of course venison has more protein, and is also much higher than other meats in many other nutritional goodies. For example, 100 grams of venison contain 3.3 grams of iron in comparison to beef with 1.7, lamb 1.4, and chicken and pork 0.7. The published levels of fat show venison with 1.6 grams per 100 grams, whole chicken 13.8, skinned chicken 2.1, beef 12.9, lamb 12.3 and pork 15.2. In cholesterol content venison has much less than other meats and only around one-third that of skinned chicken. Venison also comes top of the list in its content of that emblem of the healthy eater, the celebrated omega-3 and omega-6 fatty acids, a much-vaunted panacea for heart disease.

These figures mean that those dieting for reasons of cardiac care, or diabetics reducing their fat intake, or even just those eager to lose weight, can now eat a red meat confident that it is doing them much less harm than even skinned chicken. And of course for athletes and bodybuilders, venison is the ideal food.

On Rum, Geordie's venison had allowed us to taste the meat in all its guises; I had soon become a complete convert to the innocent delights of good food. We rarely ate lunch but thought we had deserved a good dinner. How wonderful is an appetite when you can readily satisfy it; however much abused, it always, in good health and with exercise, returns. If we are lucky enough to have food when so many are hungry then a lack of interest or care in the cooking seems to me akin to blasphemy or sacrilege. In the words of Burns:

> Some ha'e meat and canna eat,
> Some would eat that want it:
> But we ha'e meat and we can eat,
> Sae let the Lord be thankit.

And so it was that ideas for farming deer once my time on Rum was over grew stronger.

9 BASKING SHARKS AND 'SELF-SUFFICIENCY'

Looking back now it is clear that in spite of a healthy, youthful confidence in my own originality I was inevitably a child of the times. As a student I had hitch-hiked all over Europe, North Africa, and Central and North America; the hippie movement with its apocalyptic vision of a future redeemable only by renunciation of material extravagance no doubt influenced me. I have already mentioned the Reith lectures given by Fraser Darling; equally relevant was the publication of *The Blueprint for Survival* by Edward Goldsmith. To me as a biologist the scenarios depicted rang very true. At school I had read Rachel Carson's *Silent Spring*, and at Glasgow Anthony and I had had 'Ban DDT' stickers printed and distributed. This was despite forthright opposition from some of the staff who reasonably pointed out that DDT had probably saved more lives than any other chemical man had ever produced. That argument still goes on, as malaria continues to rank as one of the world's biggest killers and DDT as its most effective opponent.

There was a sense of being part of a 'back to the countryside' movement. John Seymour had had a great success with a series of books on what he called self-sufficiency. It is hard to recall now just how insecure the future seemed then but in 1973, with Mr Heath's three-day week and the Arabs' success in raising oil prices, times were exciting and any outcome seemed possible.

Another consideration was getting married. I had admired Nickie from afar as the schoolgirl daughter of my landlords for a year at Glasgow, but we only really got to know each other on a sailing weekend on Loch Fyne.

It is strange how often there are decisive periods of just a few years or months when everything in one's life can be epoch-making, vivid and important. Looking back on such times we know that nothing can ever again be so momentous.

For me such a time was the spring and summer of 1970 and it reached its exquisite pinnacle on one particular weekend. My place at Cambridge was secure; we had had our final veterinary exam results that Friday afternoon. Anthony had had a legacy a few months earlier, £500 I think, and he had, against my sober and boring advice, pur-chased a decrepit sports car which he figured would enhance his success with the girls. Within weeks of yielding to the blandishments of the dubious Great Western Road car salesman, Anthony had found himself one moment sitting behind the wheel of his superb racing machine and the next resting his bottom on that same Great Western Road. Rust had triumphed. A skilled welder was enlisted and so it was that Anthony was able to give me a lift up to Loch Fyne so that we could celebrate our exam results.

I have entertaining memories of that drive. It was a peerless night. At an early stage in the journey the exhaust system began to part company with the engine but as we roared, hood down, up the twisty road beside Loch Lomond, we revelled in the sporty sound. Midnight in June in the west of Scotland is a magic twilit time even when you are being deafened and gassed. Then quite suddenly the engine began to falter. Anthony managed to coast in under a street lamp beside a small and ancient roadside pub, and we raised the bonnet. Underneath, a very pretty sight met our eyes. The engine was suffused with a deep orange glow whilst from one of the electrical connections, a plug lead, long white sparks arced across to any piece of metal they could find. By deft poking with a bit of stick whilst Anthony sat in the cockpit, I managed to push the offending plug lead into a position where the arcing abated. Just to check the success of my 'repair' I shouted to Anthony, 'Rev her up a bit.' This he did to good effect and the countryside reverberated gratifyingly to the ear-splitting roar. It was at this moment that about eighteen inches behind and above my ear I became aware of a soft and patient voice: 'Will ye be long?' it was asking. Looking up I could see it came from a 'benightied' female form leaning out of her bedroom window, pale-faced, polite and patient. But certainly not beckoning.

Surprisingly the journey was thereafter more or less uneventful. A pause, as the name of the infamous Rest and Be Thankful Pass demands, showed that the climb had added to the brilliance of the orange glow, but still the car ran.

On arrival at the cottage Anthony went in to his lady so I, alone, taking a bottle of whisky, rowed out into the middle of the flat calm loch and lay down in the bottom of the boat. What a wonderful thing it is to have achieved something long worked for and so clear and simple as a happy exam result. There seemed no worries. For the young person privileged and optimistic there are no shadows of the difficulties that adulthood may bring, just a sublime confidence. It grew darker. I became aware of a gentle unexpected movement of the boat and a hissing as the surface of the water was broken. Reluctantly I forced myself into a sitting position and put my head over the gunwale. What I saw tested my powers of credulity, for only three or four yards away were several enormous black triangular dorsal fins each protruding one or two feet from the water and cruising around me in a good imitation of a cartoon drawing in the newspaper. Of course, as a newly qualified veterinary, I knew these were only harmless plankton-filtering basking sharks incapable of eating me even if they had had an urge in that direction; but as it was, alone in the middle of the loch in the middle of the night armed only with a half empty-bottle of whisky . . .

I rowed as hard as I could for the shore.

And it was the next day that I met Nickie. Setting off in a little flotilla, she impressed me no end by jumping into my dinghy and abandoning her boyfriend of the previous two years. Are women prey to an evolutionary strategy which inclines them to choose men who are innovators and unorthodox? I flatter myself they are. On one of the happiest days of my life, we became becalmed and entangled on a perfect June afternoon off Inveraray. The basking sharks, much less threatening in the sunshine and with Nickie to bolster my courage, were still cruising around the loch. In the distance they occasionally leaped quite clear of the water, plainly audible a mile or more away as they crashed back in again. Or sometimes they inspected us so closely we could touch them with an oar. That didn't deter Nickie from suggesting that we swim off the boat despite the absence of bathing clothes. Then a few weeks later she hitch-hiked down to Cambridge and I was very definitely impressed. Perhaps to a scientist an art student seems especially beguiling; in any event I had no doubts that life with Nickie would be fun.

We were married on 8 July 1972 in Glasgow University Chapel while I was still working on Rum and while Nickie was still studying at Edinburgh Art College to be a jeweller, with a group of crafts-men and -women friends. Indeed so talented a jeweller was she that the college encouraged her to stay on for a post-graduate year and rewarded her with a scholarship.

Meanwhile, the idea of a rural retreat and an attempt to be 'self-sufficient' became more and more attractive. Not only to Nickie and myself but to many of our friends. Tim Stead, the sculptor of wood and creator of furniture; David Kaplan and Annica Sandstrom, the glass-blowers; and Mike de Haan, the potter, all settled down in the Scottish countryside that year. And they are all there still except for the South African, Mike, who was always restless, hankering for warmer weather. He finally settled in New Zealand. We were all of a time, and establishing bases in the country was important to us all. The die was cast. Those makers, as craftsmen are now apparently called, were the cream of the art colleges, each highly talented; and while once it annoyed me, now it only amuses that the unimaginative, hidebound structure of the 'arts' establishment almost completely ignores them. Only painters, writers, musicians, film-makers, occasional sculptors and, strangely, potters seem to gain a mention, in the arts radio broadcasts at any rate.

Was it just the sixties that enthused us with an idealism? Or are all young people like that? I often encourage myself in dark moments by thinking that every time a new baby is born mankind has a reprieve, because that person is a clean canvas on which we can all start again. I suppose we felt in the sixties and seventies that rural labour was in some way liberating. It has been said that in youth we should all be socialists.

> Is there for honest poverty
> That hings his head, an' a' that?
>
> Then let us pray that come it may –
> As come it will, for a' that –
> That sense and worth, o'er a' the earth
> Shall bear the gree, an' a' that;
> For a' that, an' a' that,
> Its comin yet for a' that,
> That man to man the world o'er,
> Shall brothers be for a' that.

Even if, as we mature, and boring responsibility and the need to support our progeny and prepare for our own decrepitude intrude, and our liberal notions wane, we were once idealists, weren't we?

Meantime Nickie was developing her skills at Edinburgh as well as being given two prestigious travel bursaries. These she decided to use on a visit to Czechoslovakia to see a jewellery exhibition at Jablonec near the Polish border and I was to be allowed to go along too. It was only three years after the Russian invasion following the Prague spring and our impressions were of a country desperately subdued. We saw a Russian soldier rudely treating an elderly and tearful lady on the streets, they searched under the train and under the seats at the border. This was oppression and nothing to do with our socialist ideals. We should have known. The world is full of paradoxes: churches which preach love can create the Inquisition, or the Irish problem, or ban contraception, and now here was a socialist 'democracy' running a despotic nightmare.

With the clarity of vision of unquestioning youth, we had no doubt but that a small farm was what we wanted to occupy for the rest of our lives. For some reason that Czech trip confirmed us in our plans.

Back in Cambridge I wrote to the accomplished botanist and eminent classics don at King's College, John Raven, because I knew that he had a Highland estate at Ardtornish; perhaps he would have somewhere we could try out my deer farming ideas. He generously asked us both to spend a day or two at Ardtornish so that we could talk it over. John was tremendously welcoming and keen to help but somehow neither Nickie nor I felt that the situation was quite right either for us, or for marketing the venison, and the estate factor at that time was clearly unenthusiastic too. Reluctantly we decided to keep on looking.

While we were at Ardtornish I asked John Raven about the Heslop Harrison affair. In the 1940s a Professor of Botany at Newcastle called John Heslop Harrison had stretched the credulity of the scientific establishment by making a series of remarkable reports of plants and insects that he claimed to have found on the Isle of Rum. These all gave support to his theory that Rum had not been covered by ice during the last glaciation. John Raven, then a young research fellow at King's, had followed Heslop Harrison to Rum in 1948 in an effort to find out whether these claims could be true. John told us in minute detail what he had seen and how he had stalked the Professor. Clearly he was in no doubt that many of those discoveries had indeed been 'plants' introduced with a trowel and were fraudulent.

Later I asked the warden on Rum, Peter Wormell, what he thought of it all. Peter said that he was frequently surprised just how many of Heslop Harrison's finds had subsequently been vindicated. Nevertheless many were truly incredible. He also told the strange tale of how in 1961 the Professor, by then a very old man, had visited Rum for the last time. He had wanted to return to the site of his finding of *Carex bicolor*, the obscure sedge which had proved to be his most controversial claim. Peter had taken him part of the way and had instructed some of the children on the island not to let him out of their sight. Unfortunately the cloud had descended and the Professor was lost and made his own way down. When Peter caught up with him in the evening sure enough he had a fresh sample of *Carex bicolor* in a plastic bag. It was a very romantic story.

After Ardtornish I returned to Rum, and Nickie was charged with attempting to locate a suitable small farm and I promised to come off Rum to look at the fruits of her searching as soon as there was something to look at. My brother Paul generously offered to contribute and, because my father had passed on some of my inheritance on my marriage, we were able to hope for a very small farm. That all sounds so easy to say now and in fact it was. Land prices and house prices were still low and we were, of course, very lucky to be able to do what we did.

Deprived of her new husband, it took Nickie only two weeks to find our farm. Immediately she wrote in one of her enthusiastically illustrated letters: 'and there is a small farm advertised at Auchtermuchty ... the particulars say: "Reediehill is situated about two miles northwest of Auchtermuchty on the Mournipea Road leading to Pitmedden Forest. The farm extends to about 48 acres and it is considered that up to 40 suckler cows could be carried. The farmhouse faces south and could be developed into an attractive home." '

'Where's Auchtermuchty?' I wrote back.

10 THE DEER MOVE IN – AND OUT

We went to look at Reediehill on a wet autumn day in 1973. Two miles up a steep hill out of the royal burgh of 'Muchty we drove before the road turned and led us down to the bottom of the farm track. Five hundred yards of unmetalled rock and gravel track clinging to the side of a wooded ghyll above the little burn and we were there. Though it didn't occur to me then, that road was Reediehill's umbilicus and upon its continued existence depended the survival of the farm; there was no other way to get there. The fields were north-facing and sodden but the little house, two up, two down, was bright and dry and, as it had said, looked south. There was no garden but a fenced enclosure in front of the cottage in which a cow had just slipped a dead calf. I did not take this as a portent although I guessed that the cause was brucellosis.

We had arranged to meet the vendor who arrived in the pouring rain, got out of his car and then stood silent and stationary for two minutes. I had forgotten it was Remembrance Sunday.

We both felt there was no need to look further. Strangely without any feeling of undue moment, we placed our bids by sealed tender, in the way these things happen in Scotland. And a week later we became the owners of Reediehill Farm, forty-eight acres of north-facing grassland seven hundred feet above sea level at a latitude that puts us closer to the Arctic Circle than is Moscow. As they say, lock (the house), stock (the aborting cows) and barrel (perhaps the 'unexpired manurial residues' detailed in the sales particulars) (illustration 4).

Later, of course, we learnt much about Reediehill and its situation. Not only that Jimmy Shand, the celebrated accordionist and band-leader, and now Sir Jimmy Shand, with many gold discs and a gold heart too, was our illustrious neighbour, but that the road was a long-established drove road by which cattle had been driven between the fertile Howe of Fife on the east and Perth, Strathearn, Strathtay and the Highlands to the north and west. From the hill above us you can see from Ben Lomond on the west to Dundee's tower blocks and the coast in the east and the Highlands – Schiehallion, Lochnagar and the Angus hills – in the north, whilst to the south is Loch Leven and its island castle whence Mary, Queen of Scots escaped by night.

Nickie and I, and later Stella and Martha, have come to love that small farm with a ferocious passion, almost like a parent's for a child. When, much later, we feared that we might not be able to go on living there, the bottom really did seem to fall out of our lives. But neither Nickie nor I believed for a minute that we should spend more than a few years at Reediehill. It was, we thought then, almost inconceivable that we should still be living there thirty years on.

More important than the views from the hill were the people of Auchtermuchty. Apart from transient school and university life I had never before really been part of a community. We have always been made welcome, and considering that we came as complete foreigners, erected six-foot-high deer fences around the place and 'Venison for Sale' signs, and then when invited to give talks I sometimes forgot to go, I think we have been lucky.

My brother Paul agreed to buy half the land, which amounted to a third share of the value then, and I was to pay him a fair agricultural rent for this. It must have been the worst investment that he ever made but without his enthusiasm we should not have been able to proceed. With the land secure we could now deal with the deer.

I had become very involved with the tame deer on Rum, and as they had naturally multiplied during the years, there had arisen the question of what to do with the surplus. Someone had to pay for their daily feeding. Turning them out of the enclosure on to the island would not have worked; they would have hung around the fence and the houses making a nuisance of themselves. They were far too tame ever to integrate with the wild population. For a while their fate hung in the balance. I knew, of course, what I wanted to happen to the animals. I wanted my old friends to become the nucleus of a breeding herd. They were to be the subjects of a grand experiment. I wanted to take them off to Auchtermuchty where I would watch what became of them and let them realise their full productive potential, but first it would have to be cleared with the Nature Conservancy, as it was then, who owned the island and the deer. Fortunately, with generosity and a minimum of bureaucracy, they agreed.

The next problem was how to get the deer off the island. In the past, occasional deer such as those sent to Glensaugh had been shipped by putting them in a crate and manhandling the crate from the landing stage into the boat and then out of the boat on to the ferry and finally from ferry to lorry or even train.

I tried this once with two tame yearling hinds. The crates would not, of course, fit in the Mini Moke so I put them on the train at Mallaig. My recollection is that they came, by some quite complicated routing, direct to Edinburgh Waverley and there under the shadows of the castle I loaded them into a friend's borrowed trailer for the last stage of their journey to Auchtermuchty. How strange that idea seems now when we cannot, I think, put any livestock on trains.

Anyway, it is very clear that this experience was not very nice for man or beast. Yet this time-honoured system of individual crating had been the one used for centuries, most recently for the restocking of the Highlands in the Victorian era and onwards till at least the Second World War. During that hundred years or so countless deer had been sent up north by train in crates from English deer parks. I have spoken to an old man who recalls going with his father in a horse and cart to a rural rail halt in Yorkshire, now a tearoom; there he collected two crates of English park deer and took them back to his farm where for thirty years or so those deer and their descendants remained, occasionally jumping stone walls for a brief 'donder' around.

What a nasty shock for big English beasts, spoilt with soft life on lowland pasture, to suffer the stresses of a probably rather primitive capture, and a lengthy journey, before the sudden arrival and turning-out on to a Highland hill! There is an axiom amongst livestock farmers in Britain that you should always buy breeding stock in the north and bring it south rather than the other way round. Certainly many of those English stags must have perished without ever spawning any progeny.

Yet elderly Highland estate workers have stories of how the English park stags were turned out each autumn for the rut. They were allowed to spend a heady few weeks having their way with the Scots lassies, and no doubt struggling to fend off their smaller, fitter, less heavily antlered rivals, before making a strategic retreat to the shelter and feed of the park for the rest of the winter. Even wapiti from the United States and Canada, and perhaps deer from other far-flung parts of the Empire, were used in this way in a misguided effort to 'improve' the indigenous Scottish stock, displaying a touching faith in the value of 'blood' and breeding which I sometimes think reflects on the mentality, and perhaps even the degree of inbreeding, of those lairds of an earlier era. For undoubtedly the limiting factor in the productivity of Highland red deer is very rarely the genetics of the deer but rather the environment: food and shelter. The lesson is clear: transplants need nurturing and only if the conditions are right can they prosper.

Anyway, we didn't have enough crates; so, I reasoned, why not simply anaesthetise the deer in the bottom of the open boat? Nice dreams for the deer and, provided they didn't wake up and jump out, all would be fine. Stretchers made out of sacks and galvanised roofing struts from the old hothouse round the back of the castle, where the Bulloughs had once kept turtles, would make lifting the sleeping deer in and out relatively easy.

Nickie was bound to be a little sceptical. Just a few weeks previously I had been attempting to find a different drug cocktail for darting the stags on Rum and she had been enlisted to help. The darting went well and the inebriated stag gently subsided. I took hold of his antlers and all seemed safe so I left Nickie with the usual directions: 'Just stand astride him holding his head up by his antlers and if he starts to struggle apply a little gentle weight with your knees to his shoulders.'

I walked back up to the Land-Rover to fetch some equipment, but before I got there I was surprised to hear the rumbling of hooves from behind me. Against the blue sea and the Cuillins, Nickie was hurtling, astride a stag in full flight, towards the cliffs. Clasping his antlers like a latter-day Peer Gynt, she looked magnificent. The reality when she eventually fell off was different. As I too rolled helpless in the turf I came to understand that it hadn't been a pleasure trip; I was in disgrace and that particular drug combination was not tried again.

The deer finally came over from Rum uneventfully (illustration 6a). Gerald himself was there to help and we certainly needed him because, as we came into Mallaig harbour in the little *Sioras* from Rum, we saw firstly that it was low tide with a twenty-foot lift. And secondly, that what seemed several bus-loads of bemused tourists were gazing down from the pier on to our cargo of peacefully sleeping deer. I had rented a van: little did the hirers know what its unorthodox load was to be. In the event the tourists actually rallied round and helped us with the stretchers. I wonder if they would do the same today.

After that unorthodox sea crossing the deer seemed to settle in at Reediehill very well. For the first time in at least two hundred years red deer grazed above Auchtermuchty. They clearly relished the improved pasture and showed little inclination to pace the fences.

However, a few months after the successful installation of our deer herd our neighbour's tractorman came up to see us. After a good deal of beating about the bush and nervous shuffling from one foot to another, he sheepishly confessed the reason for his visit. Apparently, sometimes whilst walking home in the dark, he had heard a large animal following him. We said that we knew all our animals were in and so it couldn't possibly be one of our deer. Then he said, 'It made a noise like a half-dead chain saw,' and proceeded, mouth closed, to make a series of guttural sounds somewhere between a subdued roar and a moan. Now that is a perfect description of the bleating call that a tame red deer, looking for feed, makes and we knew he was right. The puzzle was: where had the animal come from? There were no wild red deer about us and we were sure that all our deer were there.

The answer came a few days later when, looking out of the bedroom window early one morning, I caught sight of our hand-reared hind

Bonnie, one of the twins, trotting back up the farm road and, scarcely slowing down or breaking step, worming her way under the gate, back home in time for her morning feed. And so I learned that a space of twelve inches under a gate is too much for a deer farm.

11 THE LAST RESTOCKING OF A HEBRIDEAN ISLAND?

There were nowhere near enough deer for the forty fenced acres but, feeling that understocking was better than overstocking, we did not initially make very strenuous efforts to find more. In any case, where could we hope to purchase them? We decided to see how the deer did, whether any problems arose, and to develop a system of deer farming suitable for Reediehill before we went out to try and increase the herd.

Nickie was soon hammering and soldering her jewellery and silver-ware in a shed across the farmyard whence emerged treasures for exhibition and commission. Soon her work was in the permanent collections of the Royal Museum of Scotland and the Victoria and Albert Museum in London, as well as Bing Crosby's private collection! Meanwhile, I was busy writing up my thesis and, though growing, the need to make money did not yet seem pressing; we naively believed we could live more or less off the land with our income bolstered by occasional veterinary locums and the sale of jewellery and eventually venison. It was an idyll.

The deer farm attracted, from the start, disproportionate publicity. I forget which publication was the first but I know that the strangely unchanging *Scots Magazine*, with a big circulation amongst the

Scottish diaspora, was early on the scene, and the *Scotsman* newspaper did something too at the beginning. There followed pieces the same year in the *Telegraph* and the *Sunday Telegraph*, the *Dundee Courier* and even *Reveille*.

Not all publicity was friendly. Two years after we started, the *Scottish Daily News*, functioning terminally as a workers' co-operative, was frankly hostile. 'Bred for the Bullet' was the headline for our centrefold piece. A simulated rifle sight was superimposed over one of the few precious Rum-born bottle-fed calves, intended for our breeding hind group. Surprisingly this did us no harm at all. In fact the only response was from a nearby local authority which asked me to help them establish a deer farm. That farm, funded entirely from the public purse, is still going strong.

There was even an exchange in the *Daily Telegraph* in which a well-known journalist, J. Wentworth Day, whose view epitomised that of the countryside establishment, expressed his disapproval of what we were trying to do. However, a riposte from Nickie's aunt, unsolicited by us, abruptly ended the correspondence to our great satisfaction. It was this and other little triumphs that taught me how, in a challenge between the small and struggling deer farmer and the pompous, powerful, self-opinionated establishment figure, we usually win in the public relations stakes. And I learnt of the pleasure such trivial triumphs may bring.

In a few years' time we were to learn just how valuable the friendship of the press could be to us in exposing injustices to unsympathetic politicians.

My thesis was now sent off and to my delight accepted, and I began to think of farming deer a little more seriously. We were already getting approaches for venison but had nothing to sell, and soon we should need to find more deer. In the meantime we had cause to be thankful to the news media for creating the publicity which gave us our first, and one of the most rewarding, deer-related jobs that I ever had to do. Although it depleted our little herd of deer, it did bring in cash and it was a challenge.

A consortium of landowners, of the enlightened category, approached me with a request to establish a population of deer on the island of South Uist. I actually viewed this political hot potato with a good deal of trepidation, and would probably consider it even more carefully now. Deer can be very destructive, and the crofters on the western side of the island, on the fertile, low-lying, cultivated *machair*, would be unlikely to welcome the depredations of deer. And, deer in the Highlands were then at least still seen as symbols of the sporting estate, absentee landlords and all those other institutions folk love to hate.

However, a walk over the area showed us that there really did seem to be a substantial part of the eastern side of the island now uninhabited by man, where few sheep lived and those that did seemed to be rarely gathered. Furthermore it was clear that wild deer would in any case eventually encroach from the north, where their numbers were high, even if we did not hasten the colonisation with a few immigrants from Fife. The problem was to ensure that any deer introduced would stay in this area.

We left it to the estate to carry out appropriate public relations by having meetings in community halls. These seemed to go well despite an aggressive editorial stance taken by the *West Highland Free Press* who, to my amusement, placed all the blame for the forthcoming introduction on the Nature Conservancy.

We persuaded the estate to construct a release pen close to the beach and of only about an acre. Into this pen it was planned to introduce the cervine boarding party and to keep them there for a week or two until, we hoped, they had come to regard it as their secure home. It was obviously absolutely crucial to the success of the reintroduction that those deer did not wander over to the west, and I believed that this release strategy would work.

There was great concern on the part of the estate that once confined to their enclosure the deer would be sitting ducks for seaborne poachers. We needed a watchman to keep an eye on the deer in their remote outpost, ten miles from the nearest house, and we cast in our minds as to who should be allotted this task since I would have to get back to Reediehill to look after things there.

By good fortune it so happened that one day we had been talking to our postie at Reediehill, and he had confided to us that he was worried about his young brother Jim who had been getting a bit bored with life in nearby Glenrothes. There had been some trouble that had landed Jim with a fine. Big brother reckoned that life at Reediehill would be therapeutic and we were happy to oblige.

Actually, as an aside, Jim's time at Reediehill was not always uneventful and, if therapeutic, perhaps not always quite in the manner anticipated. One day, while Nickie and I were away, a small group of people, interested in deer and deer farming, arrived, and Jim sensibly took it upon himself to do the showing-around. It was winter, the ground was a quagmire, and Jim, strictly against the rules, decided to give a solo feeding performance, shovelling potatoes off the back of the moving tractor, to encourage the deer to come nice and close to the visitors.

In even more flagrant disregard of all safety, he put the tractor into its lowest gear and walked along behind it. We don't know exactly how it happened, but when Jim ran round to steer the tractor as it approached a fence the inevitable happened. His foot went under the rear wheel which, of course, continued to turn whilst the little tractor was prevented from moving any further forward by the fence. Jim couldn't move either but was saved from serious physical injury by the soft mud. To the horror of the onlookers on the other side of the fence this wasn't the end of his woes, because the electric fence was switched on and every few seconds he received a pulse of several thousand volts. Springing into action, one of the more agriculturally knowledgeable visitors ran round the fence, in through the gate, and pulled the stop button on the old grey Fergie. Thankfully, apart from a little bruising, only Jim's pride was seriously damaged, and it was years before we came to hear of his narrow escape, from one of the spectators who told us it beat anything he had ever seen at the circus.

When the question of poachers on South Uist was broached, all minds immediately turned to Jim, and it was duly planned that he be stationed by the release pen in a tent about five miles from the nearest road. The idea was for Jim to stay there two weeks then release the deer and move out.

The deer were loaded at Reediehill into the South Uist estates lorry and driven through Skye to meet the ferry to Lochmaddy at Uig. On the boat I talked at length with one of the islanders. He had a dreamy eye which, cynically, I could have put down to that very real spirit of the isles, whisky. But at the time he had an other-worldliness about him which left a lasting impression on me. He told me how the deer were the cattle of the fairies and how the hinds' milk sustained the tribe of elfin, and of how their cervine steeds flew so magically they would not dash the dew from the cup of a harebell. He also told me that one day I would surely come to live in the Outer Isles. That has not happened yet but I have not forgotten; I can certainly think of no more beautiful a place. Nickie has always said I am a changeling.

Following our by now well-tested technique, the deer were anaesthetised in the lorry and carried by stretcher – still the Rum turtle-house frames with sacks – from lorry to boat and then after a short sea crossing from boat to release pen. All went smoothly with no loss or injury.

The landscape of the Outer Isles exudes melancholia. One of the boatmen told us he had been born there at our release point, yet now all that remained were a few tumbled stone shapes to indicate where the village had been. Like so much of the West Highlands the beguiling beauty of the place was sharpened with nostalgia. Hugh Miller's poignant description of the recently cleared Rum tantalised me as I wandered around the abandoned homes of Uist: 'there were fields on which the heath and moss of the surrounding moorlands were fast encroaching, that had borne many a successive harvest; and prostrate cottages, that had been the scenes of christenings, and bridals, and blythe new-year's days . . .'

Jim held out for only a very short while. Unaccustomed solitude after the bright lights of Glenrothes, together with rain and gales, probably played as much a part as those ghosts of 'christenings, and bridals, and blythe new-year's days'.

Despite his early retreat, which meant that the deer were only fed within their release pen for three or four days, the experiment was a great success. Jim tied the gate open and the deer were free to come and go as they wished yet, when Gerald and I went back there with Jim almost twelve months later, to our great delight two animals were actually in the open enclosure and the rest within a mile or two of it and calves had, of course, been born. I gather that, by and large, after an initial exploratory phase during which almost the whole little party came wandering curiously over to the west, the deer have continued to stay in the right place. In any case the crofters are entitled, I suppose, to shoot any marauding animals and put them in their freezers.

And so we had played our part in what must have been one of the last red deer restocking exercises in the Highlands and Islands following the great human depopulation of rural Scotland that had lasted from the late eighteenth to the mid-twentieth century, and which is now slowly being reversed.

12 HUMANE MEAT PRODUCTION AND A CAT'S CONSCIOUSNESS

Back at Reediehill, life was not all a bed of roses but Nickie and I were very happy.

My memories of those early days are of the cold, and strangely also of the sun. After Rum I suppose the brightness and cold would strike me. Fife has an enviable record for hours of sunshine – I believe St Andrews has as many hours of sun as London – whereas on Rum I remember it once rained every day for three months. Fife can also be very cold. My brother Nicholas, then a young doctor with a still undulled spirit of scientific enquiry, came to stay one winter and expressed his surprise after a bath. 'I didn't think it was physiologically possible to lie in hot water and whilst being warm below water level have goose pimples above.' We had no central heating of course, but there was ample firewood and the rooms were small and the ceilings low.

The deer had to start to pay their way. From the outset, of course, we had understood that they would have to be killed. I knew there would be a surplus of stags. We used only one stag to thirty or forty hinds. And we had to remove the extra stags before they became too aggressive and whilst they were at their best for eating. So at the beginning we killed at about two years of age and whenever, regardless of season, we had anyone wanting to buy. Even had the idea been remotely feasible, I had no intention of taking deer to abattoirs and, benefiting for once from the novelty of our situation, we had no legal need to do so. For unlike cattle and sheep which must be killed in an abattoir if the meat is to be sold, and which cannot legally be killed on the farm, deer can legitimately be slaughtered in the field. This has always been a key attraction of the whole deer-farming experiment. It means that a farmer can, if he wishes, create a completely self-contained and 'vertically integrated' meat-production system.

I had become accustomed to seeing deer shot on Rum, and indeed had been impressed by how humane is the effect of a large rifle at close quarters, and that had been a strong factor in deciding me to start a venison farm. Nevertheless it goes without saying that killing the deer is not a favourite job. Ortega y Gasset confesses that 'every good hunter is uneasy in the depths of his conscience when faced with the death he is about to inflict on the enchanting animal'. That is as it should be. Most societies have a token rite by which they beg forgiveness of the animal for what they have to do. It is only when we kill on an industrial scale that the procedure brutalises the slaughterman and impedes humane treatment of the animal.

As a vet the blood and gore didn't upset me, but the taking of a healthy life was an unpleasant novelty. I have learnt to rationalise it. If I don't kill the young stock then obviously I couldn't afford to keep those breeding hinds and stags which we had come to know over many years. Another option, sending the deer off for someone else to kill, was not what I wanted. The deer would need to be gathered and loaded and transported, which was stressful, and then we would need to buy the carcases back so that financially it was not sensible either. In a rather righteous way I felt that I should participate in the killing. Mankind has for the last ten thousand years or so accepted that he will eventually have to kill the animals which have been raised as a part of his household; why shouldn't I? And I have always believed that those who eat meat should understand that by so doing they are contributing to the life and death of those animals. Finally, this field slaughter had been a planned part of the enterprise from the outset.

Reediehill can produce only grass, for, being north-facing and so high up and so rocky and hilly, it is not well suited to cropping. The potatoes that we grew at the beginning are a greedy crop and need to be part of an arable rotation; at our altitude and with our rocky 'knowe heads', routine arable cropping would be madness. Like so much, if not all, of the hills and uplands of Britain we can produce only meat or give up and plant trees which would not afford us a living. If I could show that deer farming was technically feasible and then, later, that it was financially viable, I would have an alternative enterprise which beleaguered upland sheep and cattle farmers could adopt with few changes to their own grassland farms. These farmers have few options, and yet here was one which was unsubsidised and would yield a meat much healthier than lamb or beef. I therefore bought a rifle and soon discovered a surprising fact which has kept us in good stead ever since.

Feeding out the deer was a daily winter task that entailed either walking in a long line pouring feed out of a bag or sometimes, if there were two of us available, my driving the wee grey Fergie tractor while Jim or someone shovelled potatoes off the back. When it came to shooting the deer it was a simple matter to walk or drive back past the line of feeding deer, select the victim and then, at very close range – perhaps only four or five yards – shoot him (for it was always stags in those days) in the head or neck. The surprise was that, despite the very large calibre of rifle I used, and the loud explosion, the deer startled only momentarily before returning within seconds to eat within a few feet of their fallen comrade. This meant that it was simple, if needed, to shoot several deer at a time without causing any panic or distress. And as the deer were shot weekly from a large group, it was curious how the survivors, over the months, became inured to this and startled progressively less.

I have often thought that this behaviour is similar to that of the speeding motorist who sees a fatal motorway accident yet resumes speeding seconds later. Another's misfortune carries no lessons. I should not really have been surprised. I am more and more convinced that although they will avoid eating a potato 'contaminated' with blood, deer have no conception of death and mortality. The same is, I believe, almost certainly true of other animals, always excepting the primates and perhaps elephants and whales, with their large brains.

At that time legislation on animal welfare in abattoirs made a big issue of preventing any possibility of one animal witnessing the slaughter of another. This remains good practice, but for a very gregarious species the stress of isolation prior to slaughter may contribute more to their misery than seeing another animal fall. For those of us brought up with Peter Rabbit running around our dishes, anthropomorphism – attributing human consciousness to animals – dies hard.

However, no sooner have I delivered myself of this arrogant and contentious view than I call to mind a very strange story which Nickie told me about our two cats, spayed female litter mates, Tiger and Hester, one day when I returned home after a trip away. 'There are more things in heaven and earth, Horatio, than are dreamt of in your philosophy.' If it had not been Nickie telling me I should not have found it very easy to believe.

'It was Sunday morning,' she said, 'and I had planned an extra hour in bed. At about 6 a.m. I gradually came to and there was a cat wailing outside the window. It went on and on. I looked out and there was Tiger sitting looking up at the window and howling. On and on. I thought she'd been shut out, the cat flap had jammed or something, though she's never done this before. So eventually I put on my dressing gown and went down. It was a beautiful sunny morning. As soon as Tiger saw me she headed off down the drive looking back and howling. I had no choice but to follow. Whenever I stopped or made to go back she sat down and wailed at me again. So I followed. We went all the way down to a dip in the road outside Clare's garden.' (That's about half a mile.) 'And I began to feel a bit silly on the road in a dressing gown. Anyway when we got there Tiger just sat down, stopped howling and looked at me as much as to say, "There, I've done my bit, now it's up to you." I looked around and couldn't see anything untoward. But then Tiger bounded up the bank and scrambled up a tree. I followed as best I could, and as soon as I was out of the hollow and on to the bank, I could hear another cat mewing on the other side of the road in Clare's garden. And then I realised – at the bottom of the tree was Clare's dog, Yoyo, staring up the tree, grinning and panting, whilst half-way up the tree was Hester. It didn't take a minute to rescue Hester and the two cats ran off up the drive together.'

This story fascinates me. I can think of no rational explanation except that Tiger showed an actual ability to plan a rescue. The cats have never ever shown similar behaviour since, and it takes some stamina for a small cat to wake a sleeping person through an upstairs window. Eventually Tiger developed mammary tumours and I had to end her suffering; Hester seemed not in the least affected by the loss of her sibling, saviour and lifelong companion.

Nickie and I soon realised that with our practice of shooting deer in the field we were incidentally blazing a trail towards what many, apart from us, saw as a more humane means of meat production. That had always been at the back of our minds but we gradually came to understand just how important this was. We had a visit from Ruth Harrison, a member of the newly formed Farm Animal Welfare Council (FAWC) who was an animal welfarist specialising in humane slaughter.

Ruth was tremendously encouraging about what we were doing and saw us as creating a precedent that would allow small farmers to kill conventional livestock on farms. This would obviously avoid the stresses of transporting animals to the strange surroundings of an often distant abattoir. She believed fervently that this was a more humane option and Nickie and I were inclined to agree with her. Our experience of shooting the deer at Reediehill in the field to achieve an immediate death with no possible pre-slaughter stress had been very encouraging, and we had become quite evangelistic about the system.

In due course FAWC was assigned the task of investigating the welfare of farmed deer, and when it came to the matter of slaughter it was decided that they should all come up to Reediehill to see how it was done. I drove the tractor into the field and shot two deer for them, they concluded this as a humane way to kill deer and we were permitted to continue.

At Reediehill the venison in those days was hardly a volume trade. In the beginning I would shoot an occasional deer and hang it up in one of the outhouses before cutting it up on the well-scrubbed kitchen table. Then, if it was for immediate despatch, I would stitch the venison up in muslin and pack it in a cardboard box with hay to allow ventilation. Any cut bones or other likely sites of putrefaction were rubbed with ground ginger. The parcel was then committed to the care of the GPO. It was strictly a winter-time activity! But it has to be said that some of the venison we despatched south in those days I still remember as very fine.

The freezer for home sales was situated in Nickie's jewellery work-shop, an outhouse on the other side of the farmyard, where it helped her to keep warm as she worked and where customers could easily be served. Actually it is a wonder we had any customers at all, but the trickle of publicity kept flowing and I suppose that brought in the curious. Some of those trailblazing customers are still with us more than twenty years later.

We had, however, to think of a way of encouraging more sales. Funnily enough, because we certainly didn't think of ourselves as Country Gentlemen, we were nevertheless members of their Association. We had found that membership of the CGA supplied us with a useful discount on woodworm treatment of our house and we had stayed loyal ever since. In the back of the CGA magazine was a section of classified advertisements, free for members, and so it was here we first advertised.

This stimulated a stream of customers of a very friendly but fairly predictable pattern. There was one retired colonel who asked if he could have some more venison because he found it 'excellent for shooting sandwiches'. Images of a new sort of clay pigeon and a new sort of ammunition floated in front of our eyes. Then there was another delighted customer in the Channel Islands who was quite unconcerned about the delay in delivery and eventually sent us a postcard saying, 'Venison arrived today, stinking and delicious.' Not quite what we had planned.

We certainly attracted loyal and dedicated customers; they had to be to get up our track. One winter the road froze, as so often was the case then, and became completely impassable just as the venison buyers started coming to collect their Christmas joints. An intrepid consumer, John MacGillivray, after struggling up through the snow, excited by the novelty, accepted Nickie's offer of a large plastic sack filled with straw and hurtled off down the track and into the dusk, clutching his Christmas joint on this makeshift toboggan.

13 THE FIRST SKIRMISH WITH POLITICIANS

One of the best and most important things to be done at Reediehill was to start a family. Nickie seems to be very adept, I hesitate to say lucky since I am sure that there must be skill involved, in being able to pass through a very speedy and trouble-free labour. Stella, our first-born, came on the last day of February. The doctor had threatened to induce her if nothing happened within a day or two, and as there was a beautiful snowy spell Nickie decided to go tobogganing. This did the trick evidently because a hectic car dash to hospital was only just in time.

Some twenty-two months later Martha was due and Nickie was determined to have a home delivery. The doctor, after a prudent cautioning, was all-supportive. I remember sneaking a look at the notes he had written and reading with a surprised sense of self-importance: 'Husband a vet – should be OK.'

Nickie's parents and younger brother and sister came for Christmas, and just as the festive supper reached the table Martha heralded her arrival. Nickie's family wisely fled. Stella was commendably asleep and Nickie was couched in front of the fire in our little parlour. I summoned the midwife who, on account of the seasonal ice, could not get her car up the road without a push, and by the time that I had finished my pushing, Nickie had finished hers.

Stella woke to find her new sister and all was story-book perfect.

But that road continued to be a serious headache. If we were to develop a business it had to be passable at all times. We needed people to visit our shop and many were unaccustomed to off-road driving. Following our experiences with a flood in 1974, when the farm track came to resemble a white-water rafting experience, I realised something must be done to secure our road and I applied for a grant.

There existed in 1973, and for many years afterwards, grants payable to all farmers at up to 70 per cent for capital works. At that time almost all farm 'improvements' came under this heading, even such environmentally damaging ones as grubbing up hedges and orchards. The scope of these grants has been substantially reduced over the years, but in 1973 road improvements as well as fencing were certainly included.

To my genuine surprise, as we were a registered agricultural holding with a 'holding number' and received regular census forms and so on, the application was rejected. This represented a major setback. What is more, I considered it very unfair: no 'level playing field' here. My sense of justice was outraged. I had not expected assistance for our deer fences. But the roads . . .?

For the first time I understood how, by opting to farm a new species, I was placing us outside the security net which protects conventional farmers from the rigours of the market place. Agricultural support was set up, for the main part, after the war in order to ensure that the nation should always be able to provide sufficient cheap food far all, and never again be in danger of starvation in time of war. A whole host of grants and subsidies were then, and are still, provided for those who farm cattle and sheep. But now like a cold douche came the realisation that I was putting us outside the system. As a deer farm, Reediehill, it had been decided by the bureaucrats and politicians, should never share in this bounty. Any improvements that we wished to make would have to be paid for entirely out of our own pockets. That in itself I would have found entirely reasonable, but my neighbours were for the same work receiving government handouts of half or three-quarters of the cost. That was unjust. Were we not both producing meat from grass? For the time being I had no choice but to sit, think and fume.

Meanwhile the road continued to provide intermittent entertainment for many years. One winter's night I returned home with a lorry, Stella and Martha securely strapped in place, and found that, as so often, the running water on the track had frozen. Two columns of ice filled the parallel ruts like two miniature Cresta bobsleigh courses. By 'taking a run at it' I managed to complete all but the last hundred yards; lifting out Martha, I set out to carry her up to the house leaving the first-born in control of the truck. I returned a few moments later and to my horror, even with the benefit of a torch, could find no sign of the vehicle or Stella. Had she rolled over the edge? I walked and slid down the ice keeping a firm hold on those dark thoughts, and some fifty yards back down the road there it was – Stella still strapped in place and stoically sucking her thumb, oblivious of the pleasure her slide might have given had she been a few years older. Secure with its wheels in the ruts, the lorry had merely glissaded down the track.

Following my disappointment over the grants for capital improvements to the road I embarked on a campaign of letter-writing through my MP, Sir John Gilmour, a grand old knight of the shires who was extremely supportive, and also to the press. I felt that I had an undeniable case; I was not looking at that time for all the multifarious forms of production support that cattle and sheep farmers seemed to assume as their right. Even then a hill-sheep farmer's income from sales was often only half as much as the subsidy he received. But if they were receiving assistance for such items as road improvement, I could see no justice in our being denied it. We were as much a bona fide agricultural enterprise as any other. Furthermore there were already public mutterings about 'grain and beef mountains' and the like. There seemed to be no such surplus of venison. In 1976 the game dealers were offering 85 pence per pound (£1.87 per kilo) for wild venison, a price substantially greater than that of lamb, and one which probably equates to a price today of over £3 per pound (£6.60 per kilo).

At that time there was a great resurgence of support for the Scottish National Party which culminated in the referendum of 1979. I suppose my little campaign struck a chord with the Nationalists. Red deer are often seen as an emblem of Scotland and also, more importantly, it was genuinely and justifiably felt that deer farming could contribute to the Highland economy. Consequently one snowy day we were hosts to the entire SNP parliamentary party. On account of the snow several cars got stuck on our road, amply demonstrating the need for improvement. As good as their word, those SNP MPs tabled a large number of written parliamentary questions on the recognition of deer farming as a regular agricultural activity worthy of the same support for capital improvements as conventional farming systems. This undoubtedly helped to bring my campaign much-needed publicity at a time when Westminster was feeling it politic to keep those north of the border happy and quiet.

Notice of success came in a surprising way. One evening Barry Wilson, an agricultural journalist, phoned me to say that a large new deer park in the Home Counties had just been set up (by someone who, it subsequently transpired, is one of the wealthiest men in the world as a result of patents on waxed paper cartons), and the owner had been awarded support for the long deer fence around his property. I immediately phoned his farm manager and he confirmed the truth of the story.

I wrote letters to the broadsheet newspapers and got, as usual, friendly support from the journalists. Given that this had happened in England it was only a matter of time before justice prevailed in Scotland, and in the years to come we were lucky indeed to receive grants of 15–50 per cent for all improvements including, when the time came, the renewal of deer fencing (for we were obviously too late for the initial deer fence). And finally, wonder of wonders, we learnt that even our road would be eligible for grant aid. But by then we had learnt to live with, if not exactly relish, its potholes and reluctantly we decided that we could not really afford our part of the expenditure: road improvements would have to wait a while yet. But at least the principle was won.

14 PARKS AND DARTS

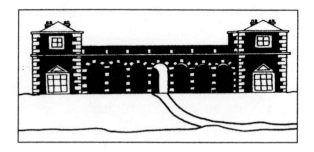

The press coverage meant that we soon found ourselves being approached by a growing band of farmers wanting to start deer farming. They believed, like us, that the writing was on the wall for subsidies for sheep, cattle and grains. Unfortunately, after the South Uist adventure, our deer herd was depleted and the choice of replacements was very limited. Thus began the long period of searching all over Britain for any deer whether wild or tame.

Soon I learnt that throughout England, in particular, there remain a great many long-established and traditionally managed deer parks. These places, of great beauty and environmental importance, are but relics of what were once a vital part of the rural scene. They were at the height of their economic importance in the mediaeval period, though in 1577 Harrison could still state in Holinshed's Chronicles: 'In everye shyre of Englaunde there is great plentye of Parkes ... in Kent and Essex only are to the number of a hundred wherein great plenty of deere is cherished and kept.' And a few years later, in 1617, Morison wrote: 'every gentleman of five hundreth or a thousand pounds rent by the yeare hath a Parke for them [i.e. deer] inclosed with pales of wood.'

We could, I discovered, procure a few deer from some parks for only about £30 and in so doing, of course, prevent them from being killed. The problem was to catch them humanely and in good condition. This is where I reckoned my veterinary experience and my time on Rum would come in handy.

About the first effort I made was at Studley Royal Deer Park beside Fountains Abbey near Ripon in Yorkshire. This became a happy hunting ground of mine and over some twenty years I must have taken about five hundred deer from Studley. But on this first occasion I arrived inadequately equipped with the toy crossbow and spring-loaded darts pioneered on Rum. I was met by Ernest Kemp, a very wonderful and experienced deerkeeper who had a deep understanding of and affection for his charges, as well as a dry sense of humour that kept me from becoming too pompous. Ernest is one of those who might sit quietly in the corner of a crowded room but will always command interest and respect.

The first thing I learnt was how much bigger were the English park deer than their poor deprived relatives on the northern hills. Our darts, cunningly designed by Roger Short specifically for work on Rum, took only half a millilitre of drug and this was generally enough for our island stags, especially if we used our home-made double-strength cocktail. Now I found to my chagrin that English park stags were fully twice as big, and also that the drug now being marketed by the manufacturers was slightly less potent.

It is among the first discoveries that one makes in working with deer that they are more easily approached by vehicle than on foot, and for darting deer this is always the first tactic to employ, especially if the animals can be coaxed into range with some feed. In those days West Riding Council were economical in their deer management, restricting Ernest's mobility to a very small, very noisy and very slow dumper truck. I lay concealed among the mangolds and turnips in this motorised wheelbarrow whilst Ernest swung the crank handle, and we then 'put-put-putted' around the beautiful Capability Brown landscape at little more than walking speed.

I soon found that the English deer were less enthusiastic about coming to close quarters than the hungry Scots hill animals, presumably because of their high living in the lush grass parkland, or because their good condition led to increased fecundity and a consequent need to cull more frequently with a rifle. Or could it be that after hundreds of years during which generations of overworked deerkeepers have been given short notice to find some venison for dinner, there has been a genuine genetic shift towards animals of a more wary nature? I often think so, for truly wild red deer usually produce quieter stock than those of park origin.

My crossbow had an effective range of only about fifteen metres. We selected the tamest stag, and by aiming about six feet over his back I managed to hit him with one shot, and then another, and another; yet it was clear that the dart's payload of drug was too small. At about 2 p.m. I encouraged Ernest to go and have lunch, and by lucky stalking through the trees I finally managed to bring that first stag to a drug-induced slumber. There he lay like Saint Sebastian pierced with many darts. When Ernest came back I was able to feel a little happier, and in his inimitable style he ignored all the problems and we set about loading the sleeping animal into my car trailer.

This may sound fairly amusing and innocuous but I was far from content. The stag had not suffered after the first injection of drug had rendered him, I imagine, 'high'. But although I was always able to reassure myself that I was saving him from death, because his useful days in the park were over and there would be the danger of him mating his daughters if he was left there any longer, nevertheless the experience had been unnerving for me and undignified for the poor old stag, and it had to be admitted that I had benefited from a good deal of luck. I resolved then and there to dart no more deer until I had thoroughly investigated some of the modern dart guns that were just beginning to become available.

By the mid-1970s the techniques of wild animal capture had progressed. The availability of M99, later to be known as Immobilon, and its antidote Revivon had meant that dart guns could be designed with purpose, and several manufacturers were now marketing weapons. I chose the American Cap Chur gun produced by a Mr Red Palmer in Atlanta, Georgia, and it has served me very well ever since. This does not mean that the system is trouble-free. A great deal of care and attention is needed to keep the barrel clean and free of grit and it requires stern resolve to renew darts which you feel might just manage another shot. I have keen sympathy with tribal hunting and fishing societies, which attach such importance to superstition. Darting is a truly hit-and-miss affair. Even after my purchase of state-of-the-art darting equipment, things could still be a little unpredictable. Two later incidents at Studley stand out.

In the first I was asked to dart and transport a sika stag to another park. Sika is the Japanese word for deer, but it has come to be used for any one of about thirty different sub-species of a family whose natural range is from the far north to the south of east Asia. Now I had never darted sika before and was unable to find any published reports of dose rates, so on the basis of sika being close relatives of red deer I simply adjusted the dose to take account of the lower body weight of sika, and off we went. In those days we had graduated from the small dumper truck and were using a tractor and trailer, with me in the trailer. This was all right except that it was so noisy that communication between the driver and his passengers was not easy. In fact, unless the driver was interested and receptive, rather than lost in his own daydreams, it was impossible. After rattling around the park for about half an hour I managed to dart the sika and in a worryingly short time he had slid quietly to the ground. Instead of ten minutes he had taken only four. We headed over to him on the tractor. 'Speed up a bit,' I shouted, to no avail. We eventually arrived, hoisted him on to the trailer and set off back to my lorry, with me sitting anxiously supporting the sleepy stag's head. Shout and wave as hard as I might, the driver, lost in blissful reverie, kept on steadily across the park. The stag seemed to be getting sleepier and sleepier and finally I could stand it no longer. He would, I felt sure, die if I didn't do something. So out with the syringe and in with the antidote. It would in any case be unlikely for the stag to respond before we reached the lorry, I reasoned. Within seconds, or so it seemed, the stag I had thought so near to death began to stir. As the lorry hove in sight, surrounded by a little party of curious visitors armed with cameras, he began to do more than this: he began to wake up. Hastily I stripped my pullover off and put it on his head as a makeshift blindfold. By now we were nearing the truck and the excited tourists, and I was spreadeagled on the poor stag who was struggling to stand up. He had got his hind legs clear now and, almost purposefully engaging a hind hoof in the belt of my trousers, kicked with all his might. In one instant my trousers opened like the proverbial sardine tin from belt to ankle. Yet still I hung on, and with Ernest's encouragement we not so much lifted him into the lorry as aimed him like a cork from a champagne bottle. The visitors, embarrassed by my undress, melted away. After that the sika stag settled happily into his new home and the only loss was my trousers and dignity.

The second misadventure I remember at Studley was potentially more serious. Ernest and I were on the trailer with a sedated stag and all was well. It had been raining and the ground was greasy, and when the driver attempted a short cut up a steep incline we became a little uneasy. Sure enough, just before the top the tractor's wheels started spinning and we began to move backwards at an increasing speed. The trailer rapidly jackknifed into the tractor and I thought it inevitable that Ernest, the stag and I would be catapulted out. Our hour had come. But instead it was the tractor that rolled over and we were left upright. Ernest made some laconic remark and we climbed off with our darted deer, none the worse, to release the shaken driver, who emerged through the horizontal cab door like an astronaut through a hatchway.

In the late 1960s and early 1970s there had been several winters when there were substantial die-offs in many parks throughout England, although thankfully, owing to Ernest's efforts, not at Studley. I remember a picture on the back page of the *Manchester Guardian* in, I think, the long, hard winter of 1962–3, of a tractor pulling a trailer piled high with dead deer from one English park. In that year Woburn Deer Park, for example, had, by dint of hard feeding, managed to contain its losses to 150, which compares with the 670 they lost in the hard winter of 1947 when feeding was not practised so conscientiously, and when in the immediate aftermath of the war less feed was available. There is no doubt that as demand for breeding stock for the farms developed in the late 1970s and 1980s most parks benefited financially and some of this was passed on to help the deer. Winter feeding standards rose and numbers of deer were kept at a sustainable level. Some diseases prevalent in parks vanished with the improved management. The same was true to some extent with the capture of Scottish wild deer; the ones we took live directly reduced the number needing to be shot, and in some cases encouraged the estates to feed the deer better.

Sadly, since those days the National Trust, no doubt nervous of any controversy, has decided to forbid the tranquillising of any deer in its parks. The consequence is that that illustrious body, of which I have been a member for many years, is deprived of a source of income, and its surplus deer must all be shot dead instead of having the opportunity to live and breed happily for many more years on farms or other deer parks. Since the removal of deer by darting is in my view a humane procedure I do not understand their rationale.

Urban man does not want to see blood shed. If there are to be parks the deer must not be allowed to breed, he says, and much effort is being expended on researching fertility control measures. I have now been approached to see if I will get involved in vasectomising stags or administering contraceptives. This I should be reluctant to do on welfare grounds. It does not seem right to me to deprive the deer of their ability to breed, and in any case there would be deleterious effects on the animals. Vasectomised males would continue to serve the females all winter with possible ill effects in prolonged rutting activity and consequent loss of condition. There would also of course be a gradual attrition of the older animals; would these be left to become progressively more emaciated until the winter took them away? Would new stock be introduced to maintain the stock numbers? Or is an attempt being made to phase out the deer herds? There would also, in all but the largest herds, be a serious logistical problem in administering the contraceptives or in capturing every single male to carry out the vasectomies. I would not much fancy the sight of a deer herd artificially manipulated so that it had no young.

Sometimes it seems as though the activists pressing for these rather bizarre measures are less concerned about the welfare of the animals than their own nice feelings.

The welfare of the deer after I had captured them was dependent on the establishment of good management techniques, but the value of deer on farms soon became so high that this was usually not a problem. We always aimed to let the wild incoming deer mix with tame animals, which I felt was important, and yet we also had to be on the lookout for bullying. Red deer are among the most gregarious of deer species and it was astonishing how quickly newcomers settled in. On balance, then, I felt that we were doing the right thing in prolonging the life of those red deer we took on to farms.

Contrarily, I find the rehabilitation of many species of wild deer after injury, usually as a result of colliding with cars, much more difficult ethically. The scale of the deer problem is surprisingly large and growing. One English rehabilitation centre already handles over two hundred muntjac per year, and in Sweden more than half the traffic accidents and a significant number of human fatalities relate to collisions with moose. Muntjac deer, introduced from south-east Asia to Woburn in Bedfordshire early this century, are thought to be increasing by about 10 per cent per annum and have been incriminated in the disappearance of orchids from one nature reserve and the decimation of bluebells in wide areas of England, as well as in the destruction of nightingale nesting habitat.

Many of these animals are subjected to heroic surgery by my talented colleagues and given all possible tender loving care by devoted and well-meaning rehabilitators, yet I wonder if in numerous cases the stresses are not more than this prolongation of life can justify. The animals' injuries necessitate frequent close contact with their carers and to mix them with other deer is not usually feasible – nor with the less sociable species would it be desirable anyway. These issues become still more complex when the background of a rapidly growing wild deer population, throughout Britain and the developed world, is taken into account. The more solitary species of deer such as the roe, and now the muntjac, which comprise the bulk of these cases have a highly complex social structure. Once removed, even if subsequently reintroduced at the same place as the accident occurred, they may find it difficult or impossible to re-enter that society. If they are placed in a new locality their problems are likely to be worse. This disappointing conclusion has been substantiated by studies of the success of rehabilitating a variety of species, in particular of birds, such as the barn owl, which have been given all possible care yet still show very poor success in readjusting to life in the wild. Hedgehogs, however, I am pleased to be able to report, apparently do well after rehabilitation and release. We urgently need more follow-up studies to establish the survival rates of more species.

The story of the enthusiastic deerstalker crawling carefully and painstakingly through the undergrowth to shoot a poor, thin specimen of a deer only to find, when he walks up to the dead beast, that it was wearing a plaster cast, is, I hope, apocryphal; but it has a point.

I have explained how, following industrialisation, deer numbers in a variety of different nations increase. In England there are now estimated to be over one million deer of all species with numbers rising strongly for most species. Increasingly people are seeing deer in their gardens, on their fields and dead beside the roads. There is no sign of this trend being reduced. In the USA in 1997 12.4 million hunters each spent an average of 860 dollars killing 6.25 million deer, yet still numbers rise. I believe that unless serious efforts are made to control deer numbers, we shall find that what we value now as a beautiful and infrequent sight will come to be viewed increasingly as a pest. The damage deer do to gardens, crops, nature reserves and woodlands is growing.

It is significant that Lyme disease, a bacterial infection transmitted by ticks and which can cause disease in people, is earning deer a bad name because that is where many ticks feed. Yet those ticks can just as easily feed on birds, mice, dogs or any other warm-blooded animal.

15 THE 'TAINCHELL' – PART OF A LONG TRADITION

Encouraged by early successes in the deer parks, but always limited by the numbers available, we took on a new challenge by attempting to recruit the much more numerous adult hinds from the Scottish hills. If catching deer in the deer parks had been problematic, then taking wild deer by darting was almost impossible unless they could be tempted in to feed. It took only one memorable, bright, snowy day to prove this point.

I am to be guided by a highly experienced stalker. We start at dawn and toil two thousand feet up from the hill road, until we are able, very carefully, to come to a suitable hind within the thirty- to forty-yard range of my dart gun. I take my time, still my heaving breast, aim as accurately as my open sights permit and press the trigger. I would have done as well with my eyes closed, for the dart, lifted by a gust of wind, misses by miles and the deer move off at a trot.

We have a brief discussion. The stalker is doubtful if such a good opportunity can come again but I have to try to prove the system works. Finally he agrees. He will attempt to outflank the group of hinds and drift them back past me, through a narrow gully much higher up, at a very slow walking speed. It will take time. I climb slowly up to the appointed ambush point and flatten myself stomach down into the wet turf. There is a timeless, clean, acid, earthy smell as I press my body close to the peat. It is almost a sexual communion but Mother Earth does not move for me as she did for Hemingway. She lies cold, inert and, through overgrazing and inclement weather, sterile. Between perishing snow squalls driven by a snell wind come periods of calm when the sun lights even the deep recesses of the glen beneath. I can see the Land-Rover, a speck on the road, and I know that within it, warm and perhaps with the wise precaution of a flask, wait the stretcher party, radios alert.

Through this glen, or one very close, must have passed, in Robert Louis Stevenson's imagination, Davie Balfour and Alan Breck on their run back to the Forth with the redcoats in pursuit. Not much in this landscape has changed since those days. Perhaps there had been a few trees then; now there are none.

Time passes. My head aches with cold and I worm deeper into the heather. As the snow flurries rush by, they leave me and the ground white. I am a part of that environment. This place is the perfect natural ambush point. Are those few stones an old sheiling or perhaps the remnant of a 'sett', placed there to direct deer up to this defile? A thousand or maybe ten thousand years ago had other men lain just here feeling the earth solid beneath them, waiting for the deer?

I have been reading recently how deer had been, if not actually 'farmed' or domesticated, then at least systematically culled, as far back as the late Palaeolithic and Mesolithic. Analysis of the refuse middens of these people, throughout Europe from the middle of Italy to Jutland, shows a most remarkable preponderance of red deer bones. In fact their remains were found at 95 per cent of 165 sites examined. This indicates that for between five thousand years in the north and fifty thousand years in southern Europe, red deer were the predominant source of meat. This venison-eating belt even seems to have extended as far east and as early as Pekin man, of whose diet, according to some sources, deer meat formed 70 per cent. It was clear that venison, especially that from red deer, had been the staple diet of at least the European for far longer than anything else.

And antler had been vitally important too. Had its use not spanned so many eras we might have had an antler age to compare with the stone, bronze and iron ages. I found in my researches the story of Grime's Graves. Here in the middle of East Anglia is a most astonishing network of neolithic flint mines. For many centuries man quarried flint here to export throughout at least England if not further afield. My interest was drawn by the fact that the tool he used for all this quarrying was the red deer antler. So many antlers were used for picks in those flint mines that it is supposed that each of the dozens of mineshafts may have required between one hundred and four hundred antlers per year. They are so well preserved that some still show the 3000-year-old finger- and handprints of the miners. Juliet Clutton-Brock has reported that the majority of a sample of 283 antler picks which she examined were from fully mature stags. Four out of five antlers had been shed and several were clearly successive antlers from the same individual stags. Her explanation of this, which seems the only feasible one, is that care was being taken to avoid these adult stags being killed so that their antlers could be collected each spring. It occurred to me that for a large group of mature stags to be retained in one area of woodland, so that their antlers could readily be retrieved, would be extremely difficult without regular feeding. Since these mines predate the growing of crops, what could they have been fed?

Why had those people over countless generations not done what I was now seeking to do: domesticate the red deer? Was there some insurmountable obstacle that I had still to encounter?

And it was not only European red deer either. Frank, my Danish friend, had recently sent me some photographs taken by early aviators in the 1920s of curious kite-like shapes in the desert. These had now been recognised as massive setts constructed for the capture and slaughter of entire herds of migrating gazelles. Bones in middle eastern middens revealed that gazelle had been the staple diet there for millennia. And the same story can be told the world over, of bison in America, for example, or caribou in the Canadian Arctic. Systematic culling of the dominant game species seemed to be the rule.

But even more exciting was the evidence unearthed by some of the archaeologists which indicated that, in the case of the European red deer at least, a surprising majority of those bones were from young males. Could this have been a deliberate culling policy? Some of those archaeologists had even argued that there must have been a degree of husbandry to allow for this selective culling. Many are critical of that theory, yet it is rather hard to see how even the most expert hunter, armed with nothing more sophisticated than spear, or bow and arrow, could accomplish such a methodical cull unless the deer had been rendered approachable to some degree.

Hard evidence for that very early husbandry is missing, but something much closer to domestication, and well documented, took place centuries later in the 'classical' period when deer parks seem to have become almost commonplace. For example, writing in about AD 65, the Roman author Columella describes how 'wild creatures, such as ... deer ... sometimes serve to enhance the splendour and pleasure of their owners, and sometimes to bring profit and revenue'. How true! He then goes on to describe how '... if the cheapness of stone and labour make it advisable ... a wall built with unhewn stone and lime is put round it; otherwise it is made with unburnt bricks and clay or they may be shut up with a post fence; for this is the name given to a certain kind of lattice made of oak or cork-wood ... in this manner you can even enclose very wide regions and tracts of mountains' and, in relation to feeding the animals in the park, 'the careful head of a household ought not to be content with the foods which the earth produces by its own nature, but, at the seasons of the year when the woods do not provide food, he ought to come to the help of the animals which he has confined with the fruits of the harvest which he has stored up, and feed them on barley or wheat-meal and beans ... in a word he should give them whatever costs the least.'

Coming forward another thousand years to the England of the Domesday Survey, only thirty-six deer parks are described, but more than seventy deer 'hayes'. The French word for a hedge is *haie* and these 'hayes' of Norman England were probably hedges or fences designed to capture deer or to allow an ambush and battue, rather like the setts and elricks of the Highlands. Such a system of driving deer towards archers or into nets was known in mediaeval French as *chace a la haie*.

I had communicated eagerly with Professor Leonard Cantor at Loughborough who claims to have identified around two thousand deer parks in mediaeval England and Wales, though not all of these were in use at the same time. This is an astonishing number given that the human population at that time was only about four million. Imagine two thousand – or even one thousand – deer parks in modern Scotland with its population of five million! Professor Cantor confirmed his findings and sent me a fistful of publications which detailed his research.

Then, nearer to home, I came across the book *Hunting and Hunting Reserves in Mediaeval Scotland* by John Gilbert. I met and corresponded with John and his minutely reported findings gave me great encouragement. It was clear that a substantial economy in Scotland had revolved around deer parks. These parks were certainly used as sources of meat, together with the dovecot for pigeons, the warren for rabbits and the stews for fish. Thus in 1503 a stalker and two men had worked in Falkland Park, only five miles from Reediehill, for twelve days to provide venison for the king's wedding.

These parks were regularly replenished, often after royal visits and the associated banquets had emptied them, by bringing in wild deer, or by taking deer from one park to another. In Scotland we find, for example, that an Englishman, Master Levisay, was employed in Falkland Park, in 1502 and again in 1505, to use nets to catch deer without harming them, perhaps for transport by horse-drawn litter to restock Stirling deer park – a journey which, even if everything went well, took a minimum of three days. Management within the parks was also quite sophisticated: hay and grain must have been fed regularly and we have records from Stirling park of payments for hay in 1288, and for oats fed at Falkland from 1504 to 1507. In 1479 two cows were purchased to supply milk for rearing deer calves at Falkland – there must have been quite a few calves to rear.

Keeping the deer in was obviously one of the biggest tasks and must have entailed substantial labour. Only the largest parks such as Linlithgow in Scotland could boast stone walls; much more usual were ditches with a bank surmounted by a wattle or wooden post-and-rail palisade, or a hedge. Deer did escape, as for instance from Stirling in

1504, although on that occasion the king was lucky since the escapee was chased back in by a 'wif'.

In England and Wales the parks seem to have flourished during the early Middle Ages, from 1066 until about 1350, after which they experienced a rapid decline. Probably this was due to the depletion of the available labour force by successive visitations of the plague and as the general movement into cities continued and even accelerated. But the economic revival of the late fifteenth century saw a growth of parks once more, though these were increasingly associated with large houses and were probably established for pleasure rather than as sources of meat.

In 1532 Henry VIII established St James's Park in London, and in 1536 Hyde Park, both as hunting parks. Henry loved hunting but still one imagines he preferred the more challenging chases outwith the parks. He sent an intimate and perhaps rather risqué note to Anne Boleyn accompanying a gift of red deer venison: 'Seyng my darlyng is absent I can no less do than to sende her summe flesche, representyng my name, whyche is hart flesche for Henry, prognosticating that here after, God Wyllyng, you must injoye summe of mine whyche he pleased I wolde were now ... I wolde we were to gyder an evenning.'

Prior to the Tudors one gains the impression that it would not have been considered quite the thing to hunt in a park for sport, that is using hounds and horseborne followers, or hunting *par force* as it was known. In his review of Scottish mediaeval deer parks, John Gilbert could only find one account of deer being killed in a park by royalty and that was of James IV in 1508 going with a certain John Methven into Falkland Park 'to stalk ane deir with the culveryn'. This also is the first record of anyone stalking deer with a firearm. In any case nearly all of these parks were far too small for anyone to hunt *par force* within them. The idea is truly ludicrous to anyone familiar with deer in parks: the effect would soon have been to drive the animals out over the inevitably rather insubstantial ditches, palings and hedges that kept them in. Probably the Tudors were obliged to hunt in parks because already around London free-ranging wild red deer were becoming rather scarce.

As in Scotland so in England there is a rich store of well-documented anecdotes describing the ways in which park deer were managed. One of the most incredible techniques used was that of driving deer from one park to another. Thus as late as 1830, Stonor Park at Henley-on-Thames was stocked by the expedient of driving all the deer from Watlington Park five miles along the roads to Stonor. Even more remarkable was the feat of Joseph Watson, park keeper at Lyme Park in Cheshire, who for a wager of £500 drove twelve brace of red deer stags from Lyme Park to Windsor, perhaps two hundred miles. Watson died in 1753 at the age of one hundred and four, having been keeper at Lyme for sixty-four years. Shirley, writing in his valuable *Deer and Deer Parks* in 1867, cites another, undated, account from Playford's *Introduction to Music*: 'Travelling some years since, I met on the road near Royston a herd of about twenty bucks following a bagpipe and violin, which, while the music played, went forward, when it ceased they all stood still; and in this manner they were brought out of Yorkshire to Hampton Court.' Those of us who have trained deer to come to call for feeding will find such accounts believable, but only just.

In any event, the numbers of English deer parks grew dramatically in the late sixteenth century and by 1577 William Harrison wrote of England, 'The twentieth part of the realm is employed upon Deer and Conies already ... the owners still desirous to enlarge those grounds do not let daily to take in more.' Yet only twenty-five years later in 1602, Carew in his *Survey of Cornwall* describes how a great many parks 'within the memory of man have been disparked, the owners making their deer leap over the pale to give the bullocks place.' And Morison, in his Itinerary of 1616, wrote: 'every gentleman of five hundreth or a thousand pounds rent by the yeere hath a Parke for them inclosed with pales of wood for two or three miles compasse. Yet this prodigall age hath so forced Gentlemen to improve their revenewes, as many of these grounds are by them disparked, and converted to feede Cattell.'

This decline in the number of deer parks was further accelerated by the Civil War and the Commonwealth of Oliver Cromwell. Come the Restoration there was some revival of interest in parks as witnessed by Johannes Kip's famous engravings of country houses (1709), almost all of which show deer in the foreground. There were indeed several importations of deer from mainland Europe to make good the losses of the Civil War and the Commonwealth. With the advent of the parks of William Kent, 'Capability' Brown and Humphry Repton, deer became part of a carefully contrived landscape and this notion has persisted, through the Victorian love of the decorative, to the present. During those years deer came and went in the parks, but reached an all-time nadir during the twentieth century when the depredations of the world wars and the requisitioning of so many stately homes took their toll.

Why, I muse, as I lie stiffening with cold, did domestication not progress any further? Why was a species that was of such crucial importance as a food source for many thousands of years abandoned when cattle and sheep came along? Why did all those deer parks decline? If it is accepted that deer were at least available for domestication, and already emparked on a considerable scale a few hundred years ago, why were they later 'overtaken' by cattle and sheep? In historical terms that was a very recent development.

I grow numb and my thinking becomes ponderous.

Just five miles from where I lie, with the cold now really penetrating, Mary, Queen of Scots had been present in 1563 at a deer drive organised by the Duke of Atholl. No doubt on his mettle to impress, the duke had gathered two thousand red deer as well as fallow and roe. The bulk of the deer broke back, killing two or three of the beaters, but 360 deer and five wolves were slaughtered. And long before that, before the Normans and into prehistory, huge tainchells were organised to drive deer into the elricks. The early twelfth-century Gaelic poem 'The Enchanted Stag' describes how one thousand men, one hundred women and one thousand dogs killed two hundred deer. Later Gaelic poems describe the deeds of Finn and his dog Bran, with the numbers swollen to three thousand men, each with two dogs, killing six thousand deer.

Even allowing for exaggeration, such drives required powerful leaders and it was probably small groups of hunters with coursing dogs who claimed the most deer over succeeding centuries, aided later by firearms. Deer numbers dwindled; but long before that had come the cattle, with centuries of raiding between feuding clans and then the trade in cattle born in the Highlands and Islands, slowly swum across the narrows and lochs, and driven along the broad drove roads to the trysts at Crieff, Falkirk, Dumfries and . . . and thence eventually, after fattening in Norfolk, as far as Smithfield. Reediehill was once on a drove road, I muse, and the ruins of a drovers' halt still remain. The cattle had been shod with metal shoes for those long journeys; skills and trades proudly developed and now all gone.

While I lie there dreaming and musing I watch and listen, with senses taut as a hunter's bowstring. I concentrate on the point at which the deer must surely soon emerge. I struggle to keep my hands warm and the dart gun's mechanism dry. How could those stone-age bowmen have been so effective in restricting their cull to young males?

And then suddenly there they are. A group of hinds with well-grown calves slowly grazing upwards. I have to discipline myself to wait until one hind is standing stationary across my line of fire so that the dart doesn't bounce off. The range seems tremendous after the relatively easy shots in grassy parks.

The stalker's patience after my first effort had been commendable but frustration at the miss was inevitable; set alongside the incredible accuracy of the modern high-velocity rifle normally used at between one hundred and three hundred metres, the blundering failure of my weapon is bound to make him doubt my competence. My reputation is on the line and it is now or never.

I am forced to risk a wild shot from a very long range. I aim a good twelve feet over the hind and the gamble pays off. The dart describes a parabola to end up perfectly placed on her shoulder. A great fluke. She runs off until at the top of the ridge, silhouetted, she pauses, stands and then quite gracefully lies down in the snow. I am jubilant and when we reach her, thankfully warmed by the climb, I take a momentous photograph. In the snow we are able to slide her carefully down to the burn; there the rest of the party meet us with a stretcher and eventually, as the shadows lengthen, I can drive my prize home to food and shelter. But never again: I could not expect that much luck to strike twice.

16 DARTING BY APPOINTMENT

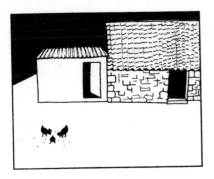

The realisation came that, unlike deer which have been fed into range, ambushed or stalked deer will run when darted, and that in any case it is extremely difficult, given the limitations of the dart gun and dart, actually to stalk close enough, say thirty metres, to place a dart at all precisely. This is a difficult message to convey to anyone used to rifles, but for a dart to fly in a straight line, horizontally, without dropping, it has to go quite quickly; and yet if it is not to bruise or injure an animal, it must not strike too fast.

The quick-witted fallow deer, alerted by the report of the gun, sometimes spots approaching darts and dodges them! It requires fine judgement and regular practice for the marksman to judge his range so that the dart neither falls short nor hits the animal too hard. An alternative, now much used, is to employ a light plastic dart but, in Scottish conditions at least, these usually blow around too much in the wind. The need to avoid injuring the deer is not a problem shared by bow hunters who can be effective at much greater ranges. Sir Ralph Payne-Gallwey, the nineteenth-century toxophilist, reckoned that 'a skilful archer with his longbow might quite possibly pierce a galloping stag with an arrow at a distance of seventy yards'.

I suppose that to the uninitiated the idea of firing a dart at an unsuspecting deer sounds barbaric, but it has to be said that in very many cases the deer do not even notice that anything has happened until they feel an uncontrollable urge to lie down. Nevertheless it does require practice to dart deer successfully. I must have darted some five thousand over many years, yet still I learn.

In the early days of darting, Roger Short and I were the object of a BBC *Tomorrow's World* programme. The film crew came all the way to Rum, braving seasickness, and then embarked on the very rough twelve-mile Land-Rover trip to reach Kilmory. All I had to do was dart one of the stags. Everything that could go wrong did, but the crew were patient and when I saw the edited piece I realised why it is that everyone imagines darting to be so quick and straightforward. All my misses, underdosings, darts bouncing off and so on had been skilfully erased.

Not all producers are so kind. When I darted a stag more recently for another programme, the entire sequence was left intact as a sort of *cinéma-vérité* with my suppressed oaths and ignominious searches for lost darts and all. Given the problems of tranquilliser rifles and darts, to call the guy with the gun a marksman is a bit of a misnomer; he can only use his experience to minimise the variables, aim and hope.

As the demand for deer grew we had to look at ways other than stalking with a dart gun and we soon found that, as on Rum, many landowners feed their deer during the winter and darting these was much easier. On some of these estates, such as that on the Isle of Jura, cattle were being fed the famous 'draff', which is the waste from the whisky distillery once the alcohol has been washed off the fermented barley. The deer were just interlopers snatching a snack from the cattle. On other estates winter feeding was thought to help the stags stay on the property and keep them in better condition so they would produce larger antlers for the sportsman the following autumn. Certainly stags are usually greedier and more aggressive than hinds. So the females, which we wanted, often did not come into range; but if all went well and if a number of feeding sites were employed we would usually get between three and ten 'feeder hinds' in a day.

It was about this time, in 1979, that I received a request from

Balmoral to see if we could help them by darting hinds to send down to Windsor. Windsor Great Park had had deer in it from the early thirteenth century until the Second World War, when the herd was dispersed. Now the Queen had proposed that it would be interesting to restock. It was suggested that it would be a good idea to use solely Scottish deer, and although not everybody was entirely supportive it was nevertheless agreed. From my viewpoint it was a thoroughly good plan. I had always been fascinated to know how well Scottish deer would perform in good lowland conditions, and this was the ideal testing ground.

Years later we found that in body weight they compared favourably with 'indigenous' English deer, and though the Scottish stags' antlers never matched those of the English, their temperament and body conformation for meat production were better. Anyway, I had a number of enjoyable days at Balmoral, starting with sighting the gun in on the front lawn and then working with the head stalker, Sandy Masson, and his cheerful crew. Sandy had started his time as a rabbit trapper and keeper around the coal mines of industrial Fife and this, combined with his army experiences, made him an ideal head stalker who always commanded respect and set an example. Sandy was invariably forthright and, I imagine, happy to trade curses with Prince Philip. He loved life at the top and would tackle any job if it provided a challenge. His fund of stories never ran dry. It was Sandy who, perhaps as much as any, changed Prince Charles's attitude from one of reluctance to shoot any deer to a more realistic appreciation that the numbers must be reduced to prevent serious environmental damage and to reduce spring mortality among the deer themselves.

It so happened that in those days our bank manager in Auchtermuchty was Sandy's cousin, and he suggested coming with me on a deer-catching expedition. It was a glorious sunny day but there was quite a depth of snow at the end of Loch Muick, and we had to drive up between a track cut through the drifts by the snowplough. There were two or three Land-Rovers, my little van, and a Snowmobile or two which were ideal for retrieving the anaesthetised deer. We got on famously because the snow had brought the deer down nicely and they were hungry enough to feed very well. Old John Robertson lived there and he had an ancient tractor with an adapted fertiliser spreader which spewed out pellets of feed to the impatient masses of deer. I sat precariously on the back of the tractor attempting to dart the hinds. We had one or two battues, and about fifteen or twenty deer were lying comfortably asleep for collection by the Snowmobiles when the wind began to get up very stormy. The loose snow started to drift and it was soon clear that the track home would be impassable.

Sandy phoned up for a snowplough and in due course late in the afternoon there arrived in succession two snowploughs and a snowblower. Unfortunately the depth of snow was now such that these stuck too, and we were all obliged to pass the night in John's cottage. The deer were by this time all ensconced in deep straw in my truck enjoying better shelter than their friends on the open hill. In the cottage, despite the hospitality, there was a substantial shortage of beds and floor space, and for a while I thought I might be sharing a bed with my bank manager.

When the first lot of deer got down to Windsor they were turned out into the park outwith my control and without anyone thinking to treat them for warbles. Needless to say, deer on farms are easily cleaned of warbles by treatment on arrival and subsequent restriction of access to wild deer and their warbles. The obvious concern at Windsor was that we might create a pool of Scottish warbles in the Scottish deer but fortunately it hasn't happened like that. Perhaps jackdaws came and gobbled up the larvae, delighted at the strange feast.

Having established the hinds we needed a stag of independent breeding. Lord Dulverton, President of the British Deer Society, decided it would be a fine idea to contribute a really good stag from his Scottish estate at Glen Feshie as a gift from the society to Prince Charles, and he asked me to come and dart it.

The stag Lord Dulverton had in mind was a particularly handsome chap by Scottish trophy standards. It would have been completely impossible to approach him close enough except by attracting him in to feed, but unfortunately he could only be lured in to feed in the bottom of the glen at dusk. The idea was that, since it was early autumn and quite dry, we would use His Lordship's Jaguar car as our approach vehicle. We waited impatiently all afternoon. I made up my dart as dusk approached and we waited on. Finally in virtual darkness the beast arrived. The laird, who had previously been rather on tenterhooks, swiftly became the man of action and we swept down the glen at a terrific rate, leaving some paint and gaining a dent as we crossed the bridge over the burn. Across the rocky boulder field towards the stag we sped. The poor car crashed and bounced along and I slithered from side to side on the slippery leather of the back seat. 'Where is he? Where's he gone?' Astonishingly the stag stood his ground while I fired a hasty dart. It missed. I commanded a strategic retreat in order to load another dart in the darkness with deadly syringe needles all about me.

Conscious that Lord Dulverton had run the Army Sniping School during the war, I was on my mettle now. It was so dark that the gun flashed and the foresight was quite invisible. For five agonising minutes we waited unaware of whether the dart had gone home; and then to my immense relief the stag lurched a couple of times and lay quietly down.

Darting should in my opinion be recognised as a veterinary procedure; after all, we are administering a general anaesthetic by remote injection. But it is rarely if ever included in the overcrowded veterinary curriculum at our six British veterinary schools and vets have shown little interest in becoming involved. Instead there are a number of laymen equipped with dart guns who must obtain their drugs from the vets, and who carry out most of the darting.

I find myself called upon to dart a variety of runaway animals but most often cattle. Almost invariably this is very straightforward, humane and quick. It is generally a simple matter to approach the animal close enough to place a dart. Also the massive haunch and thick hide of a cattle beast can absorb darts more safely, so that one doesn't need to be quite so careful about firing the dart a bit more powerfully. Usually the poor animal has been pursued by the anxious farmer assisted by the police with attendant blue flashing lights, and by the time I arrive has found sanctuary in somebody's garden. Urgency sometimes dictates that I too should arrive escorted by more flashing blue lights. Often it is dark and the scene is illuminated by spotlights, making the whole enterprise rather surreal. I make my approach stealthily through the neighbour's vegetables and carefully take my shot over the garden fence, watched from a number of windows. As the drug takes effect the animal will normally begin an uncoordinated shamble which on one occasion I remember flattened a greenhouse. In any case it all seems preferable to the use of a heavy rifle, which is the usual alternative where busy roads or railway lines are concerned.

Darting deer is more difficult since they are quicker to scent someone and their visual acuity is better. Also we are often asked to dart several animals at the same time, which makes the job much more demanding. Surprisingly, though, if one hides up a tree deer will pass below and rarely notice the unusual sight: this must have been a very common ruse for early hunters, along with stalking-horses and other tricks.

In any event, the Glen Feshie stag settled in well and sired many calves in the unaccustomed lush pasture of Windsor.

17 HOW NEW ZEALAND BEAT US TO IT

The Glensaugh project had started in 1970, and in 1974 the first report of what was grandly called the Strathfinella Improvement Group was published. The first chapter was, even more grandly, called 'Genesis and Its Accompanying Vicissitudes', and I think that encapsulates the feeling of all us early deer farmers that we were engaged in something epoch-making. The members of the group were those who had played a part in setting up the pilot deer farm. Because it had been established as a joint endeavour between the two institutes, Sir Kenneth Blaxter, Director of the Rowett Research Institute, and Ian Cunningham, Director of the Hill Farming Research Organisation, headed the list of authors. Years on, its optimism reads refreshingly; it made a lasting contribution to our understanding of red deer. A second report was also eventually published in 1988; by then the project was not so shining new, but what the second report lacks in novelty it makes up for in scientific content.

In, I think, 1978, Ian Cunningham went to New Zealand and on his return I listened to a lecture of his about New Zealand deer farming. What particularly struck me were his stocking-density figures; that is the numbers of deer carried per hectare of New Zealand farmland. Perhaps over the years my memory plays me false, for it is a terrible thing to suggest that such an eminent agriculturist, who has always been a good friend to me, could possibly have made an error. Nevertheless I believe that Ian actually did make a mistake in converting acres to hectares, and the figure he gave in response to a question from the audience increased the stocking density by a factor of two and a half when it should have been *reduced* by that factor! In any case Ian's talk whetted my appetite – those stocking-density figures were truly amazing – and I went to a bucket shop and bought a ticket to Fiordland at the southern extremity of New Zealand, where at Te Anau in 1979 the New Zealand Deer Farmers' Association were having their annual get together.

As soon as I got off the flight in Auckland I realised the New Zealand advantage. The climate was perfect. The stags had just finished their rut and our hinds were about to start calving; it was May, and when I phoned home Nickie said she had six inches of snow. Such a late snowfall is a rarity with us but in New Zealand much more so. On my farm we have to feed the deer for two hundred days at least. Few New Zealanders need to feed for more than one hundred days. Their advantage is the grass; it grows almost all year on very productive volcanic soils that have been cropped for only a century. Perhaps Ian had not made a mistake about stocking density after all.

It was a very exciting meeting. Far more delegates attended than had been anticipated and we were bussed around the conference in a convoy of fifteen charabancs. They even managed to show us helicopters emerging from the bush with drugged deer slung underneath them in nets ready for release on to deer farms. At that time the helicopters were catching about ten thousand deer a year for the new farming industry. Deer farming, it seemed, had really come of age in New Zealand. Whilst, like most British, I was shocked to see the way in which these wild deer were being shot or darted from helicopter – so very different from the meticulously careful individual rifle shooting which is supposed to be practised in Britain – I soon learnt the reasons.

The story of New Zealand's deer industry makes a fascinating tale. When the Europeans arrived in New Zealand there were no mammal species except, I believe, seals and perhaps a bat. Because of its isolation from the largest land masses the evolutionary breakthrough that the mammals represented had still not reached New Zealand. However, in naive simplicity, for sport or conceivably meat, but mostly perhaps for plain nostalgia, red deer, along with a terrible list of other animals and plants, were taken out from Europe to exact their toll on the delicate native flora and fauna. Red deer probably throve better than just about any species except rabbits, or the opossums introduced from Australia. The deer also did just about as much damage as the others. It is difficult to grasp what a huge environmental impact these grazing animals inflicted on a uniquely rich ecosystem which had evolved with no need for protection against herbivores.

In other ecosystems worldwide, plants have developed a whole battery of defence mechanisms against browsing: they synthesise chemicals to make themselves poisonous or indigestible or simply to taste unpleasant, they have learnt to coppice, that is to sprout up again with several shoots when they have been grazed down to ground level so that bark stripping is less likely to kill them, and they have spines to provide mechanical protection. But such mechanisms were less developed in the New Zealand bush. There were many species of birds unique to that habitat, some of them, like the kiwi itself, being flightless; they had no need to fly in the absence of predators. Many, owing to destruction of habitat and the introduction of mammalian predators, have now become extinct or desperately endangered. The deer thrived and the population exploded and colonised more and more of the bush. Soon deer were even being blamed for erosion as the forest was reduced. Something had to be done.

Within twenty years of the last introductions of red deer to New Zealand, the State Forest Service had realised the awful mistake and strenuous efforts were soon being made to control the animals' spread. Stalkers were provided with free ammunition and paid a bounty on deers' tails. For a period around the war the skins made good prices which encouraged many hunters, and the tally of deer killed rose, but not enough; still the population increased. And then, with the post-war growth of the German economy forcing venison prices up world-wide, came a change. In the 1960s, when the same set of economic factors prevailed globally as those which were eventually to lead to Glensaugh's establishment in Scotland in 1970, namely high venison and low lamb prices, Kiwis started thinking of new ways to extract the venison. Inevitably their minds turned to helicopters, and in April 1963 Tim Wallis and a few friends hired a helicopter and made the first effort to use it for venison shooting and recovery. Soon the use of helicopters from which to shoot the deer and retrieve the carcases became widespread. In the very rough terrain of much of New Zealand it was the only practicable solution.

To sporting deerstalkers in Britain this seems heresy but, as in all such issues, one must look at the options. In this case the alternatives were particularly stark: it was death by rifle and not always a perfect shot, given a moving deer and a helicopter, or it was sit back and watch the destruction of the ecosystem. Reducing deer by traditional stalking had proved ineffective, and poisoning was barely feasible, as well as being inhumane and wasteful. For let no one misunderstand the ecological imperative – if deer numbers had not been reduced in New Zealand the native bush would have vanished, leaving only a few vestiges of a wonderfully rich flora and fauna on offshore islands. Loss of that unique habitat would have meant the end of many species of plant, bird and animal, including ultimately most of the deer too.

Only the New Zealanders could turn a potential ecological catas-trophe into a valuable new agricultural industry, but that is what happened; New Zealand's deer farming can be looked on as a by-product of saving the ecosystem, I suppose. A substantial industry grew around the sale of wild venison to Germany: requirements included helicopters, fixed-wing aircraft, jet boats, ships, factories and chillers. Wild deer numbers began to fall and thoughts turned to the farming of deer. In 1968 the first deer-farming trials were set up at Lincoln College and proved successful. And then in 1975 the German auth-orities imposed much more stringent sanitary regulations, and consequently the costs of procuring wild venison rose dramatically. The trickle of new deer farms became a flood and in 1977 the first auction of live deer was held. The New Zealand Deer Farmers' Association was founded in 1975.

One of the factors accelerating the development of the New Zealand deer-farming industry was the presence of eager investors called, after Auckland's business quarter, 'Queen Street farmers'. Encouraged by favourable taxation regulations, these businessmen entered into 'share-farming' arrangements with the farmers and dramatically speeded up the industry's growth.

The price of deer for breeding shot up and more and more helicopters were enlisted to catch live deer. Within six months ten million dollars' worth of helicopters were imported into New Zealand with the sole object of capturing live deer. This was achieved first by the simple if ruthless expedient of jumping out and wrestling the animals into submission, then putting them in a net and hauling them out. Later came the less exciting but much more humane technique of shooting them with a dart gun, then finally – and this is the technique that has stood the test of time – shooting a net over them with the so-called 'Gotcha Gun'.

The ethics of capturing wild deer in the manner favoured in New Zealand in those days, and even of shooting them from helicopters, are bound to be controversial, especially in more urbanised societies such as England. For the animals it must certainly have been a profoundly shocking experience made only slightly more acceptable by the use of tranquillisers. Nowadays the 'live capture industry' has all but vanished and very few deer are caught by helicopter. In its heyday, perhaps twenty thousand deer were caught in a single year and for several years the annual catch remained around ten thousand.

New Zealand has close ties to the Far East, and Korean buyers had for many years been visiting to purchase antler from the shot deer. The importance of 'velvet' as a by-product of deer farming was clear to New Zealanders from the beginning.

The velvet antler as consumed by the traditional Chinese medicine taker is the whole growing antler. During the period of regrowth the antlers are said to be 'in velvet' and are soft, covered in fur and full of blood, nerves and cartilage. As the velvet antler reaches full size, after about four months in red deer, it starts to harden and the furry skin or velvet peels off to leave the antler as 'hard horn', actually bone.

It is this velvet antler which has, for at least two thousand years (since we have a silk scroll from a Han tomb dated to 165 BC testifying to the use of velvet antler), been credited by the Chinese with pharmaceutical powers. Second in importance only to ginseng in the traditional Chinese pharmacopoeia, it is used particularly as a tonic for invalids and children and for old men with declining potency. Velvet is thought to strengthen the 'yang' aspects of the consumer, that is the masculine, active, ascending elements. As providers of velvet, deer have actually been 'farmed' for at least a few hundred years in eastern Russia, China and parts of southeast Asia. The international trade in velvet is large and centres mostly on Korea, but also on Hong Kong and Singapore, where frozen antler is sent for drying, and Taiwan, where fresh velvet is especially prized. Dried velvet is traded in China and other markets. It is a multi-million pound industry worldwide, as New Zealand was not slow to realise. In the 1980s one of the most successful entrepreneurs in this business even flew the world in his own jet, buying velvet antler from reindeer in Alaska, elk in Mongolia, Manchuria and Canada, and even red deer in Scotland (illustration 7b).

New Zealand deer farmers found Koreans beating a path to their door, and the farming of deer for velvet as well as meat soon came to be an accepted practice in New Zealand. Incredibly, in a country with a human population not much more than half that of Scotland, by 1983 there were nearly two and a half thousand deer farms, and between 1991 and 1997 New Zealand exported annually between about 150 and 200 tonnes of dried velvet antler, worth over $US30 million per annum, a sum usually equal to about a third of their venison exports.

The financial crisis in the Asian economies which began in 1998 damaged velvet production but within twelve months recovery was well under way, demonstrating the resilience of the trade. There is some indication from New Zealand scientists that velvet antler has genuine pharmacological activity, and the New Zealanders are endeavouring to expand their markets by selling velvet products through health-food outlets to occidental customers in the United States and elsewhere.

My visit in 1979 coincided with a boom time for deer farmers and especially velvet producers, and it was exhilarating to be there. Even if, the New Zealanders reckoned, velvet prices fell, there was an ongoing demand for venison; indeed it is probably fair to say that most Kiwis always looked to the venison trade as the ultimate reason for keeping deer.

It was a time for heroes and one such was Tim, now Sir Tim, Wallis, who was the man with enough conviction to start using aircraft first to cull deer and then to catch them live for the fledgling deer-farming industry. As the helicopter cull began to reduce deer numbers, Tim bought an old tramp steamer, put in a refrigeration plant and a helicopter landing pad, and was then able to work in the difficult terrain of Fiordland. The *Ranginui* could carry six hundred carcases in her refrigerated hold and it took two helicopters only three days to fill her up. When the live capture business took off the *Ranginui* was fitted up with stalls and used to accommodate newly captured live deer.

Tim Wallis has been an inspiration to deer farmers everywhere. His personal courage is an example to us all. Like many of the helicopter pilots operating in the New Zealand deer business he has had several flying accidents. Until recently the worst took place in 1968 when he was taking hay up to sheep in very heavy snowfall and poor visibility and he contacted high-tension power lines. He broke his back and was paralysed from the waist down. Told he would never be able to walk again, after months of recuperation not only did he learn to walk unaided but incredibly he managed to get back into helicopters once more and take up from where he had left off.

Travelling the world to keep his various businesses in good shape, Tim is known to almost all deer farmers and universally admired. He has developed the most successful and humane capturing systems and has used his helicopters to catch animals worldwide to assist conservationists.

Tim's hobby has been the collection and restoration of Second World War aircraft, and it was while flying a Spitfire that he had an accident in 1996 which put him in a coma for many weeks. No one expected him to survive, but at the World Deer Conference in Ireland in summer 1998 there he was, being promenaded in a wheelchair by that other deer-farming pioneer and knight of New Zealand, Sir Peter Elworthy. Interesting that Sir Peter, the first Chairman of the New Zealand Deer Farmers' Association, had also been President of the nearest equivalent to our National Farmers' Union; imagine our British NFU headed by a prominent agricultural diversifier! It could not happen. Tim's mind is as acute and perceptive as ever and rumour had it that he was swimming thirty lengths every morning in the hotel swimming pool.

Helicopter capture is fast and efficient. It has to be because of the costs, and because, if overstressed, deer will not make good farmstock. Just how fast and efficient I found out when I was taken up by a pilot. Strapped in the back of the minute machine, unable to see much through the crazed perspex, I soon threw up. Fortunately I had a small bag of films with me and was able to put it to good use and avoid disgracing myself. After that I felt much better. Within the first ten minutes of hectic searching we had located a hind, swerved in, and a minute later shot a net over her. The shooter leapt out to secure the animal and give her an injection to quieten her while we flew off to land and prepare the strop, then back again for a hazardous hover about a metre above a tree top for two or three minutes to secure the netted, sedated creature and re-embark the shooter, who was able to scramble aboard from the top of the tree, and off again to the farm where the hind was lowered into a darkened shed. So within less than fifteen minutes of being sighted, that hind was in rehabilitation.

The skills accumulated by these capture teams were awe-inspiring. A number of crews were killed, and at times competition for deer-rich areas was fierce. A hangar was thought to have been burnt by a competing company and several farmers strung cables across narrow valleys to deter the choppers. Poaching of farmed deer by helicopters became for a period almost common.

As a naive, well-brought-up boy from another country I dropped into this frontiers world in 1979 and rubbed my eyes. The first night I was asked to give a brief talk to the meeting about United Kingdom deer farming, and got a good response when I told them they didn't have much to worry about in the way of competition from the UK in the foreseeable future. I was right. Only two or three British farmers had followed me at that stage. I was treated with such courtesy and welcomed with such open hearts wherever I went, that it was all very humbling.

One thing I did on that first trip was to stop in Hong Kong on my way back and chase up some of the velvet buyers. When I came home I found that many Scottish stags are shot in late summer during the early part of the stalking season when they are in full velvet. This velvet I was able to buy and freeze. I then invited my Hong Kong friends over and they paid me enough to cover my trip with some besides. I still have the photo of three smiling Chinese posing outside Reediehill after they had examined the contents of our little chest freezer. 'I go home now and immediately open LC for you.' This was my first encounter with the 'confirmed irrevocable letter of credit', opened this time on the Hong Kong and Shanghai Bank: the romance of trade!

Back in staid old Britain I began to think about the velvet business. Two things seemed clear. Firstly the ethics: I was not too keen on the idea of keeping deer simply for the purposes of amputating a piece of live tissue each year, and I was equally sure the British public would not look kindly on it either, even if it was done under anaesthetic with veterinary supervision. If it had been crocodiles or rats it might have been acceptable, but the Bambi syndrome is well developed in Britain. And as I was soon to find out, those susceptible to the Bambi syndrome had strange but powerful bedfellows in the landowning, deerstalking lobby. I had come into deer farming to promote lean meat, not to deal in a substance whose merits, or production ethics, seemed unlikely to withstand close scrutiny.

Secondly, I thought that velvet prices would not be sustainable. The market would soon be saturated, and westernisation of the velvet-eating peoples would lead to a gradual decline in consumption. But now, twenty years on, I wonder if perhaps I was wrong; time will tell.

So when I was asked to speak to the British Deer Society shortly after my return from New Zealand, I aired the subject of velvet production quite thoroughly. I made no value judgements but I remember saying that it was to be expected that someone would take my comments to heart, and that is just what happened. Within a year velvet production in Britain was declared illegal on welfare grounds.

18 HUSBANDRY BEFORE DOMESTICATION

As the newspapers and television continued to show an interest in deer farming, and as we became more of a feature at agricultural shows and in the media, I was asked to give more talks. These were usually to farmers in one guise or another, but included the usual round of Rotary and Probus clubs. I also had a short innings with the Scottish Women's Rural Institute, but was only asked once for the simple reason that I forgot to go on the appointed night.

I remember Nickie and I were enjoying a peaceful supper by ourselves, or more accurately were about to enjoy one, when the phone rang. 'Are you coming'? they said. 'We're all ready.' Seized with terror, I leapt into the car and drove like Ben-Hur thinking the whiles about what I should say. No chance to select slides, they would have to look at me for forty minutes while I tried to entertain them. On arrival, there was the village hall with the upturned, expectant, and by now actually rather angry, faces. I hastily judged the 'Dressed Coathanger' competition, which no doubt further alienated all except the winner, and then I was off on a long rambling discourse. Without the benefit of slides, which require the lights to be doused so that those who have had a busy day can at least slumber unnoticed, a speaker becomes all too clearly aware of the impact, or lack of it, that he is making. The poor speaker who, in my case, had himself fallen under the influence of Lethe earlier that evening can but envy the sleepers and try hard to shock them out of their reveries.

Shamefully I have to say that this experience was but the first of several. Usually preceded by a series of verbal requests for the talk, and notwithstanding my efficient entry of the date, time and place in the diary, for some reason that awful plaintive phone call – 'Doctor Fletcher? We're all sitting here waiting, Doctor' – still happens. It isn't, so far, the talks at distant conferences or the teaching appointments at universities that have been forgotten, but always the local organisations. Why is this? It must reflect some flaw in my psyche, and those good people, whom I especially wish to be nice to, must think very badly of me.

The last time this happened was mid-morning on 1 April. The phone rang and, since the venue was actually in Auchtermuchty, they generously allowed me ten minutes to put some slides together whilst they concluded their own business. That, and by now accumulated years of experience in giving these talks, coupled with the surge of adrenaline associated with the element of guilt and surprise, meant that I actually gave an adequate performance. The generous voter of thanks even managed to gloss over my rude delayed appearance by convincing some of the audience that it was all a carefully contrived April Fool's joke.

On the more normal occasions I can generally be relied on to stimulate some questions, and one of the commonest – usually emanating from a cocky, complacent and well-heeled sceptical farmer who probably banks a subsidy cheque of at least £50,000 each year – is: 'If it's such a good idea to farm deer, why wasn't it done before?' Yes; just the same question that continued to bother me.

I felt duty-bound to try and answer this conundrum to my own satisfaction. If I couldn't, then perhaps I should be asking myself what I was doing farming deer in the first place. I devoted quite a lot of time into researching and thinking out an answer to this really very obvious question, and eventually I developed a thesis that satisfies me.

I had already established that, to a surprising extent, deer had been husbanded in parks over the last thousand years. Long before that, we had the unexplained fact that mesolithic man had somehow learned to selectively cull the young male deer, thus maximising the production of their local deer population. How could they do this without some degree of husbandry? Yet in turn, how could a society with no crops possibly even tame the deer, let alone 'domesticate' them?

Suddenly, to my great delight, I came across a possible explanation. Excavations and pollen analysis of mesolithic dwelling sites showed puzzlingly high levels of pollen from ivy. The only explanation was that substantial quantities of ivy were being hoarded. Why on earth was ivy being collected in such quantity? The archaeologists proposed that it was being harvested as a winter food for deer.

I remained sceptical of this interpretation until my father-in-law showed me a passage from the diary of Celia Fiennes. This redoubtable lady, born in 1662, rode around England recording things which interested her, in 'a spirit of pure curiosity', as she declared. And one of the sights which spurred her to take up her quill was foresters using browse to tempt deer into a park on a winter's day in the New Forest in southern England

> ... what is peculiar to the New Forrest and known no where else are these Brouce Deare; at these severall Lodges the Keepers gather Brouce and at certaine tymes in the day by a call gathers all the Dear in within the railes which belongs to each Lodge and so they come up and feed upon this Brouce and are by that meanes very fatt and very tame so as to come quite to eate out of your hand; all the day besides they range about and if they meete any body, if it be their own keeper, without the pail of the Lodge will run from him as wild as can be; these Lodges are about 4 miles asunder and its a great priviledge and advantage to be a Cheefe Keeper of any of these Lodges, they have venison as much as they please and can easily shoote it when the troop comes up with in the paile ...

Celia Fiennes' observations had bridged the gap between the Meso-lithic and our own experiences at Reediehill; a way in which these prehistoric hunters could selectively cull out the young males had been staring me in the face. For, at feeding time, it is a simple matter to select an individual animal and despatch it instantaneously without upsetting even its friends. This could certainly have been the way in which the people of the Mesolithic managed to cull their deer selectively. I believe that with a bow and arrow, or even conceivably a spear, it would have been eminently feasible. Was it farming? It seemed rather similar to what Nickie and I were attempting.

This brought me face to face with those who have for centuries been debating what exactly constitutes domestication. I found that first of all, for archaeologists, the index of domestication has to be the first point at which they can see definite change in the size or shape of the bones of a species. This is not surprising, since the skeleton is almost the only material the archaeologist has had to work with, at least until very recently. Consequently the accepted definition of domestication amongst archaeologists is the point at which a species has its breeding under the control of man and no longer has access to breed with its wild relatives, for under those conditions it will soon change its physical form.

This definition seems to me unsatisfactory. For example, it excludes elephants which have been used from the earliest historical times as fighting machines, for transport, for work and for ceremony. Those elephants are surely, in the eyes of most of us, domesticated. And yet they are always mated by wild bulls since the bull elephant is too dangerous to handle in *musth*. Similarly, camels have by most common-sense definitions been domesticated for many centuries; and yet, because they still interbreed with wild camels, there is virtually no physical difference between the wild and domesticated populations. And what about reindeer? May they not be mated by wild reindeer or caribou over much of their range? As a result, the reindeer, the elephant and the camel closely resemble their wild relatives and are usually classed as undomesticated by archaeologists.

'Isn't this all rather academic?' you must be thinking. I suppose you are right, except that the crucial importance of the process of domestication is not often realised except by the specialists. In his book *Guns, Germs and Steel*, the American physiologist and biologist Jared Diamond recently reviewed the literature on this subject and drew some fascinating conclusions.

It has long been recognised that in the slow, painful, halting, progress of mankind from the stone age to modern technology, one of the first steps, and perhaps the most crucial of all, has been the domestication of crops and livestock for food. Through the development of systems of food production, it is estimated that an acre of land could be made to yield between ten and one hundred times more food than in its uncultivated state. The story goes that this allowed our ancestors to abandon a nomadic way of life, for the most part, and to settle down. Anyone who has been on a camping holiday will know the advantages that brings.

The domestication of livestock allowed the production of manures so vital to crop yields and health, and the animals could be used to till the ground and produce milk, tallow for candles, and wool and leather for clothing. Meat must have been of secondary importance. By being able to anticipate annual harvests and gluts and times of shortage, and relieved of the necessity of hauling food around, early farmers were able to develop systems of food storage; and although they probably worked even longer hours than their hunter-gatherer ancestors, their patterns of work became predictable and a hierarchy was established which did not simply give all accolades to the most successful hunter. Associated with the hierarchy was the creation of a leisured class: writing, philosophy, politics, religion and so on could all become much more sophisticated, and so bands became tribes, tribes clans and clans nations whilst villages became towns and towns cities. No longer were the daily and weekly rounds of societies dependent on the vagaries of wild animals, but feasts and festivals could be precisely timed around the harvests and the sowing of crops. Settlement created possessions. Even wives became chattels to be jealously guarded, since with them and their progeny passed ownership.

Expansionist ideas took hold, and wherever peoples that had successfully domesticated plants and animals encountered hunter-gatherers they prospered at the expense of the more traditional societies. Jared Diamond points out that this was due not only to their often more advanced technologies (writing, the use of livestock for haulage and in war, food storage, etc.) but also, crucially, to the support of an unseen ally: disease. Unlike the hunter-gatherer way of life in which infectious diseases were probably non-existent, aggregation of the population in settled villages opened the door to epidemics. These diseases, like most if not all infections, have their basis in the livestock. Peoples living in close proximity to their animals, often sharing the same houses, soon developed resistance to these bacteria and viruses but, as Diamond explains, when they came into contact with peoples that had never previously encountered those infectious agents the results were devastating. When Cortés conquered Mexico with only six hundred Spaniards, the population of some twenty million Aztecs had already been nearly halved by smallpox which had arrived a few years earlier, borne by an infected slave from Spanish Cuba. Similarly Pizarro, reaching Peru in 1531, found that the Incas had already been decimated by smallpox which had arrived overland around 1526.

Is it stretching the point too far to say that, conversely, as modern man loses contact with livestock and becomes thoroughly sanitised and urbanised he becomes more susceptible to animal-borne disease such as Escherichia coli 0157? We know that increasing levels of asthma, for example, are associated with diminishing exposure to bacteria in early life. Certainly many scientists would agree that the way forward is not through progressively more sterile food, but that some more realistic alternative must be found to protect us against pathogens.

The questioning farmer has by now either lost track of my argument or is looking just a little more respectful.

19 HOW OUR TABUS PREVENT PROGRESS

Archaeologists have been puzzled for a long time by just how few species of animals have been domesticated compared to the very large number of potential domesticates. Thus, of the herbivorous animals over an arbitrary one hundred pounds' body weight, Diamond lists only fourteen which have been domesticated. Why were so few used? It was Francis Galton, that extraordinary mid-nineteenth-century polymath and cousin of Charles Darwin, whose musings led to a list of criteria which he considered rendered an animal suitable for domestication. (Incidentally it was the same Galton who wrote so enthusiastically about selective breeding that he was deemed to have strayed into eugenics. It has been argued that his work provided the Nazi party with a spurious scientific basis for their crimes.) Writing in 1865, Galton listed

> ... those conditions under which wild animals may become domesticated:
> 1. They should be hardy
> 2. They should have an inborn liking for man
> 3. They should be comfort loving
> 4. They should be found useful to the savages
> 5. They should breed freely

6. They should be easy to tend

It would appear that every wild animal has had its chance of being domesticated, that those few which fulfilled the above conditions were domesticated long ago, but that the large remainder, who fail sometimes in only one small particular, are destined to perpetual wildness so long as their race continues. As civilisation extends they are doomed to be gradually destroyed off the face of the earth as useless consumers of cultivated produce.

In other words Galton states that every species not yet domesticated must by now have been tested countless times and been found wanting. This argument has been accepted by all subsequent writers on the subject up to the present. Diamond even points out that the latest evidence suggests that cattle were domesticated independently on three separate occasions – in south-west Asia, in India and in north Africa. That seems to strengthen the argument that cattle were particularly suitable for domestication and that any species remaining undomesticated must have been left alone for good reason.

Thus Diamond cites and agrees with the archaeologist Juliet Clutton-Brock and the behaviourist Valerius Geist in saying that red deer, simply because they have not previously been domesticated, are not susceptible of domestication. This seems astonishing given that around two million red deer are on farms within New Zealand alone, and that, even using the archaeologists' own strict definition of domestication, these deer are absolutely domesticated or at least well down that road. Not only are the deer used for breeding selected as carefully as are sheep and cattle, but there is widespread use of artificial insemination and even embryo transplantation. No longer is there any interbreeding with wild deer, and indeed some degree of change is already apparent in the body shape of farmed deer compared with their wild relations: after all, even in English parks the antlers of red deer stags are quite different from any seen elsewhere in the world. In fact red deer appear to be the perfect candidates for domestication: they are gregarious and they eat grass; two vital prerequisites for a new pastoral domesticant.

If Galton and his successors are wrong in suggesting that all species as yet undomesticated are intrinsically incapable of domestication, we are still left to produce some alternative hypotheses as to why so few species were ever domesticated. As someone who has spent his life attempting to sell the idea of husbanding red deer to a conventional farming community, I feel that I have some of the answers. I believe that the stability of societies is ensured by rituals, tabus and traditions whose strength may often be underestimated by biologists. The connections which a society makes with its principal sources of food are deep. Opposition from a powerful lobby of established livestock breeders and hunters, invariably supported by politicians, in modern societies is, I believe, an expression of that tradition – and one with which modern deer farmers worldwide have become very familiar!

After all, why should a society well supplied with existing domestic animals such as cattle and sheep wish to domesticate any new grazing species for meat production? Until very recently it would have been highly expensive in time and resources, and the speed of genetic improvement would have been such that nothing as productive as cattle and sheep could ever have been produced without long selection. Deer, for example, could never in less than several hundred years yield the milk, fleeces, traction, fat or other products of existing domesticates already selected by man. Crucially, I suspect, cattle were also favoured by the relative ease with which the new tame strains could be genetically isolated from their increasingly rare wild relatives, forcing inbreeding and speeding up selective breeding.

Deer, on the other hand, offered principally meat, leather and antlers – items for which no selection was required. If culling could be achieved by the simple expedient of supplying browse, such as ivy, during the winter there would have been no pressure to carry the procedure further.

One day I was reading about the seventeenth-century 'naive' paintings of English sheep, pigs and cattle. To my eye the paintings illustrated seemed not only naive but absurd. Huge rounded bodies on minute thin legs. Reading on, I came to understand that these 'naive' painters travelled the country taking commissions from farmers who expected their stock to be represented as they wished them to appear. In other words the stockmen wished their animals to be fatter than we can possibly imagine. The fat was very desirable. And, with selection, cattle and sheep soon came to provide prodigious quantities of fat. Tallow was not so much a by-product as a co-product valued as highly by most people as the meat, since in the form of candles it allowed the day's work to be prolonged by light. And of course dietary fat would always be popular in a society with no heated houses and most of its work manual. Even the deer were especially valued if they were fat, as Jane Austen makes clear in *Pride and Prejudice*: '. . . venison roasted to a turn; everyone said they had never seen so fat a haunch.'

Now, although much progress has recently been made by breeding for leanness, our conventional domestic animals remain very fatty. Not only that, but the constitution of those fats is particularly injurious to human health. This fat is now identified as a major source of disease. We need to look at healthier meats. Our needs have changed and we need to broaden our search, beyond cattle and sheep. The time is ripe for a new grassland domesticant.

While it may be correct for Juliet Clutton-Brock to suggest as she did, as late as 1981, in describing the progeny of the hand-reared first generation of the Glensaugh deer, that they 'cannot really be counted as successful domestic animals', it is surprising that at a time when the New Zealanders were already farming several hundred thousand red deer, she should have made so much of the difficulties of sawing off the antlers – 'a difficult task and not practical for a large herd' – and felt impelled to state that 'the hinds can also be untrustworthy and aggressive'. The same can still be said of cattle despite their ten thousand years or so of domestication!

Diamond also ignored the New Zealand farmed deer herd, which was over one and a half million strong by the time he wrote the following in 1997: 'modern efforts have achieved only very limited successes' and 'one never sees . . . tame deer . . . driven in herds like sheep' (but see illustration 8c).

Clutton-Brock also cites the Canadian behaviourist Valerius Geist as saying 'that man can associate with wild sheep and goats in a way that is not possible with red deer . . . the reasons for this are that the deer are territorial animals which although they live in groups or herds do not have a social structure that is based on dominance hierarchies'.

These comments perhaps demonstrate the tabus and prejudices associated with one of our society's deepest-rooted traditions. It is extremely interesting that the strongest reaction to farming deer always arises among hunting communities, with the established livestock-breeding bodies following close behind. There often seems no rational basis to their complaints. Their voices make it more difficult for any far-sighted bureaucrat or politician to extend the scope of agricultural support beyond the traditional. The hunting lobby in Denmark, for example, has successfully pressurised the government to make it illegal to house even the introduced Mediterranean fallow deer during the winter, thereby creating an inevitable threat to the animals' welfare!

But to be fair, the hunter may also feel something else. I return to Ortega y Gasset: 'the domesticated animal is a degenerate one, as is man himself ... domestication partially de-animalizes and partially humanizes the beast. The domestic animal is an intermediate reality between the pure animal and man.' The hunter wants to glimpse the wild animal from afar: alert, and ready for flight with its senses perfectly acute, a challenge to the stalker. I was not blind to the beauty of the deer but wanted to get closer, to help it, to let it relax and to admire and understand its physiology.

The availability of readily domesticated cattle and sheep must, for centuries, have removed the incentive for anyone to domesticate further grazing species. Also, the development of rituals and traditions in a society serves to fix a pattern and create a culture. This inhibits innovation. In every generation the elderly decry the modernism of the young. It is the role of tradition and ritual to stay the rebellious. Domestic animals are a crucial part of the culture of farming societies, and to challenge the status quo is bound to create controversy. We have seen how some of the Scottish landowners greeted the Glensaugh experiment. Each society has its own ways of ritualising practices, often through established religions; in the late twentieth and early twenty-first centuries bureaucracy is perhaps the establishment that deters new ideas.

In Britain the National Farmers' Union has a near-monopoly of input into the government's agricultural policy and has, at least until very recently, shown itself quite hostile to grazing animals other than cattle and sheep. This has been a perfect instance of bureaucratic enforcement of tabus and rejection of new ideas.

It is not just in Britain that powerful forces of conservatism encourage cattle farming in situations where game animals would seem to offer greater benefits. Over very large areas of Africa the tsetse fly spreads disease, *ngana*, to cattle making many areas impossible to farm. Cattle were introduced into Africa south of the Sahara quite recently by the Bantu as they migrated south between AD 500 and 1000, and they have still not developed resistance to *ngana*. The many different species of game animal, however, remain unaffected and can safely colonise those areas. Nevertheless cattle occupy so vital a position in the culture that massive programmes to eliminate wild game in an effort to remove the tsetse fly's hosts and so control the fly have been undertaken by government hunters. In what was then Southern Rhodesia, around 700,000 wild animals were shot during the first half of the twentieth century. Nothing was gained, many rare species were damaged and millions of pounds' worth of meat was destroyed. Were it not for cultural considerations it would have been vastly more logical to crop the game in a sustainable way and leave the cattle behind.

Nickie and I found that students, journalists and so on relished our deer-farming ideas whilst the older more sedate conventional farmers often either mocked or felt threatened. But the real obstacles to our plans were set by the bureaucracy – subsidies were restricted to cattle, sheep and conventional crops. This was a strong disincentive for anyone to invest in deer farming. Furthermore, legislation took no account of farmed deer and required rewriting in many details, and this was often controversial.

It has become a cliché to say that the English are good at ideas but that the establishment is frightened of innovation. Babbage, who created a mechanical device that is often considered to be the forerunner of the computer, had similar trying experiences. 'Propose to any Englishman any principle ... however admirable, and you will observe that the whole effort of the English mind is directed to find a difficulty, a defect, or an impossibility in it. If you speak to him of a machine for peeling a potato, he will pronounce it impossible. If you

Summer, and stag
in full velvet box

Aristotle in the
laundry at Kilmory

The dead stag on
Rannoch Moor
that started it all

Warble fly larvae
in the partially
skinned carcass

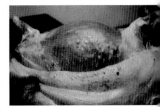

Fiona Guinness
filming on Rum

Above The wild hind, Crottal, by the Mathieson family grave, Kilmory, Isle of Rum

Right Scott, the hummel from Mar Lodge, wallows

Below Friction and Manfred fight for hinds

Reediehill in 1974

. . . and in 1999

Top left Five minutes after antler casting the wound bleeds

Top right Ten days later the new antler is in full growth with the healing wound still visible

Centre Early summer and the velvet antler is forty days old

Right Late summer and the fully grown and hardened antler is cleaned of its velvet ready for the rut

A boatload of sleeping deer

Sandy and her twins Bonnie and Clyde immediately after the birth

Nickie feeding a stag at Reediehill

Antlers for sale in a Chinese medicine shop, Hong Kong

Above The author pours a bucket of water over Ferox at the Royal Show

Right A red deer stag is helicoptered out of the New Zealand bush

A herd of deer is driven to market along a public road in New Zealand, confounding the experts

peel a potato with it before his eyes, he will declare it useless, because it will not slice a pineapple.'

Only in New Zealand, where the country is so young that change is itself a part of the culture, could deer farming really take hold. There, agriculture is still the nation's major industry and attracts innovators who in more industrialised nations might gravitate to cities, commerce and manufacturing. Or is it that those new countries, such as New Zealand, Australia, Canada and the USA, took all the most radical thinkers, the most innovative and entrepreneurial of our society, and that two or three generations on we still feel the loss? Watching the All Blacks rugby team, recruited from a population half the size of Scotland's, one might be forgiven for thinking so! Did the talents of those settlers behave like John Donne's violet transplant: 'The strength, the colour and the size, all of which before was poore and scant, redoubles still, and multiplies'?

New Zealand remains an agricultural economy. The thrusting entrepreneurs of Auckland, with business interests often rooted in the very different cultures of south-east Asia, are keen to retain a link with their rural background and seek a stake in new farm enterprises. The arrangement works well. The successes of the kiwi-fruit industry, the wine and deer-farming businesses, say something. A young British entrepreneur is unlikely to invest in an agricultural enterprise, or, if he does, he soon finds that subsidies discourage diversification into new schemes and that the dice are heavily loaded in favour of cattle and sheep where grazing options are concerned. In New Zealand, on the other hand, deer farming has risen in twenty years to be an industry adding $NZ200 million per annum to the country's balance of trade and with a farmed deer population of over one and a half million.

As well as cultural traditions that discouraged innovation there were obvious practical constraints. For the earliest people who contemplated domesticating deer, perhaps five thousand years ago, they must first of all have been difficult to enclose. Even much later, when deer parks were established and represented a vital part of the mediaeval rural economy as I have described, keeping up the pale must have been onerous. And when the Black Death killed a quarter of Europe's population between 1346 and 1352, and as the feudal system declined, and with growing urbanisation, the mediaeval park surrounds, mostly a ditch and hedge or wooden paling, could no longer be kept in repair. Merely containing the animals must have become a problem. And deer, unlike cattle which no longer had wild relatives to slow up their selective breeding, were still wholly subject to seasonal factors. Once deer have lost their fear of man and have become tame the stags can be dangerous, especially during the autumn rut. It would have taken a very determined and long-term strategist to domesticate deer in historic times when cattle and sheep were already yielding milk, wool, leather and tallow from grass.

But times have changed now. Saturated fats, ideal for candles, are modern man's biggest killer: if he is to eat meat it must be lean. Our physically active ancestors needed a lot of fat in their diet to keep warm, and as tallow for lighting; now our needs are different. Few of us live a very energetic life and we use fossil fuels to provide warmth and light and locomotion. Consequently we are becoming very fat, and heart disease is without question the epidemic of our time and society.

The modern western diet is lethal. Soon the British will be as fat as the Americans. Dominated by dairy produce, our diet seems to be associated not only with heart disease but also breast and colonic cancer, multiple sclerosis, diabetes and arthritis. One in four men will have a heart attack or stroke before retirement age in many western societies. Colonic cancer and a host of other conditions have been linked with obesity, and are becoming more common as we grow more overweight. Nor is obesity solely a disease of the developed world; it is rapidly becoming a problem in the urban centres of developing nations, too.

There is another point which I think is of vital importance. Scratch the skin and we are all hunter-gatherers, with the behaviour and physiology of our forebears. All the evidence indicates that our brains, and presumably much else besides, have remained unchanged for hundreds of thousands of years. Domestication of both animal and plant food sources only took place around twelve thousand years ago, so that the consumption of these foods is a novelty. As for the fatty meats taken from animals bred for fat, they have formed a significant part of our diet for only a few centuries. It is reasonable therefore to argue that we have not yet made the necessary physiological adaptations to that fatty diet and may be suffering the consequences.

The nutritionist Professor Michael Crawford has pointed out that because man has, for nearly all his existence as a species, eaten more wild meats, especially venison, than any other meat, his body is best adapted to that meat. He argues that '99.8 per cent of man's life has been spent eating wild food' and that 'man is still a wild animal not yet adapted to eating other than wild foods'. In other words, he argues, we have still not become habituated to the meat of cattle and sheep which we have, in the biological scale of things, only been eating for a very short time. This may seem a little far-fetched, but the fats of domesticated animals are not only more substantial in quantity – in Britain we now eat enough animal fat to power all our light bulbs – but also very different in structure from those of the game species.

There are many fatty acids, the constituents of fats, which are vital parts of our diet: the essential fatty acids (EFAs). They are, for example, essential in building the brain. These structural fatty acids are the polyunsaturates, notably the omega-3 fatty acids. Along with fish, game animals such as venison are rich in these acids. It may be relevant that for long before cattle and sheep began to be domesticated, fish was a key element of man's diet; indeed, worldwide, we still derive as much of our protein from fish as from meat. On the other hand, the fat of the domesticated animals we eat is rich in the injurious saturates.

Crawford points out that in game meat the fat is predominantly structural and intracellular, high in polyunsaturates and made up for the most part of essential fatty acids (EFAs) which are vital, as their name suggests, to the proper functioning of the body. Among these are the larger-molecule EFAs, the omega-3 and omega-6 fatty acids. Dairy products, like the meat of the animals from which they come, are deficient in such acids. Crawford notes that cows' milk contains more protein than human milk but far fewer EFAs; this makes it better suited to sustaining body development, whilst the milk of women, being abundantly supplied with essential fatty acids, is adapted to nourishing the growth of neural tissue: brain versus brawn.

I reason, therefore, that instead of trying to breed cattle and sheep to be thinner, we should widen our horizon and look at the species which are already lean. Venison is, after all, dark red because it has less fat, and more iron, than the paler beef, lamb, pork and chicken.

There remains, of course, the danger that by domesticating our deer, selecting unwisely and feeding cereal-based rations, we breed too much, and more saturated, fat into the deer. Certainly that is a risk but, alerted to it, the modern farmer can surely avoid making the mistakes of our ancestors who were, after all, eager for fats.

And by this time that well-heeled farmer has assuredly taken himself off to the bar.

20 HUMMELS, POLITICIANS AND ABATTOIRS

On 30 November 1978, The British Deer Farmers' Association (BDFA) was founded. The first issue to be handled was the legality of velvet harvesting. The Farm Animal Welfare Council (FAWC) had just been set up by the government to examine various procedures involving livestock, and in a move not unrelated, I think, to my talk to the British Deer Society on my return from New Zealand, the very first topic they addressed was 'velveting', as it came to be known. In 1980 they found against it; legislation was quickly pushed through and I was relieved: now we could concentrate on producing venison.

In fact it is not quite so simple. Most British deer farmers still remove the hard dead antlers from their stags in the late summer, and although the deer cannot feel this it does involve handling them. It would be extremely satisfactory, for both the farmed deer and the deer farmers (although not for the trophy hunters), if we could breed 'hummels'. These are antlerless stags which occur quite commonly in the wild in Scotland, probably as a result of a period of poor nutrition at a critical phase of their development. Congenitally polled cattle used to be called hummels, as Samuel Johnson noted in 1773: '... some are without horns, called by the Scots "humble" cows, as we call a bee an "humble" bee, that wants a sting.'

There is a myth amongst Scottish deerstalkers firstly that hummels are abnormally well grown, secondly that they are particularly effective during the rut in defeating antlered rivals, and thirdly that hummels beget hummels. On Rum, with Roger Short's help, Gerald had set about attempting to breed hummels, and when we came to Reediehill the programme continued. In fact those deer which went to South Uist had a considerable amount of hummel blood in them. The first hummel we used was captured by Roger at Mar Lodge and named Scott after the head keeper at Mar (illustration 3). He behaved impeccably in the enclosure behind the castle and sired many progeny including Bonnie and Clyde, all the males of which in due course became antlered. Even breeding him back to his daughters yielded antlered staggies. Although an impressive beast, Scott was never successful in competition with antlered stags – but of course the conditions in our enclosure were very different from those on the wild hill.

At about this time one of the Nature Conservancy scientists did a check on all the hummels whose weights had been recorded in the game books of sporting estates. He could find no significant heavyweights amongst them. It was a little disappointing. Perhaps when we see hummels on the hill they seem larger because we are unconsciously comparing them with the similarly antlerless hinds. And maybe in the hurly-burly of the rut the antlered stags make the same error and fail to chase the hummels away from their harems because they think they are females to be courted. This is all very speculative. We concluded that hummels remain without antlers because they are, for a crucial phase of their development, exposed to particularly straitened circumstances; they are in fact stunted. It is no coincidence that we rarely see hummels anywhere except on the most impoverished of Scottish deer forests.

I became Chairman of the BDFA in 1980 and was almost immediately thrust up against the fact that legislation continued to be drafted without taking any account of deer farming. In this case it was a new Scottish Deer Bill. If enacted as it stood, this would prevent Nickie and me and the other small band of Scottish deer farmers from killing deer except during the three-and-a-half-month hunting season. It all hinged on a slight change of wording which had, I suspect, been inserted by someone who specifically opposed deer farming and who was, as we were now accustomed to finding in our most implacable opponents, a hardened deer hunter. By good fortune someone noticed this threat the day before the bill was to go through its critical third reading. I decided that we had to make a stand.

My MP was still Sir John Gilmour who continued to show helpful interest in our unusual enterprise, and when I phoned him he immediately put me on to Sir Hector Munro whose bill it was. He suggested we meet. I flew straight down to Westminster and after twenty minutes of friendly and businesslike discussion it was agreed he would include an exemption for farmed deer. A clause, 'Clause 7', was introduced, and despite entrenched opposition from John Farr, MP, and Lord Northfield it was incorporated into the legislation. For the first time the words 'farmed deer' appeared in British law. Under the heading 'Deer Farming' it reads: 'This section does not apply to the killing of deer by any person who keeps those deer by way of business on land enclosed by a deer-proof barrier for the production of meat or foodstuffs, or skins or other by-products, or as breeding stock ... provided that the deer are conspicuously marked to demonstrate that they are so kept ...' In this way we found ourselves with a legal definition of a deer farm, and in the absence of anything better this has stood the test of time. The bill received royal assent on the 28 June 1982.

Following our success in having close-season regulations relaxed in Scotland, the legislation in England eventually caught up and at last deer farmers throughout Britain were no longer constrained by close seasons that had been designed for hunters.

Meanwhile a growing number of deer farmers were showing interest in having their animals killed in abattoirs. In New Zealand this had been done for years. Specialised abattoirs, known as 'deer slaughter premises', were constructed so that venison could be exported from New Zealand into Europe as game meat and to avoid the stranglehold that the unions had on sheep abattoirs. All New Zealand farmed deer are killed on such premises, and this entitles the New Zealanders to pay a game-meat tariff of only 3 per cent on the farmed venison they export to Europe instead of the much higher tariff of 14 per cent payable for lamb, beef and even, astonishingly, domesticated reindeer imported into Europe. We European deer farmers have campaigned for years to have this anomaly removed for the benefit of the European economy. Such a move would be of tremendous value to Europeans selling game venison as well as to us farming deer. Strangely the EU bureaucracy seems reluctant to act.

Many deer farmers felt quite reasonably that deer farming could only grow to what they considered a worthwhile-sized venture if their beasts were sent off to an abattoir. After all, most farmers in Britain, whether producers of grain, meat or whatever, have for years simply concentrated on farming to a very high standard; they have left the marketing, promotion and processing to other specialists. Few farmers in the conventional meaning of the word want to become involved in meat processing; far from it! The last thing most farmers want to engage in is the slaughter of their stock on farm. I have always felt differently, at least from the ethical viewpoint, since in principle I think farmers, like consumers, should understand that what they do, whether producing meat or eating it, has its downside of slaughter.

As chairman of the deer farmers at the time, however, it was my job to do what we could to ensure that legislation would allow deer farmers to use abattoirs, as well as to continue to kill deer in the field. In fact, because in England the legislation listed those animals which cannot be killed in slaughterhouses and in Scotland it listed those that can, and since neither list included deer, the anomaly existed by which deer could be taken off for slaughter in English abattoirs but not in Scottish! By this stage I had come to understand that deer can be transported easily and in suitable vehicles with plenty of space and bedding, and that perhaps abattoirs had improved since my student days.

FAWC had decided in 1982, following the Scottish exemption of farmed deer from the close-season legislation, that they should consider the general welfare of farmed deer including their transport and slaughter. They immediately undertook to prepare a report. We in the BDFA co-operated as best we could. So FAWC came up to Scotland to witness deer being killed in an abattoir, and were for the most part content with the way it had gone. I had actually been present on that occasion, and one notable and intelligent animal welfarist subsequently wrote to me saying he had been very impressed, and that the deer had appeared less stressed than many sheep he had seen being slaughtered.

Since many sheep, especially off the hills, are handled much less than farmed deer this was perhaps not too surprising; but one must remember that deer have not had any significant amount of breeding for docility and tractability whereas for some ten thousand years, albeit rather haphazardly, sheep and cattle have.

Anyway, FAWC could not make up its mind unanimously on this hot potato; although the majority found no fault with the idea of deer going into abattoirs, a minority, including Ruth Harrison, found the concept repugnant. Along with the rest of the council she had been to Reediehill to watch me shoot deer in the field with a rifle, and evidently preferred this in-field slaughter to the abattoir alternative.

Since that time deer have regularly been slaughtered in specially adapted abattoirs in England, Scotland and Wales, as well as in Ireland, and legislation has been amended where necessary to make this procedure legal. No particular problems have emerged, and although Nickie and I still prefer to kill the deer at Reediehill in the field we accept that for other farmers abattoir slaughter is the only way to kill significant numbers of deer, and that it can be carried out in a well-controlled and humane way.

My two-year stint as BDFA Chairman was over. There were inevitable schisms and factions among such a disparate group of individuals and I was happy to pass the baton to Alan Drescher, a cheerful but tenacious pig farmer from East Yorkshire who had diversified into deer. Alan was typical of the best new entrants into deer farming, who had been moved by endless discussion in the media and encouragement from politicians to believe that agricultural support would decline and that 'diversification' was the thing. Many of these new deer farmers were large arable farmers who were interested in deer and were also highly competent stockmen, with abundant assets in the way of arable by-products such as straw, and fodder beet for winter feeding, and also very often in possession of redundant farm buildings that made good winter housing. These people were invaluable assets to the embryo deer-farming industry. They had joined us in response to the bland-

ishments of successive governments to diversify into market-led indus-
tries in readiness for the removal of subsidies. They were to remain
disappointed.

21 EXPORTS, SWISS CHALETS AND VEAL

I suppose that eventually an order from overseas was inevitable, and when it came it was very welcome. Our early unexpected successes in attracting publicity had been gratifying, and naturally a lot of the magazines and broadcasting snippets went abroad. Soon foreign agricultural journalists came specifically to interview and photograph us and we became quite blasé about seeing ourselves in Dutch, Swiss and Italian magazines. But you don't necessarily grow wealthy from seeing your picture in the papers. The few sales of deer to embryo British deer farmers helped and the venison sales were growing, albeit from a very low base. Nevertheless the need to make a living at Reediehill was becoming more insistent.

It was as a result of one of these features that we received an unannounced visit one afternoon from a young Swiss farmer. Max Bürgi was everything a man from the mountains should be. His very voice made me nostalgic for my old Gum Club holidays climbing in the Alps. He moved and spoke with the quiet deliberation that comes of pacing your way up the mountain and planning every footfall. His accent had a beautifully soft and measured rise and fall; his posture and gestures were redolent of snow, sun and rock. Of course, we asked him to stay the night and next morning came the proposition. Max had, it seemed, successfully inspired the government in his local canton – the Jura – to try an experiment. 'I am looking for a way to make those small farms in the Alps survive. We all have cows and that's OK, but we need a new local enterprise if we are to continue without being so dependent on grants. Venison is very popular in Switzerland; we could produce it like you do here.' How often I was to hear that story. 'Great,' I said, 'but where can you get your animals from?' 'I have persuaded the authorities in Basle to help ten farmers set up deer-farming operations using in some cases fallow and in others red deer. I want to buy the deer from you. This spring you bring some red deer?'

Although livestock transport was not, in the late 1970s, the emotive procedure that riots twenty years later were to make it, this business nevertheless already gave me much food for thought. For me it was important firstly that the deer were for breeding and that their higher value meant that they could be allowed a lot of space and ample bedding, secondly that I could go with them and ensure tender loving care throughout, and thirdly that I should be happy that Max would treat them well in Switzerland.

I had never transported deer anything like so far before, but I reasoned that when I did move them they always seemed to travel well enough and that if I gave them plenty of space and fed them well on the journey they should do fine. And so it was decided that Nickie and I would set out together with the deer as soon as Max phoned to tell us that the road was clear of snow. We wanted to move quickly so as to give the hinds plenty of time to settle in before calving.

Impatiently Nickie and I sat in Scotland as the days rolled by. April passed and we couldn't believe there was still snow. We phoned Max for a progress report. 'There is still two metres on some parts of the road but I will dig it away with the tractor. I think you can come next week.'

The sun beat down as we spun through the north of England and then greyed as we entered the grime of the Midlands and southern England. There was no M25 then, and by the time we finally pitched up in Dover it was dark and about midnight.

I commented to Nickie, 'Wonderful. No queues, we should get on the first ferry.' Yet as we followed the signs to 'Freight Departures' I began to realise, green though I was at this game, that something was a little odd. Everything was closed. The docks were all but deserted. Eventually I found someone and asked what was happening. He looked at me as if I had come from another planet. 'Don't mean to tell me you haven't heard about the customs strike? Don't you have television up there?' Well, I suppose he wouldn't have believed me if I told him that we didn't. I had actually heard about the strike but had not imagined, in my blithe innocence, that it would pose any problems. Evidently the boats were sailing, but they would not carry me unless I had the appropriate pieces of paper. Nickie and I retreated to the lorry cab for a council of war. It certainly seemed desperate. To find local accommodation for the deer in Dover while we awaited an end to the strike was unthinkable. What were we to do?

Ever the man of action, I strode off to the shipping office and delivered an ultimatum. 'Tell whoever is in charge of the strike that unless we get our papers now I shall telephone all the national papers and tell them that it was his absence that caused the death of twenty red deer.' It worked like magic: the power of the press. Within an hour the Chief Customs Officer was out of his bed and, with perhaps justified ill grace was stamping our papers. 'Where do you want to clear customs?' he asked. 'I haven't the faintest idea,' I said, 'but I suppose at the end of the autobahn at Basle.' 'OK,' and he wrote: 'Basle Bahn.'

We were soon aboard and slept well on an empty boat, waking refreshed. The journey through Germany was uneventful. I remember picking branches from some trees, which down in the south were in full leaf, and feeding them to our passengers. The first green leaves they had eaten for six months. The deer did wonderfully. They lay down on their straw beds and almost seemed to enjoy the journey, looking out inquisitively or lying quietly cudding as we swept along.

In due course we arrived at the end of the autobahn at Basle and the frontier. We showed our documents to the uninterested customs officer who waved us through and told us that since our papers were marked 'Basle Bahn' we couldn't clear customs with him but must go to the railway station. This seemed rather unusual but we did as requested and made our way to the station. Here the deer attracted some attention from curious passers-by. Eventually a very helpful railway official arrived and when I showed him the papers he set off determinedly with me in his wake. For a good half-hour we went from office to office, nobody showing the slightest interest in my papers. Reluctantly, with his goodwill a little tarnished, the helpful rail worker turned to me: 'I think it is hopeless. You must continue.' Jubilant, I hurried back to Nickie and the admiring crowd and off we zoomed.

Once more the sun shone; never have the Alps looked more exhilarating. As we drove, I instructed Nickie to tear up our redundant papers in very small pieces and throw them out of the window. It was a catharsis.

Within two hours of leaving Basle railway station, we had crawled up precipitous narrow lanes between walls of melting snow, turned the deer out to look around them in wonderment at the mountains and the pristine green grass, and then, with our knees under the Bürgi family dining table, were downing spätzli, that delicious fried-noodle/pancake/pasta product, prepared and cooked by Max's wife Helena.

It was during this memorable meal that I came to realise one of the more unusual perils of life in the Alps. Their chalets are constructed on steep hillsides, and good use is made of the incline so that hay can be loaded for the long winter at the rear of the house at ground level directly into the loft which extends over the entire cowshed and human dwelling space below. It can then be easily forked down to the beasts. The resulting dung is then wheelbarrowed out at the front of the building, along an elevated plank, and built into a midden downhill from the chalet. Between mouthfuls of spätzli, Nickie and I both noticed, in the kitchen ceiling above us, an irregularly shaped area where Max had evidently replaced some of the pine boards recently. 'What happened there?' I asked. There was an embarrassed silence as the Bürgis looked at each other a trifle abashed. Finally Max came out with: 'It was a cow.'

'A cow?'

'Yes, in the middle of the night, it wandered into the loft above and down it came through the ceiling.'

Apparently unharmed, Max had been able to lead it out of the kitchen, but Helena had not been as amused as we were.

We stayed on a few more days trying to understand the economics of the Swiss alpine farmer. Twice a day Max would take his single-legged milking stool, strap it around his waist and proceed to hand-milk some ten cows. Infinitely precious is traditional alpine dairy farming to the Swiss culture, and through tourism, to its economy. An alp must either be pasture grazed through the summer or a meadow with the grass cut for hay; without grazing or mowing, it slowly reverts to scrub and eventually woodland. Without cows no one would cut hay: ergo no cows, no alps, no skiing, no tourists. And so rich is the Swiss nation or so keenly does it treasure the alps, that the subsidies are sufficient to allow each farmer to survive with only a handful of cattle. This system ensures that the grass is cut for hay as neatly as ever, using specialised tractors and mowers that can operate on grassy slopes that would be difficult to walk up but which were previously scythed. In Max's tractor was a glass-covered saucer with a ball to indicate the level of tilt and warn the driver if he is being over-ambitious.

One evening Max took us to see his neighbours. We walked through the spring grass and wild flowers for a mile or so. He wanted, he said, to show us a truly traditional alpine farm. I remember in particular the solitary veal calf. Proudly reared to yield the truly finest veal, this animal was tethered in the depths of a huge, beautiful and very ancient wooden chalet. In almost complete darkness he had drunk his milk copiously all winter and was now substantial. In order to satisfy his craving for fibre he had also gnawed through some bulky timbers. Here, I thought, light years away from a 'factory farm', exists this miserable creature with all around him the most exquisite rural idyll. Yet you cannot eat the scenery, and life was hard for these people and even harder for their veal calf. Of course, having never known any other way of doing things, and because of the demand for white veal,

Max's neighbours were doing as their forebears had for centuries and any accusations of discomfort, let alone cruelty, would have shocked and hurt them. It was in an effort to change all this that Max was seeking to establish a new pastoral industry and we were being enlisted to help.

With a great sense of relief after the rather stressful delivery, we took off for a few days' break to enjoy the Swiss lakes and mountains in springtime. We hired a rowing boat in one of the lakes and swam from it. It was a perfect day and we were very happy. We drifted past a landing stage belonging to a rather smart hotel, in fact a veritable *schloss*. I have always had a weakness for opulent hotels beyond my means, and on impulse I ran up the steps to the imposing, brilliantly painted white edifice and into the hall. I stood at the reception desk dripping wet in my swimming trunks, and booked us a room. That evening we ate on a terrace to the accompaniment of a piano, and the next morning took a chairlift up from behind the hotel.

We ascended slowly and silently through the green forest canopy. As we climbed we looked back over our shoulders. 'Look, there's the hotel.' Sure enough it was easy to see its showy whiteness dominating the pristine Swiss landscape. 'Which is our room?' 'There it is and . . .' Nickie's voice trailed off in horror. Her new blue jeans, washed for the first time and left to dry on the balcony, had made their mark. Descending for two floors was a broad blue stripe on the hotel's newly painted wall. Sheepishly and guiltily, but quickly, we descended and checked out.

That wasn't quite the end of our Swiss adventure. Several months later an official-looking letter written in German arrived for me from Basle. I was comfortably home again by then, it was winter and all our reports from Max indicated that the deer were revelling in their Swiss sunshine and alpine hay despite the deep snow. In fact the snow was so deep that the fences were completely submerged and the deer were free to come and go as they wished, but the lure of Max's sweet, herb-rich hay was enough to keep them. It all seemed a far cry from the rain of Scotland and the daily pressures of running the farm at Auchtermuchty; I was not inclined to take a long tract of German from a distant bureaucrat very seriously. It lay quietly and accusingly on my desk. Christmas passed and Hogmanay arrived. Our dear polyglot Luxembourgeoise friend Maggy Stead came to stay and I thought of the letter.

'Oh, Johnny, you are in deep trouble!' said Maggy. 'You are due to appear in court in Basle on 20 January and it says that unless you respond and put up a good defence for the illicit introduction of livestock to Switzerland you will never be able to visit Switzerland again without being arrested.'

I thought of the green pastures and snowy alps and knew that I did want to go back some day. So I wrote a long letter explaining the whole saga, how we'd done our best at the railway station, and pleaded ignorance of all the regulations – after all I was only a vet not a professional lorry driver. Maggy laughed and said my letter was very British, by which I suppose she meant unashamedly amateurish and incompetent. Anyway she nobly translated it and we posted it off. Again the months passed and finally, finally, I was officially exonerated.

And so much for my European exports. I could write of the frustrations of being delayed by ships whose skippers would not take my deer in anything more than a stiff breeze, of my early ignorance of paper requirements so that the French customs told me that I should have to kill all my deer and throw them in the docks, of delays due to absurd and unnecessary veterinary requirements which can do more to compromise the welfare of the animals than to control disease, of my delaying ships by failing to wake on arrival, so precipitating a full-scale search of the whole ferry, of stowaways, of fires on ship and much more besides. Of deer formally released, in the full glare of the media, on to a Dutch polder in front of their Minister of Drains to help transform that reclaimed seabed into a national nature reserve. Or of Scottish deer taken to French agricultural research colleges to pioneer new enterprises in the Massif Central. Through it all there have been kind, helpful people who have enabled me to treat my deer with patience and care.

I am as keen as the next man to condemn the export of live animals for slaughter; indeed I have for many years been a paid-up member of Compassion in World Farming, and why else would we go to such lengths to kill our deer on the farm here rather than have them hauled off to an abattoir? I believe that my deer, on beds of straw with plenty of space, deserve the chance to live longer lives as breeding stock in good conditions overseas. And, of course, I do go back to visit them and find them happily established.

With the benefit of hindsight, I can enjoy all these adventures now. There can be few experiences so abidingly pleasurable as the release of the deer from their long incarceration into the mild European spring after the cold privations of a Scottish winter. Fresh grass weeks early, and the silence and sweet smells, as the deer walk slowly away into the woodlands: those are the best memories.

22 VENIBURGERS, VENISON AND CHEFS

Right from the start, venison sales had been the objective. Nickie and I were united in the knowledge that deer meat was tasty and healthy and that we must get this message across so that more people would try it. I had modestly planned at one stroke to reduce the excessive and fast-growing Highland deer population, develop a new Scottish industry in *farmed* venison and improve the nation's health. And so far it seemed we were on track.

The demand for breeding stock was gratifying and certainly necessary to create a new agricultural industry, but perhaps it sidetracked us from our main goal of increasing venison consumption. Though growing, venison sales remained small; we needed to encourage venison eating on a grander scale.

What was needed was a way of broadening the market. There would always be a small nucleus of venison eaters who had been obliged as children on summer holidays in shooting lodges to gnaw their way stoically through old stags and had eventually developed a taste for it. But in fact many others had in this way been put off venison for life; after all, who grills steak from old bulls? Only the young lamb, heifer or steer is good enough for the dining table; the cull or cast breeding animal should end up in a sausage or pie. What surprised us was not so much that people came all the way up to the farm to tell us their dismal experiences, but that they were prepared to give it a second chance. This was encouraging. Over the years, Nickie's books, firstly *Venison, the Monarch of the Table*, devoted entirely to venison, and then *Game for All*, dealing with other types of game as well, created a following and were successful in disseminating simple and foolproof rules for the cooking of venison. We began to see new-style eaters coming to the shop and could see the scope for growth.

Somehow we had to extend this small group, to seduce potential new venison consumers with the meat of young deer. We knew how good it could be. To do this we needed a simple product which anyone could cook, and that we could grill and sell direct to the consumer, allowing us to talk to them at the same time so that we could tell them what venison actually was, and, crucially, how to cook it. When we stood at agricultural shows most people had not the foggiest idea what we were trying to sell. 'Venison? Wha's that?' They even confused it with veal.

Then along came a whirlwind of youthful energy and chaos, brimming with bright ideas, in the form of Alasdair Darroch. Studying agriculture at Edinburgh University, Alasdair, like so many students, became seized with the idea of farming deer. Alighting on us at Reediehill, he immediately started some trials for his Honours thesis, helped us while we extended the farmhouse, and brought his friends for jovial weekends when Nickie, Stella, Martha and I basked in their goodfellowship. As Alasdair's time at Edinburgh came to an end everyone became enthused with venison promotion. We plotted; we schemed.

The answer we came up with was a venison burger. This could be made easily and sold cheaply. It had, if not actually a downmarket image, an air of being generally available, faintly trendy and, of course, undemanding of culinary skills. What is more we could sell it at shows for people to eat immediately. Nickie went to work on the development and the 'Veniburger' was born. The name was obvious, and though the *Guardian* was later to quip that they should have been called 'Bambiburgers', we were happy.

We reasoned that those agricultural shows would be an appropriate testbed and the Royal Highland Show in Edinburgh was chosen as the place for the launch. The Deer Farmers' Association had secured a site suitable for exhibiting two or three tame deer and we judged that these animals could make our message even more emphatically. No doubt a few squeamish souls would cavil at the idea but we knew that the deer wouldn't mind; I have never been one to resist the temptation of rumpling a few stuffed shirts, and we would have a chance to explain things to the squeamish.

We embarked for Edinburgh and the Royal Highland Show in June 1983 and set up a small marquee with some trestle tables, a kitchen area and a small domestic gas barbecue. Some signs reading '*Quarter Pound Veniburger in a Sesame Seed Bun with Salad and your choice of Dressings, 80p*' were produced and off we went. The response was phenomenal. We had not realised how deprived the poor Highland Show-goer must have been. By lunchtime on the first day, queues were twenty yards long and they never diminished all day. As the show went on, word got around and demand grew.

We had a cheerful write up in the *Financial Times*, Veniburgers' first publicity, and then a live studio broadcast for BBC and so it went on. Each day our noble gang of workers became more and more exhausted. Around lunchtime when we were going flat out, the fat from the burgers would regularly ignite and send flames rushing up into the branches of a sycamore, adding to the brio of the occasion. Eyes reddened and eyelashes melted. We became regulars at the First Aid tent. St John's Ambulance stalwarts were rewarded with well-grilled burgers.

On our return we held a council of war. How to capitalise on our success? It was clear that the first thing we needed was a small team of helpers to make the burgers. We advertised, and in this way we found Barry Burns who, nineteen years on, is still here. Sharing many of the

attributes of his famous-namesake Rabbie, Barry is redoubtable. His
intelligence and quickwittedness have not been blunted by too much
education and he retains a great capacity for organising and remem-
bering things, but, above all, he remains a highly skilled and very fast
butcher; what we would have done without Barry it is hard to say. He
knows everyone, and now that his reputation as the stud of Newburgh
is becoming a memory and the prospect of his settling down no longer
seems laughable, he keeps regular hours and we are very happy. It was
not ever thus. I got distinctly fed up with having to haul him out of
his bed in the mornings, being obliged on one occasion to climb a
ladder to rouse him through the window only to find that he was
generously sharing his bed with two ladies. And there was the night
when the police rang to tell me that I had better come to Newburgh
to collect my tractor. Barry had put a large round bale of straw on the
foreloader at the front and driven it up the High Street before, in
parking it outside the pub, he had removed their rainwater guttering,
or as we say here, rhones.

Flushed with the Veniburger's success at the Highland 'launch', we
set off to shows all over Britain. Especially successful, five hundred
miles away, was the Kent Show where, in amongst the cherry and
apple tents, stood our deer. The Duchess of Kent politely told us she
didn't like venison and I immediately classed her as one of those who'd
been obliged to eat an overcooked old stag once too often.

As we became more professional we had to employ a bigger and
bigger group of folk and our sales speeded up. We reached an all-time
high at the national Game Fair at Romsey near Southampton in July
1984 when we sold nearly four thousand Veniburgers a day for three
days. Our teamwork was phenomenal: one person slit the rolls, another
stuffed them with sliced-up salad and wrapped them in a napkin, a
third took the napkin and held the roll open to receive the cooked
burger and hand the ensemble to the customer, and the fourth took
the money. Once a rhythm had been built up we could go at a great
rate and the queue would shuffle past at a walk. On one occasion Barry
was taking the money so fast that he had people's change ready before
they had even ordered. He was holding out a roll with burger and
salad packed into it when one unassuming country gentleman said:

'Do you mind awfully if I don't have any cucumber? It doesn't agree with me.' Quick as a flash Barry said, 'Nae cucumber? Nae problem,' and, whipping the cucumber out of the bun and into his mouth, handed over the roll, burger and change. The customer was past and we had probably served another ten before he knew what had happened.

Eventually the principal caterer must have decided we were becoming too popular, to the detriment of his pocket. We were pushed to the side and he surrounded us with what we considered downmarket hot-dog stands, candyfloss sellers and so on. Sadly we had to reduce our presence each year until it was no longer sense for us to go. The shows are the poorer, because 'charcoal-grilled Veniburgers' were what the showgoers wanted. Also, for many years, even at game fairs, our venison was the only game visitors could buy.

After our successes at the shows we naturally wanted to expand into other sales outlets. Pubs and shops were singled out. We purchased, second-hand, a little van and had it painted with the Veniburger logo (antlers on the letter V) and '*They're not just any burgers they're …* *Veniburgers*', and set to work delivering. Our full-time salesman Dougie, his technique honed by the high-pressure selling of American vacuum cleaners for which he had won prizes, worked as hard as he could driving the van all hours.

As a result of the publicity from the shows we were astonished to find ourselves the subject of a full twenty-minute film made by BBC Northern Ireland. Television cameras followed our van and filmed Dougie as he delivered into a shop in Auchtermuchty. Finally there was a sequence of Nickie and myself having a candlelit dinner of roast venison with a glass of red wine, actually filmed mid-morning but with the curtains drawn, while the presenter gravely asked us questions of great pith and moment. We were being depicted as the ideal farm diversification, taking no public money yet employing four or five people on a very small farm: it was all very flattering and gratifying.

Alasdair's optimism was unquenchable, and as month succeeded month he remained resolutely cheerful. But things were not going well. Our original idea with the Veniburgers had been that by choosing a 'downmarket' type of product we would explode the myth that venison was a habit pursued only by the ruddy-cheeked port-drinking classes. In this way we would introduce a wider eating public to the delights of this healthiest of all meats. Instead of 'Wa's tha' then, eh? Nae thanks' we looked for 'Oh, aye, venison, aye, Ah like tha'. Gie's a bi' o' tha'.' We were really quite successful at that, but when we came to try and increase sales by venturing away from our captive show market to compete in the real world of commercial burgers, we found things a little more tricky. Our main difficulty lay in the catering trade.

Despite the entreaties of salesmen wishing to get us hooked on coloured hamburger fillers and extenders, we naively yet honourably used proper red meat whilst 'the trade' generally used a mixture of fat and 'mechanically recovered meat'. It was the case then, and probably still is, that you could sell a sausage or a burger into the catering trade without putting any 'meat', as we know meat, into it at all. At least the products sold in shops must have a declared minimum meat content. As you might expect, we had designed our Veniburger to have lots of meat and taste good, something indeed that would not shame us. Not for nothing did we call them 'the honest burgers of Auchtermuchty'.

However, when Dougie took them along to a fish and chip shop, for example, the proprietor would frequently show great interest and might even occasionally risk tasting one, but as soon as the price was discussed he would fall about laughing. We were looking to sell our burgers for about 20p each and they were buying their 'beefburgers' for about 2p! The other quality demanded by the discerning fryer was elasticity. 'Och, nae use that, gie it a wee waggle and it's a' in pieces.' By which they meant that the process of dipping the burger in batter was traditionally followed by a brisk shake to remove surplus batter before immersion in the deep fryer. Our Veniburger lacked the necessary measure of elasticity. In fact I doubt whether any burger with a normal complement of red meat could pass the waggle test without the incorporation of some high proportion of latex or similar binding material.

Dougie would not give up, though, and soldiered valiantly on; but eventually there were days when the van returned without a single sale. The time finally came when I had to go with Alasdair to the bank and say enough was enough, would they please lend us no more money. Dougie was laid off. Alasdair was devastated and we had a series of stormy meetings, sometimes with accountants officiating, but usually just the three of us, until eventually we reached an amicable agreement and have remained friends to this day. We were chastened, a lot poorer, and our first failure was behind us.

Nevertheless lessons had been learned, and one of them was that the catering trade was not for us. All but the few elite restaurants will buy whatever is cheapest; virtually none say where their ingredients come from and thus there is no premium paid for good quality or local products.

Fortunately, all this time sales of live deer for breeding were holding up well and indeed growing. I was kept increasingly busy at home and abroad with sales and some consultancy work. Prices were fine and we were not dependent on venison sales. And just in case there was any danger of our becoming too modest, it was about this time that BBC Radio Four with Sonia Beasley chose to devote a full length *Enterprise* programme to me. It is everybody's dream to be able to talk about oneself with a friendly presenter on the radio or television and I cannot deny how much I enjoyed the experience. Once more everything was going our way, and the Veniburgers had become merely a necessary episode on the road to what we still never doubted would be eventual success, fame and glory.

Over the years, Nickie continued to promote venison in a whole variety of ways. Apart from her own two books, she compiled another for the Deer Farmers' Association; she gave venison- and game-cooking demonstrations, lectured at conferences, featured on television and radio programmes, encouraged school and student projects and talked tirelessly to our customers, both on the telephone and in the little shop. We were both touched and delighted when she was chosen to be the recipient of the very first Scottish Food Awards lifetime achievement award.

Of all these activities, the most crucial was liaison with journalists, since they could spread our message for us. Those broadcasting from Reediehill on the subject of venison have included Derek Cooper,

Sophie Grigson, Loyd Grossman, Marguerite Patten, Jancis Robinson, Oliver Walston and, of course, the Two Fat Ladies. Even the late brilliant Jeremy Round visited and wrote of us. Our pile of newspaper and magazine clippings is a deep one.

We had two main messages for the journalists. One was the lean and healthy aspect of venison. It never ceases to astonish me how often chicken is recommended for those on low-fat diets. Is there a hidden agenda here? After all, environmentally, chicken production has to be more damaging than a grass-fed product, nor do we feed our deer antibiotics. A growing number of people on low-fat diets who become bored by chicken and fish are delighted to realise that they can eat venison as a red meat since it has even less fat than skinless chicken. And as for cholesterol, venison has about one-third the cholesterol of skinned chicken.

The other message we had to convey was that, contrary to what many believed, good venison needn't be dry or tough. You could cook it gently for a few hours in a low oven as a pot roast like we used to do in the Raeburn on Rum, in which case the liquids kept it moist. Or you could cook it very quickly at a high temperature and serve it rare. No marinading, no larding necessary. A short period of resting will leave the meat pink and moist throughout. It is physically impossible for pink meat to be dry.

This was perhaps a forgotten message; it was hardly new. Over a hundred years ago, the celebrated chef, Alexis Soyer, who did so much to improve military catering during the Crimean War, knew all about cooking venison. In the *Gastronomic Regenerator* of 1846 he wrote: 'Venison must be underdone, red in the middle, and full of gravy.' And again: '... even after all that nature has done in point of flavour, should it fall into the hands of some inexperienced person to dress, and be too much done, its appearance and flavour would be entirely spoilt, its delicious and delicate fat melted, and the gravy lost.'

At last some understanding is beginning to take root; this simple secret is becoming recognised more widely with the improved avail-ability of farmed venison of a known and guaranteed youth. Wild venison responds well to this treatment as long as it is from a young animal, but it is extremely difficult if not impossible for the cook to know what she has when she buys wild venison over the counter. Sadly, game 'venison' could be anything from African antelope to locally shot roe deer or even kangaroo. This is arguably correct, since historically the word venison merely means the meat of a hunted animal. Nevertheless it does not make life easy for the would-be gourmet. After all, the antelope is more closely related to cows or sheep than to deer, and there is as little connexion between red and roe as between cows and sheep.

Most cookery books, with very few exceptions, do not assist in resolving this confused situation. It is usually clear that the authors themselves know next to nothing about the seven or eight different species of deer that can provide the British cook with wild venison, or about the seasonal difficulties created by the differing rutting seasons or the legal close seasons. Roe deer, for example, are only distantly related to red deer; they are also only about one quarter the size, and are in season at very different times of the year. To further irritate the aficionado, most cookery writers get the nomenclature quite wrong as well, hopelessly muddling red deer (stags, hinds and calves), roe (bucks, does and kids) and fallow (bucks, does and fawns). All very trivial maybe, but for those who know deer, as important as not calling lambs kids and so on.

However, there have been some notable conversions. Quite early on, the late Jane Grigson wrote an article about venison for the *Observer*, and sent Nickie the draft to read through. It contained many of the old chestnuts and Nickie agonised for days. How could we presume to correct someone whose integrity and writings we admired so much? Eventually Nickie sent in her corrections, all backed up by evidence, and, with professional grace, Jane Grigson completely rewrote the piece.

As for chefs, for an example of just how successful we have been in explaining what we are trying to do, and that farmed venison is a safer bet than wild, I can quote Raymond Blanc. In *Cooking for Friends* in 1991 he wrote: 'Try to avoid farmed game which is much cheaper, but not worth buying, with the exception of venison'; and again in the same book: 'I rarely recommend game that has been farmed, but farmed deer is one of the exceptions.'

Although Nickie's efforts were crucial to the development of a taste for venison we were also undoubtedly benefiting from the vogue for new food products that has come with increased wealth and affluence. Awareness of the product has changed dramatically in the few years we have been taking trade stands. The comments are generally informed and enthusiastic; a far cry from the Veniburger launch. It has required a great deal of hard work but the results have been rewarding.

There was always the danger when we started promoting farmed venison that people would think of it as inferior to wild when in fact, of course, the reverse is more likely to be the truth. Even now there are still a few dinosaurs of journalism trotting out this unfounded prejudice, usually without having tried both types of meat. There is a romantic appeal about the wild which is wholly understandable, and if there is a complaint about farmed venison, it is invariably that it will be bland. This is often heard from people who have always eaten marinated venison. We were able to demonstrate through blind tasting trials that it is not possible to tell the difference between wild and farmed venison – you can have bland, or well-flavoured, or marinated, or over-strong versions of either. It is merely that farmed is more consistently good, more reliable.

After a great deal of trial and error at Reediehill we found that maturing our venison for two to three weeks gave the best balance of flavour, and this is what we have done here ever since. The meat is hung as a whole carcase, without its skin, in a refrigerator. Some people are surprised that we hang it for so long, but Nickie and I believe that one reason for the general decline in meat-eating is the complete tastelessness and watery texture of much meat exposed for sale. The old butchers used to hang their beef for a very long time and we believe that, although it is expensive to do so, it is worthwhile. For many years we milked a cow at Reediehill and once reared one of the calves for beef. We hung that huge fatty carcase for five *months*, after which time it had grown a rind like a Stilton cheese; but once trimmed, the meat inside was quite extraordinarily delicious.

Large meat companies supplying supermarkets, who now take 70 per cent or more of the retail meat trade, cannot normally afford to hang whole carcases for long. They would lose up to 10 per cent of the carcase weight through drying-out, there would be a loss of cash flow, and it would require large, expensive conditioning rooms. This is one reason why our venison is more expensive than that available from other suppliers. The New Zealand venison processors, who use an electric current to tenderise their meat, obviously think we are completely unhinged to mature our meat in this old-fashioned and wasteful way. But fortunately our discerning customers appreciate the service.

It is not easy for anyone new to the farmed/wild venison debate to understand fully the complex issues, and I often refer to our product as being simply that of the deer park. After all, what we produce is only the same as the mediaeval park was attempting. The plethora of deer parks at that time cannot possibly have all existed to provide hunting grounds. Most were too small anyway. They were, in my view, like the hundreds of doocots which are liberally sprinkled over Fife, intended for meat production, and so were respectable forerunners of the twentieth-century deer farm. I should be very surprised if the mediaeval parker did not aim to concentrate his cull on two-year-olds in order to maximise his production – after all, the mesolithic hunters had.

23 AN ARABIAN INTERLUDE WITH ENDANGERED ORYX

While Veniburgers rolled on, I was making frequent deliveries of hinds to people, mostly in France, who were starting to farm deer. Over the next few years I calculate that I assisted in the establishment of around thirty new deer herds in France alone. And there were beginning to be more glamorous but less frequent trips outwith Europe, lecturing and doing some consultancy work. It seemed as though everything was on the up; we could do no wrong; whatever we touched came right. We didn't see the demise of Veniburgers as anything more than a temporary setback.

One winter evening as Nickie and I settled down to supper with the wild rain lashing down, the curtains shifting in the draught through the ill-fitting sash window and the cat flap hovering at the horizontal, the telephone rang. 'Ees that Dr Fletcher?' It was a foreign voice loaded with drama. 'Yes,' I replied. 'This ees the household of Sheikh Zayed, Ruler of Abu Dhabi. His Royal Highness wishes to discuss with you a problem with his deer. He would like to see you in London tomorrow.'

By remarkable good fortune I had to go to London the next day, so this arrangement suited perfectly. It was agreed that I should go to the upper floor of a private hospital. This hospital belonged to Sheikh Zayed and he had taken over the top floor for a period in which to hold court while his teeth underwent some work. After a short wait I was escorted in.

There were, I remember, double doors held open for me, and as I entered I was confronted with the raised buttocks of the previous appointment leaving backwards on hands and knees. Nevertheless my welcome was cordial and I was bade sit next to His Highness on a couch and share some fresh dates with him. Even with the limited language resources that we shared it was fairly obvious that the 'deer' were actually antelope. Now antelope, if I may remind the reader, are actually bovids related to sheep and cattle; they have horns which grow continuously and they are not at all closely related to deer with their antlers which fall off and regrow each year. Anyway, evidently the antelope were in his private park and were lame. But there seemed to be something else too. After a good deal of prevarication and embarrassed gesturing on his part and equally embarrassed guessing on mine, it became clear that the animals were further afflicted by a swelling of the testicles. Since the lameness was also apparently accompanied by a swelling of the joints the likely diagnosis was simple – brucellosis. This, I explained, would need to be confirmed by laboratory tests of suitable samples and appropriate treatment of the outbreak instituted.

'Good,' he said. 'Go there now and see to it. You may take your wife and family.' The interview was obviously over. I explained to his secretary outside that I would need to collect some things from Scotland, in particular my dart gun, as well as rearrange my diary. But they were adamant we move quickly, and I agreed to fly up to Scotland that night and thence from Edinburgh to the Middle East the next day. I would not be taking my wife and family.

The prospect of this trip at such short notice was exhilarating, as I had only just started winning overseas consultancies. I was easily impressed. The tickets were of course, first class, and as I sat in the first class lounge at Schiphol Airport, Amsterdam, not only the champagne but everything else went to my head. With the unaccustomed leisure I was avidly devouring the daily papers and thinking of

Nickie back home shovelling potatoes to the deer off the back of the tractor. An item caught my attention and I was soon scribbling a letter to the *Telegraph* and another to the *Guardian* and thinking myself a great swell. It was only when I got back that I saw both had been published. Since then I have found it easier to understand how the supposed makers and breakers of our society find time to write and read in a busy schedule. There is nothing more conducive to constructive thought than sitting in a half-empty aeroplane being plied with food and wine.

On my arrival in Abu Dhabi there was a flurry of excitement as my suitcase was opened to reveal that I was carrying both firearms and drugs; that is my tranquilliser gun, ammunition, syringes and tranquillisers. They were all confiscated. I was booked into a magnificent hotel and left there. The next day I made every effort to retrieve the darting equipment and by judicious use of Sheikh Zayed's name succeeded, but still nothing happened to indicate when my pleasant, though sober (it being Ramadan), interlude at the hotel should end. Daily I phoned the palace explaining that I had been told that I was on a matter of great urgency and that I had greatly inconvenienced myself by coming out at the drop of a hat. Each afternoon I swam, sunbathed and wrote by the pool, occasionally windsurfed on the sea and generally carried on as I thought befitted a consultant. There was nothing else I could do; I had no idea where the antelope were.

Finally word came. A car would collect me the next morning. And so I was driven south into the desert. Like most young boys I had been captivated by the romance of the desert. I had read *The Seven Pillars of Wisdom*, seen the film *Lawrence of Arabia*, and read Thesiger and others about the Empty Quarter. To be there now myself and comprehend the extraordinary revolution which had, within a decade or two, turned the races that had lived the most austere existence on our planet into the most affluent people on earth was a great privilege.

After a few hours' drive across the desert we came to the huge oasis of Al Ain. I was reinstalled in another air-conditioned palace of a hotel to await developments. All around I could see the most astonishing pieces of modern architecture that I have ever come across. The owners of these lavish palaces were for the most part sitting outside in the sand on rugs, eating from low tables. We joined one such group and were given camel to eat. Many parties had huge television screens erected in front of them. What a strange concatenation of the old and the new, I thought. Most of those of more than middle age, now living in these vast, extravagantly designed concrete palaces would have been brought up in tents in the desert. No matter if many might not be able to read or write, they must have a huge wealth of inherited desert lore and it would soon vanish for ever.

I was privileged to be taken to the royal falconry mews, where rows of falcons were perching on their blocks awaiting hunting expeditions. Each hawk and falcon was kept in precise condition to ensure maximum performance on the appointed day. It was explained to me that the sheiks would travel into the desert on motorised hawking and hunting safaris several times each year. This, I reflected, was a continuation of the regime that had brought extinction to the free-living Arabian oryx, of all grazing mammals the best adapted to survive in extremely arid conditions. In the nineteenth century it ranged through most of the interior of peninsular Arabia, but hunting progressively eroded the population until in 1972, around 18 October, the last six wild Arabian oryx were killed. Now no oryx survive in that region except for the few still preserved in zoos and private collections, and for those being reintroduced into Oman in a project funded by His Majesty Sultan Qaboos bin Said of Oman and his government.

As soon as I arrived in Al Ain, I realised that I was only some fifty miles away across the desert and mountains from a great friend of ours, Mark Stanley Price, who, with his wife Karen, was living in the desert in Oman actually carrying out this reintroduction of the Arabian oryx, mostly from San Diego Zoo. Mark and Karen spent seven years there and he published an excellent book about it all when he left. The main strategy was to encourage the local tribe of *bedu* to view the oryx with pride as a part of their heritage, and to follow each animal day after day so that its habits became known and any risk of poaching or predation was minimised.

Mark and Karen had been to stay with us at Reediehill during breaks from Oman and we had followed accounts of their project with fascination. So well adapted is this magnificent animal to its arid habitat that it can even lactate without drinking, using only its fat reserves and scant dew as sources of moisture. The loss of these beautiful white animals through extinction would indeed be grievous; there is so much more that we have still to learn from them. It is therefore thoroughly satisfactory to be able to report that the Oman oryx project has been a resounding success and a brilliant example of how such reintroductions can work if the habitat is intact and if the people living in that habitat are sympathetic to the ends of the scheme. There are, sadly, not too many other examples in place as yet.

Still, I remain optimistic. The Arabian oryx had declined to virtual extinction as the human population rose, firearms and vehicles became available and technology developed. Now the oryx are gradually increasing again following their well-planned reintroduction. This story mirrors the red deer model I had observed on Rum and the Scottish mainland. There must be some hope in this for other endangered wildlife.

Back at Al Ain, the next day I was taken a few miles further to see the affected animals. The Ruler had certainly been accurate in his description: the antelope were in dire straits, but even more of a surprise to me was the fact that these poor creatures were not, as I had expected, just the normal gazelles of the region or even imported African animals – they were the highly endangered Arabian oryx. They were sharing their enclosure with a large number of gazelle but it seemed to be the oryx that were most seriously affected. They were in pain, their testicles enormously distended and their limb joints swollen so that walking was difficult, and it was simple to catch two or three of them to take blood samples and administer some antibiotics.

The pattern of disease was absolutely typical of brucellosis. I asked the driver to drive me round the enclosure and I was interested to see a large flock of fat-tailed sheep and goats penned in on the other side of the fence on a piece of ground slightly raised above the oryx and gazelle.

I collected what samples I could and went away to think about it. On the way back to the hotel, I fell into conversation with the driver, who was from India. I had just seen the film *Gandhi* and asked him if he had seen it. 'Oh, yes, sir. We thought it was a little unfair to the English.' I was very surprised to hear this but suitably gratified, and we talked on. He said that his father was forever bemoaning the departure of the British from India. And then he said, 'Why don't you go to see the English vet at the zoo?' This was the first that I had heard of the presence of a compatriot, let alone a co-professional, so I thought this sounded a pretty good idea and suggested we go there right away.

At the zoo, which was, of course, new and lavish, I was astonished to see some red deer sitting under a tree in the heat. It transpired that these had come out from one of the English parks and were apparently coping remarkably well in one of the hottest places on earth provided they had adequate shade and water and good feeding. And the man charged with supplying these needs to the deer and all the other animals was none other than Chris Furley. I had known Chris's partner at Cambridge and so we were able to have a very useful exchange about the 'antelope'. Chris had been to see them himself and had already confirmed the diagnosis and instituted treatment. 'It happens every time it rains,' he said. 'Whenever it rains – which doesn't happen often, like once every three or four years, but when it does it's usually pretty torrential – all the detritus from those sheep and goats gets washed down into the oryx and gazelles. We know all about the brucellosis.' What he meant was that the dirty bedding and dung from the sheep, who had probably more or less come to terms with their infection and so showed no signs of clinical disease, were washed down into the oryx enclosure to contaminate their pasture and spread the infection to these endangered animals.

We discussed the situation further. The remedy was so simple it was really hard to believe that nothing was being done to prevent a recurrence. 'Last time this happened he brought consultants from all over to have a look, and the one whose advice was taken was someone who supplied some brightly coloured powders and left instructions that these were to be sprinkled on the ground at the full moon.'

I had just one chance to speak to the Ruler's brother that night before I returned to Scotland to prepare a report. It was an anticlimax. Whilst he was very gracious to me, it was clear that, try as I might, I was not really making an impression. My admiration for Lawrence of Arabia soared.

Back in Auchtermuchty, I wrote quite a short but detailed report making the obvious suggestions. Nickie even did beautiful sketches of the Arabian oryx on every page. I also went further and indicated to him that he might wish to consider a programme for eliminating this disease from the entire country. That would be a tall order but the technology was available. The months went by and became years and I heard nothing.

24 TOKYO, CHERNOBYL, PARISIAN MICE AND THE QUEEN'S AWARD

Venison sales were growing steadily but we were still dependent on the income from setting up new deer farms. We had, by virtue of our early start, been privileged to sell deer throughout Britain and our reputation stood very high. At one time I had sold deer to every single member of the eleven-strong BDFA council. France had also been good, but we were now competing with herds in the south of England that we had ourselves established and who now in turn had stock for sale. They had a five-hundred-mile advantage over us so that competing on cost was difficult. Also, deer on the hills of Fife never grow as quickly as do deer in more favoured locations further south. Although they are certainly not genetically disadvantaged it is not always easy to convince customers of the truth of this. I therefore reasoned, encouraged by my Swiss experiences and one or two French trips, that we should, in the true entrepreneurial spirit of Thatcherite Britain, be looking further afield – outwith Europe even.

Thus when a man from the ministry came along to tell us that the Department of Trade and Industry were sponsoring a British stand at an agricultural show in Tokyo, this seemed ideal. We had had previous enquiries from Japan, and though these had come to nothing we were attracted by the prospect of our deer, in a highly suitable climate, adorning a Japanese park. Deer are the perfect complement to the carefully designed, symbolic yet informal Japanese landscape. Besides I knew that their indigenous deer, the sika, occupied a privileged place in the Shinto religion. So, impulsively, with none of the expensive and time-consuming market research which we are told should always accompany a launch into new markets, I decided we would take a stand.

Two calves, imaginatively named Jamie and Willie, were carefully bottle-fed and manicured for the publicity, and preparations put in train. Nickie, as usual, dreamed up brilliant and economical graphic design panels and these were laboriously translated into Japanese. I wrote explanatory pamphlets and these too were translated.

It was at about this time that a pleasant little bombshell landed at Reediehill. The New Zealand Deer Farmers' Association wanted me to address their annual general meeting as keynote speaker. Critically they would also pay all my costs, and the day of the AGM coincided to the hour with the opening of the Japanese trade fair. What to do? I wasn't going to throw up this chance. We racked our brains and a solution soon materialised. Frank Vigh Larsen, a previous super-student from Denmark, was infinitely adaptable. Was he available, and how much bribing would he take to accompany Nickie as my 'envoy'?

A phone call and an instant decision from Frank and our plans were laid – I would fly off to Auckland. The two calves, by now very good friends and very spoilt, would be required to spend a few days before the show in quarantine, courtesy of the Japanese Ministry of Agriculture, so Frank would go out to Tokyo for a few days prior to the show to look after them and prepare the way. Nickie would zoom in at the last minute to create our stand (which was to be highly sophisticated despite being accomplished on a shoestring). Frank and Nickie would man it together. I would rendezvous with Nickie at Bangkok on the way back and we would spend a few days in Thailand relaxing before flying home. We were assured that there would be no problem in finding a buyer for Jamie and Willie together. We certainly did not want to separate them.

After several false starts we found that Jamie and Willie were to travel in style on the inaugural direct, non-stop flight from London to Tokyo. The aircraft was to be a 747 combining people and freight. Apparently many animals, especially pigs, had travelled in this way in the past. But the human passengers had had their blithe insouciance rudely shattered when the air-conditioning on one flight 'mal-functioned', pumping strong agricultural odours into the first-class cabin.

It all worked out ... eventually. There were several very nerve-racking bureaucratic hurdles to be jumped, and we had to load the two calves at Auchtermuchty on and off the lorry several times before we could finally set off down to London to put them on the plane.

The stand in Tokyo was a triumph. We established good and loyal agents, indeed the same as supply the imperial household, a number of sales resulted, and we even took on a charming Japanese stockman in Auchtermuchty for a training period.

And what, you may be asking, happened to our hand-reared Jamie and Willie, that Frank had taken out and looked after so well? They were sold to a wealthy Japanese who insisted on paying us the four million yen in cash. Now according to Japanese law such transactions must be witnessed and the money checked at the time of sale. Con-sequently Frank was required to count the yen with quite an audience of British diplomatic staff as well as the prestigious purchaser and his party. Frank was given a table and chair and set to work surrounded by the smiling faces of the onlookers. As he finished his embarrassing task, Frank looked up very gravely and said, 'I am afraid there must be some mistake.' Dismay and horror were writ large on the normally inscrutable faces of the Japanese. Then Frank with immaculate timing dropped his punchline: 'You have given us one yen too much!' After a moment's silence the Japanese rocked backwards and forwards in laughter and relief.

The deer throve in a climate not very different from that of central Europe, and when I went to see them all a few years later they had settled in excellently and were being looked after in great style.

My New Zealand trip went well and as usual was highly educational for me. Afterwards Nickie and I met up in Bangkok and travelled to Phuket Island for a week in the sun. We went on a very small boat to an idyllic little offshore island only to find we had to share our beach with a group of Americans. And did they have news for us? Yessir, they sure did. Hadn't we heard about the nuclear explosion in Europe? European details were scanty – they were clearly more worried about the possibility of fallout in California. We watched the sand crabs scuttling to and fro, ate some more lobster and agonised about our two poor little girls left behind in Scotland with Tim and Maggy Stead. It turned out that this was Chernobyl.

Amongst the less talked-about consequences of that disaster was the collapse of European venison prices due to concern in Germany about the levels of radioactivity in reindeer meat. In the event, and despite a rather unhelpful press release from the Ministry of Agriculture effect-ively warning everyone not to eat venison, we were able to demonstrate on our return that our venison was not contaminated and that its becquerel rating was fine. The ministry was compelled to recant and Chernobyl left our business pretty well unscathed, though the wild venison trade was seriously damaged.

Encouraged by our successes in Japan we began to look at more active promotion in France. There is, held annually in Paris, a huge agricultural show. In fact, as befits such an agricultural and gastronomic giant as France, it was Europe's largest. We knew of course just how many French farmers were looking at alternatives to cattle and sheep and it seemed a good chance.

We soon became hooked on those Paris shows and went to four in a row. How we used to enjoy them, hard work though it certainly was! One of the five or six colossal exhibition halls at the Salon d'Agriculture features regional stands, each with its own restaurant. Customers share benches at trestle tables and eat oysters on the Brittany stand maybe, or on the Toulouse stand cassoulet, or perhaps on the Savoie stand cheese fondue. All is exhausting for the servers, a non-stop four-day party, but for the consumers it is the perfect release from tramping around the show. If only we could aspire to something like that in Britain; many Parisians must attend the show solely for that treat, and come away with feelings of bonhomie towards the farmers and food producers and loyalty towards France's regional food.

One night as we returned from a jazz club to our little hotel for a few hours' sleep before the next day's session, we found ourselves admiring a display of bread in a darkened baker's shop window. It was a very smart shop in a fashionable *quartier* – all fancy breads, not your good old *baguettes* and *ficelles*. As we stared vacantly, we suddenly realised that we weren't the only things interested in the bread. In a scene redolent of Beatrix Potter's *Three Bad Mice*, and oblivious of us, many minute rodents were industriously nibbling away the inside of loaves to leave the crusts intact. It was a brilliant accomplishment. Next morning the apparently pristine bread was still on view while the mice, who were presumably sleeping off their nocturnal excesses in the loaves, were now invisible to the smartly dressed passers-by. Only a few tell-tale droppings gave the game away to us initiates. We watched them every night, and the next year they were still there; but when we came back two years later to show Stella and Martha, all had gone.

By 1990 overseas sales were going really well. Further deer farms were set up in Japan; we sold a consignment to a very friendly man in Minnesota, but above all there seemed a never-ending stream of French farmers. They were, no doubt, encouraged by seeing us at the Paris Show with all the ensuing publicity – indeed one year we won the Prix d'Innovation for our stand. They were, like us, concerned to explore new ways of making their farms work since there was widespread belief that the Common Agricultural Policy was not going to sustain them indefinitely.

Soon I found that my little lorry was not large enough, and I began to employ bigger trucks from a firm of professional hauliers whom I could trust. We would load the juggernauts at Reediehill after first bedding them with abundant straw and after that a good covering of potatoes or carrots. And then I would travel out in my small vehicle in convoy with the large one. The deer travelled extraordinarily well, thank goodness, and I had great confidence in the drivers, whom I could readily appraise from the level of fellow-feeling they expressed towards the animals as we loaded them up. My dictum remains that good bedding and plenty of space are the key ingredients for the safe transport of deer; and, of course, we must remember that all our animals are destined for breeding, so that not only can we afford to take care but it would be folly not to do so. I used to look at the other livestock trucks on the docks and ferries with a great deal of sympathy for the sheep and calves they carried. There really is no excuse for taking animals hundreds of miles just to slaughter them on their arrival. Such a system is demeaning for the drivers and stockmen and horrific for the animals; its very existence must be a bureaucratic anomaly and it should not be beyond the ingenuity of our politicians and civil servants to think of ways of making this trade unnecessary.

The pinnacle of our foreign successes was reached with the prestigious Queen's Award for Export Achievement in 1990. It was interesting in retrospect that the award came our way when it did. There seems to be some sort of pattern with these awards. It has become a cliché to say that a business award generally precedes a collapse. In many cases awards are based on turnover, and a company that is selling very strongly is often underpricing, with the inevitable consequences. Or perhaps, growing faster than it knows how, it becomes overgeared, or maybe simply manages just to develop too big an idea of its own importance. In our case it was actually none of those things. It was simply that we had been part of a little boom, and before the Queen's Award application had even been processed – let alone before the junketing had begun – I knew we were in for hard times. Winning the award was a matter of great excitement. We were the smallest company ever to win the thing, and it was a huge morale boost for our entire little team just when we needed it.

The Queen's Award for Export Achievement is given to companies which can show a sustained growth in export earnings over three years. Our figures were indeed good; we had much more than doubled our export earnings each year. This was entirely made up of my consultancy services and the exports of deer breeding stock.

We were presented with the award by Lord Elgin, the Lord Lieutenant of Fife, and we put up a marquee. I was determined that the deer should be part of the occasion, so we let them run around and into the marquee in the field during the proceedings. We had to stop the tamest from eating the food. It was a beautiful day, Nickie of course cooked a magnificent feast, and lots of friends came over. When I gave my speech of acceptance I probably cast rather a pall over the occasion when I said that I couldn't imagine this unique type of business ever being successful again, as New Zealand farmed venison imports were growing and the British government showed no sign of doing anything to help deer farming compete on the same terms as sheep and cattle.

But then a few weeks later we all went up to Buckingham Palace and, perhaps because I was wearing a kilt, we were singled out for a lengthy chat with the Queen and all was celebratory.

25 EDUCATING THE WORLD
– A VENTURE INTO TOURISM

The gradual growth in trade at our minute farm shop (only two or three can fit in at once), as well as the steady development of the mail-order venison sales, was proof of Nickie's success with her books, articles and broadcasts. The occasional customers grinding up the hill to visit us and purchase venison had become a steady trickle. Since their journey demands a two-mile detour from the main Edinburgh to St Andrews road, and that uphill all the way from Auchtermuchty on a narrow track, this remains highly gratifying. Nevertheless I pondered, as the years went by, that if we had a base down on the main road away from the farm this would allow us a good deal more peace at Reediehill and would surely increase sales. I was still apprehensive about our continuing dependence on sales of breeding stock. I did not believe that those sales would continue indefinitely, nor did I want them to.

Also, less prosaically, I had a yearning to tell people about deer. To me they were the perfect means of introducing all sorts of educational subjects, not just biology, although there was plenty of that at all levels, but also the history of our forebears and their dependence on deer, human nutrition, cooking, agriculture and many other disciplines.

For several years I had been strongly of the opinion that there was a hidden value in deer as a tourist resource. This was rooted in our experience of taking stags in full velvet antler to shows all over Britain. The attention they attracted and the pleasure I had from answering questions about them were compelling reasons for wanting to go on with this. 'No, they don't grow a new point on their antlers every year so you can't tell how old they are from the number of points.' 'Yes, it is true that their antlers fall off each spring and yes, they do grow all that again each year. Those antlers have grown in six weeks; nearly an inch a day, the fastest-growing mammalian tissue.'

I also wanted to demonstrate that deer were not mysterious and uncontrollable wild beasts, but had the same need for care and attention as cattle and sheep, and that given good husbandry they would thrive in a farm environment – and that they produced a delicious and very healthy meat which was easy to cook.

I wanted to share my own fascination, to explain that the stag's antler cycle was synchronised by day-length: the antlers growing in the spring, hardening in the summer and losing their velvet as the days draw in so that they are ready for use by the stags in their crucial competition for the hinds – that contest between the stags to sire as many calves as possible that is the autumn rut. I wanted to show that this is evolution in action. Why was it all organised by day-length? To achieve a calf drop synchronised to make best use of the short period of grass growth – didn't the hinds yield two litres of milk a day for those fast-growing Bambis? And so on ... and on ... and on.

When we took stags to shows they genuinely seemed to relish the attention. Our particular stars were dear old 'Number Eight' and 'Ferox', both of whom would walk sedately up the ramp into the lorry in anticipation of going to the show, and who would approach people so that they could be stroked through the fence. When I took groups of people into their pen they seemed to revel in being the centre of attention. Number Eight was Scottish through and through, whilst Ferox was a magnificent, blue-blooded English park stag from Normanby Park near Scunthorpe (illustration 8a). At no time did any of the stags ever threaten visitors by standing on their hind legs and boxing, which would have been their natural defence in the summer.

Once, I had arranged a bed in the back of the lorry for Nickie on our homeward run from a show. Nickie, exhausted after a series of cookery demonstrations and going down with a cold, had slept fitfully and watched how the stags would lie down, or stand up, or chew on some hay, or look out of the ventilators as much as to say, 'Only Manchester – another five hours yet.' They seemed to travel like the seasoned professionals they were.

My experience with the stags at shows confirmed in me the belief that a permanent site could work. I developed a vision of a deer farm close to a main road and centres of population, where people could come and see the deer, stroke their antlers during the summer (that was very important), and learn a little of the magic that held me in its thrall.

I envisaged school visits where, through the deer, students could learn of the biology of survival, evolution and much more besides. They might discover the importance of antler as a material for making tools, and of the mediaeval deer park; they would find out how hunting had been so much a part of our ancestors' daily lives, and how the deer had eventually been almost banished from even the Scottish hills until, with the advent of the clearances, came the sheep and then the sporting estates; and they would hear of the role of venison as a staple meat nourishing man for nearly all this time. And then the visitors could go and taste venison in the restaurant and buy it in the shop. Our enterprise would become the centre for enquiries about deer, where we could develop a library, a cookery theatre, a directory of deer herds and much more besides.

In the wildest ramifications of my scheme we would have a butchery where, through a plate-glass window, visitors could watch the skinning and evisceration of carcases and the skilled craft of meat-cutting. My theory was that the present century is the first since man came out of the trees in which he has not been a frequent witness to the slaughter, disembowelling and dismembering of his meat. I believe this unfamiliarity is a factor in the rejection of meat, and for the grass-growing regions of the world, including Scotland, a decline in meat-eating would be a catastrophe.

I knew from the many visitors to Reediehill that young children are invariably unperturbed and fascinated by this novel sight that had always been so much a part of the lives of all our ancestors. It was only their elders and the media that brainwashed them into the irrational 'ugh'. There is nothing repulsive about the sight of fresh meat, organs and viscera. On the contrary, they are, as Rembrandt and other painters of an earlier age recognised, beautiful; familiarity with such things is a good basis for a better understanding of what makes us all tick. It is only when flesh rots that it becomes disgusting; presumably a long-developed adaptation to ensure the avoidance of unhealthy food.

As a way of making this point, in my early years at Auchtermuchty I had even dreamed of hiring a room during the Edinburgh Festival in which to exhibit cases of meat and possibly even whole dead deer. From beautiful pieces of fresh meat, these would slowly decompose, aided by the summer flies, so that, between the opening and closing Festival parties, the enticing red meat would be reduced to shrivelled remnants with only the brown shells of the flies' vacated pupae to show what had happened. I wanted to confront this tabu, with its attendant shock and disgust, head-on. The display would also, of course, have symbolised the waste of deer dying in the wild each spring because they haven't enough food, and more ambitiously, the universality of death and corruption. Dream on, Damien Hirst! Your shows are but a pale imitation of what I had in mind.

I realised naturally that the commercial possibilities of these more extreme ideas were very limited, but I was sufficiently encouraged by the public's interest in deer, as demonstrated at the shows, to believe that it would be possible to create a deer-based tourist venture in Scotland. The 'add-ons' of merchandising, catering, children's play areas and so on would be fundamental to the financial success, but the principal summer attraction would be the chance for visitors to have hands-on encounters with the deer in the presence of a guide. This was to be the Scottish Deer Centre.

I painstakingly drafted a business plan. It soon became obvious that the hackneyed tenet of all retailers, hoteliers and others – that the three secrets of success were 'location, location, location' – was also true of deer-based tourist centres. In the absence of a site, in vain I touted my business plan around various investors who showed no trace of interest. And then, at a dinner party one night, we met some new neighbours who had recently purchased a property about five miles from Auchtermuchty. It had some farm buildings close to the Edinburgh–St Andrews road near Cupar which I happened to know rather well, for I had used them for several winters to house our deer from Reediehill.

When our exports of deer had been at their height and before we had constructed our own shed, we had rented farm buildings all over Fife to house deer through the winter and as quarantine premises. One site had been those roadside steadings. The new owner asked what I thought he should do with them and I told him of my plans for a Scottish Deer Centre.

Meetings were held, and having formed a partnership we rushed ahead to open for the spring. The Scottish Tourist Board helped, the buildings were renovated, the fences erected and the deer installed. My project for an on-farm butchery and viewing chamber was not incorporated! But we did install an audio-visual theatre and a walk-through exhibition. In the exhibition I chose to work backwards. Firstly the present situation of Scottish red deer with numbers still climbing, the resultant conflict with farming and forestry, deer dying in the spring, the difficult job of the professional stalker, and then the history – the sheep walks, the 'great sheep', preceded by the Highland clearances with sheep displacing man and deer forests, and before that the deer parks as exemplified by that at nearby Falkland Palace. Finally we installed a man in the mouth of a cave by the embers of his fire, dreaming of the deer he hopes to kill in the hunt as he stares up at the constellation of Orion the hunter. Nickie contributed many pieces, including some facsimiles of antler tools copied from the many in the Royal Scottish Museum of Antiquities. In the first year we had around forty thousand visitors.

The audio-visual script was also written by me, and I supplied photographic slides from my own collection and begged others from friends. It was intended to demonstrate the yearly round as exemplified by deer. Slides of Callanish, the huge stone circle on Lewis which long predates Stonehenge, began the show, accompanied by a piece of music by the contemporary Scottish composer John Maxwell Geddes entitled 'Callanish', which had been its inspiration and whose score lies buried by the circle. It is thought that Callanish was used, by aligning stones with the sun, to time events in the calendar of its constructors and my point was that the deer also timed their life by the sun. Photoperiodic control is fundamental to the success of seasonal breeders such as red deer. I wanted to convey the urgent need for the deer to drop their calves so as to make best use of the early summer grass for the hinds' lactation.

I was determined that we should use the name Scottish Deer Centre. I envisaged it, probably correctly I still believe, as being a point of contact for people interested in any aspect of Scottish deer and their husbandry. I wanted them to feel that we were the 'one-stop shop'. The word Scottish was a protected name and we had to use lawyers to overcome the opposition to its being used as a business name.

In haste we appointed a manager, but at a very early stage it became obvious that things were going wrong. A week before opening, the manager told us that our partner, who had recently broken his leg in a car accident, had attacked him with his crutch. Whether true or not, it was clear that tensions were running high.

We struggled on for two or three years and visitor numbers reached 85,000 a year, but the partnership was not a happy one. Peace of mind and such simple pleasures as a good night's sleep are worth any cost, and reluctantly Nickie and I decided to leave, abandoning our substantial investment and three years of hard work. It was a huge waste of a part of our lives and there had been much acrimony and no enjoyment. For the first time since Veniburgers, something big had gone wrong – and at least with Veniburgers there had been buckets of fun.

Nickie and I felt the loss of our involvement in the Deer Centre project very deeply, but even in such a fiasco there were benefits. We had both learnt a lot about managing deer-based tourist projects. I got a job investigating the feasibility of such a scheme in northern Spain, which was interesting and lucrative, but I was especially keen to try again in Scotland. By dint of asking landowners, we did find another site – probably the very best situation for a tourist project in

Scotland. Here the proprietor was willing at least to entertain the idea. We were commissioned to carry out a project to investigate the viability of the site. The result was encouraging and the cash-flow projections looked very promising. The proposal was put to the directors in our absence. We understood that the board was strongly in favour of progressing the scheme, but the elderly landowner vetoed it.

We had been paid a fair consultancy fee for our six months' work, and as the weeks passed by I became calmer. I felt that finally I had got the idea of deer-based visitor centres well and truly out of my system. Nickie was relieved: 'Surely we can just keep it small and at Reediehill?' And so we resolved.

That was always assuming that we could remain solvent and keep the farm. For now the financial ramifications began to tell: interest rates were rising fast and our overdraft suddenly seemed an unscalable mountain. But before we could concentrate our minds on whittling down the debt, we had to experience another blow.

26 AN EPIDEMIC AND MORE MYOPIC POLITICIANS

The origins of the calamity lay in Sussex. It had all begun when I was engaged by a company of New Zealand stock agents called Dalgety to help them locate and quarantine deer of good quality for export back to improve their bloodlines. This task was to last several years and was made pure pleasure by the buccaneering nature of the Kiwis. I remember one night driving a load of deer down Park Lane en route to Gatwick in the days before the M25 motorway. My companion was a young 'cocky', a New Zealand deer farmer, who had recently inherited a remote property and with it a huge debt. In effect there was no chance of his ever being able to trade his way into solvency. Until, that is, he started to catch the wild red deer by feeding them on to his land. So valuable had farmed deer become that after one great night's work, daylight showed that he had enough hinds to clear his debt with some to spare. He sent a card to his grandmother telling her that he had just driven some deer through London and down the famous Park Lane. When he got back and saw her she said in her strong New Zealand accent, 'Good heavens, boy, they must have fine dogs to be able to drive deer through the middle of London!'

The focus of our activity was the London airports, and when someone called Carl Wheeler expressed an interest in starting to farm deer near Gatwick I was immediately interested. The farm and house were beautiful. Though it was so close to London, Carl's father had managed to have every phone and electric cable hidden so that from the garden a view of tens of miles of Sussex countryside was uninterrupted by anything man-made. I was very keen to become involved and took to Carl straightaway. He was obviously a highly competent farmer, the land was good and above all I enjoyed his company. The conversation went something like this:

'Carl, if you go deer farming, I would like to join in.'

'OK, how about a fifty-fifty partnership?'

And I don't recall that we ever put anything in writing.

At the start the scheme was a great success. I darted hinds from the best of English parks that by now I knew so well, and delivered them in sixes and tens. We aimed to run 150 hinds on the fifty acres and in a couple of years we were there. The deer throve. We soon had sales to Italy, New Zealand, Ireland and France and all was going well.

A lot of this success was due to our stockman, Janice. I have never met such a human dynamo. Accustomed to running a dairy herd, Janice soon got to know all the deer with their foibles and eccentricities. In order to effect real improvement in a herd of animals of any sort, you need to know precisely, with no room for error, which mother produced which offspring. Without this information you cannot select the bloodlines that you want to cultivate as being nearest to your ideal. This is the sort of genetic engineering that man has been carrying out for many millennia in livestock and crops. When it came to spring and the tricky, time-consuming job of identifying the mother of each calf as it was born, and weighing, sexing and tagging the calves, Janice was peerless. She drove set routes through the field in her own Land-Rover every morning and evening feeding the deer and noting those ladies who did not rush forward to join in. Then she would slowly move about the field until the truants were noted, and like as not they would be in labour. The carefully set routes were necessary to prevent any chance of driving over young calves hidden in the grass, and the Land-

Rover itself was a wise security measure, providing a point of refuge in case hinds became over-protective.

Hinds, like some breeds of beef cattle, can be fiercely protective of their young. I had noticed years before that the most dangerous hinds were usually those that were tame enough to have lost their fear of people – but not, interestingly, the hand-reared hinds, who in my experience are always quite oblivious to human presence as they pass through labour and will tolerate their calves being handled without any sign of concern.

Meanwhile I had to work for the New Zealanders. As their deer-farming industry grew, demand developed there for different blood-stock. The genetic base of the early introductions had been very small and there was something of a rush to breed the perfect deer. We had a whale of a time touring Europe from Sweden to Yugoslavia. East European deer were all the rage on account of their being so large – many deer farmers have what I like to think of as a latent Texan syndrome.

Although I didn't much like their leggy characteristics, it did seem that Carl and I should at least give them a trial. Accordingly, when we were approached by a New Zealander with a deer farm in Essex who wanted to sell three German stags we agreed to proceed. It was a fatal mistake.

The stags arrived just in time for the rut, and when one of them failed to recover condition after his strenuous round of mating we didn't take it too seriously. We buried him on the farm. Subsequently we lost a hind. Now normally deaths in the Sussex herd were an extreme rarity, so we had an autopsy done.

Carl phoned me up: 'They think it might be TB and they've sent samples to the ministry for culture.' That meant a wait of many weeks while the lymph glands from the diseased deer were carefully treated in an attempt to grow the bacteria they contained. Smears from the glands would be made on a choice of growth media in different mixtures of gases. Then the bacterial cultures would be subjected to a variety of tests to see if they really were the mammalian strain of tuberculosis. The weeks passed, during which time we lost another deer and then came the verdict: positive.

It was only gradually that the awful significance of this dawned on us. Although I was a vet and knew all about TB in cattle, and that it was a 'notifiable disease', there were no regulations with regard to deer; perhaps through some protective instinct I didn't grasp the implications for our precious herd. In other words we did not immediately start to panic.

Nevertheless, as soon as we had had the initial report, even before the culture results came through to confirm the diagnosis, we had, fearing the worst, started to make a plan for the deer. With the last year's calves, we had about three hundred deer on the farm, and that number was set to grow to 450 by the next spring. We aimed to create three groups: one which was known to have spent a lot of time with the German stags, a second group which had had some contact, and a third which had never encountered them.

In addition, as soon as the positive diagnosis was made, we started testing. The test we used was the tuberculosis skin test designed for cattle. This has been used for seventy-five years and has been wonderfully successful in eliminating tuberculosis from cattle. Moreover, by thus reducing the contamination of milk it has also saved many hundreds of thousands of human lives. It is one of the greatest achievements of the veterinary profession, although sadly it is being eroded as the levels of TB in cattle and badgers are rising so quickly now. The test consists of injecting a non-infectious extract prepared from the bacteria into the skin. Three days later the site of the injection is re-examined, and if it has swollen up the test is considered positive. This procedure had been developed for cattle but the New Zealanders, in the face of quite high levels of tuberculosis (often spread by opossums – which they had imported rashly from Australia – in the same way that the unfortunate badger spreads TB in Britain), had found that this skin test also worked reasonably well in deer. So we set to work to use it on our herd. We were helped in this by vets and scientists from the Central Veterinary Laboratory who were keen to learn something about TB in deer. We tested and we tested and we tested . . .

It was a slow job. We got results, but it was hard work for man and beast alike. Each test required the deer to be handled once for the initial injection and then again two days later to read the test. We could only repeat the test every two months or so because there was some evidence that it lost sensitivity if the interval between tests was too short.

I have not explained in enough detail the predicament that confronted Carl and me while all this was going on. As soon as the diagnosis had been suspected the ministry had served upon us a 'Form A'. This made it illegal for us to remove any deer from the farm – as if we would have wanted to anyway – until it could be shown either that tuberculosis had not been confirmed or that the disease had been eliminated, when a Form B would be served. This legislation had been created for cattle and, as we were soon to find out, deer were treated very differently. In the case of cattle, farmers are compensated for animals presumed to have TB which are then slaughtered. We deer farmers were told we would receive nothing; there was no legislation in force. We were in a terrible limbo.

And that was not all. There had been regular movements of deer from the Sussex farm to Reediehill. Consequently there was a distinct risk that the TB had spread to the Auchtermuchty herd. The Scottish Department of Agriculture was obliged to serve a Form A on our Scottish farm; now we could move deer neither on nor off Reediehill.

For Nickie and me this was crippling. We still had a good overseas trade, and that Form A effectively prevented us using the farm for any sales. Since there is no recorded instance of tuberculosis being spread by the eating of meat from infected animals, the venison sales could continue; but coming after the blow of the Scottish Deer Centre, and with no prospect of anything but expense from Sussex, those meat sales were nowhere near enough.

I agonised for about one month and then took the decision. We would have to slaughter all our precious breeding herd built up so slowly and carefully from the Rum nucleus, with all our old friends known to us for up to twenty years. If I didn't do this, we should have had to sell the farm and still lose the herd. There was really no choice. I often think of the cattle farmers faced with compulsory slaughter of their herds and I sympathise, but at least they receive compensation. We would not get a penny for this Reediehill slaughter. But what else could I do? It seemed likely in any case that the deer might have tuberculosis. Testing would take at least a year, and probably much longer, during which time we would have little or no income. Delay would be fatal. There was no sign of any reparation forthcoming from the government.

The department was helpful and sympathetic. We carried out the grisly affair over two days with help from a game dealer friend. On the second day I made sure I was away. It was too much. Then the farm was silent and empty; all our stock had gone.

We left the farm unstocked for six months and reseeded the paddocks. It was very lonely. Two months after that desperate week the department phoned to tell me the supremely ironic and surprising fact that of all the samples taken from the slaughtered animals, none had proved positive for tuberculosis. All our deer had been healthy.

Meanwhile in Sussex our problems seemed no nearer resolution. Carl and I, with Janice's blood and sweat, had built up that deer herd as well over several years. Janice especially had made friends with many of the animals whilst Carl had spent long hours recording the herd and working out with me our breeding strategy. They were the progeny of my hand-picked English deer; we cherished those animals, and the fact that science seemed to have no solution to our problems, and that the government which had encouraged us to diversify had allowed German deer to be imported with tuberculosis, took a little getting used to. Undoubtedly the Ministry of Agriculture, it could be argued, carried some of the blame. Those deer had been imported under regulations drawn up by the ministry specifically to exclude such disease, and it bore some responsibility for ensuring that imported livestock was healthy.

It was now clear that if we bowed to the seemingly inevitable and simply had our deer shot, I at least would be bankrupt, and I would also have been responsible for getting Carl into a most unholy mess. Not that Carl even at the most desperate moments ever hinted that he felt I was to blame.

For Janice the blow might not be financial but it would be even more heart-rending. To her had fallen the crucial job of relating dam to offspring, tagging the newborn calves, and all the daily feeding. Her involvement with the deer was bound to be close. During all the testing of the deer she was the one to hold their heads as we shaved the sides of their necks. Although no case of TB being passed from deer to man had ever been reported at that time, we thought it advisable to check that everyone working with the deer was still healthy. They went off to be tested themselves and we awaited the results.

In the meantime I was trying to think of strategies to save at least our precious bloodline, and also to secure some compensation from the government such as we should have received if we had been one of the growing number of cattle herds compulsorily slaughtered after a diagnosis of TB. We had several meetings with the Chief Veterinary Officer and also with successive Ministers of Agriculture, but it was the height of Mrs Thatcher's austerity and they were implacable.

'You might as well forget any possibility of compensation. The Treasury is absolutely determined not to allow any more expenditure on livestock farming.' And, conveniently forgetting their encouragement to diversify: 'Nobody told you to go deer farming. Don't expect any assistance from us.'

There are drugs available for treating TB and, at least in man, they have been extremely effective, although now the disease is becoming increasingly resistant to most of them. Vets, especially in the livestock industry, have to control the disease rather than save the individual. Historically, serious infectious diseases in animals have always been eliminated by the identification and removal of diseased animals rather than by their treatment. In the hard world of meat production, treatment is expensive and the protection of the health of the national herd paramount, so the veterinary profession has learnt over the years to sacrifice the few to preserve the many. Thus it is only in a few valuable zoo herds that treatment of tuberculosis has been attempted. The classic approach is to treat the pregnant females and, on the assumption that they are then less infectious, 'snatch' their calves from them as soon as they are born and rear them on the bottle in isolation.

Well, I reckoned if it was good enough, and evidently successful, for zoos, why not give it a try? Carl was in agreement and we started to search for the drugs. Nothing was available in Britain in sufficiently large quantity but we eventually ran some to earth in Finland. It was flown into Gatwick. But that's as far as it got because the government, keen to prevent us treating our animals, refused us an import permit and the whole lot had to be destroyed at the airport – at our expense.

Nevertheless, even without the safeguard of treating the pregnant hinds with drugs, we determined to press on with our plans to 'snatch' the calves. We decided to collect about forty female calves from the hinds in the group we reckoned least likely to be infected. A helper was found to assist Janice in the colossal labour and Carl had some ideal pens which would allow the calves to be isolated from each other. In the event, the weaning and rearing were a tremendous success. Fed on milk from Carl's adjoining dairy herd, the calves thrived mightily. Each litre of cow's milk was enriched with an egg, a teaspoonful of cod liver oil and a tablespoonful of glucose. Of thirty-eight calves, only two failed to make it and they had been very poor things to begin with. Those thirty-six were the best hand-reared calves I have ever seen, and how Janice and her colleague did all that work for two months, never sleeping for more than a few hours a day and up several times each night, I shall never know.

In November that year came an unexpected development. Edwina Currie was reported as stating, albeit inaccurately, that most British-produced eggs carried salmonella, thus precipitating the first of the food hygiene panics that have punctuated the nineties. Egg producers went out of business and there was a huge rise in imported eggs carrying even more salmonella than the home-produced ones had. We were told not to make mayonnaise and that eggs should only be eaten 'piping hot'. Mrs Currie resigned and the government was clearly on the defensive. Excited journalists hunted around for more stories along similar lines and soon came up with one on listeria in soft cheese.

Here at last was our opportunity. As the government did not seem even remotely sympathetic to our plight, Carl and I decided that the only resort left to us was the press. It was at this juncture that Janice came back from a visit to the consultant with the disturbing news that she had evidently contracted tuberculosis from her cervine charges. She was prescribed a six-month course of antibiotics and the prognosis was good. We asked if Janice would mind if her story was given to the press. She agreed without hesitation. In the space of a few days we did several television and radio programmes and many newspaper pieces.

It wasn't many more days before the government succumbed and passed legislation which granted deer farmers 50 per cent compensation in cases where their deer herds had to be destroyed as a result of tuberculosis. That is to say that the Ministry would value the deer and pay half the agreed valuation to the farmer before having them compulsorily slaughtered. Cattle farmers at that time received 75 per cent compensation and this was increased to 100 per cent in 1998, whilst the underprivileged deer farmer still only receives 50 per cent.

It was nearly two years too late for my herd at Reediehill, but Carl and I felt that 50 per cent was as good as we could hope for. Because we had been prevented from treating the disease we were now losing deer and there was no choice. We received what in the circumstances was a generous valuation and the grisly business of disposal of our old friends began. In two days that too was all over.

So what lessons might we learn? One is that the media, whether or not they are always accurate, are an effective check on the government. This is the democracy of our children's time and perhaps it's not such a bad thing. We know no other. In the often arrogant lack of response we encountered in successive Ministers of Agriculture – Donald Thomson, John Gummer and David Curry – were the seeds of the Conservative Party's overwhelming defeat of May 1997. Governments need at least to appear sympathetic.

Those German deer had been imported with a standard of health status sanctioned by the ministry. Might we have been successful in a court of law on that issue? Who knows? A more sympathetic approach at the outset would have saved taxpayers' money and the government's face. In terms of cost–benefit analysis the government acted very stupidly.

There was one closing feature to this horror story: the hand-reared calves. In retrospect, perhaps they stood no chance. The ministry, in its bureaucratic way, could not risk taxpayers' money by offering them a reprieve. As it was, they had us skin-test the calves and imposed so stringent an interpretation that it would have been difficult to conceive of them all passing. Of the thirty-six, three were deemed inconclusive using a test that required us to measure skin changes to half a millimetre. They were all killed; our precious bloodline was lost.

After this we believed tuberculosis was bound to prove a serious problem in farmed deer, and deer farmers set to work to monitor the situation minutely. With the passing of time, however, it has become clear that our fears were largely unfounded. There have been no more serious outbreaks in farmed deer, and deer seem no more susceptible to the disease than cattle. But wild deer, especially the fallow and sika, have not been so lucky. Almost certainly related to the rapidly growing badger population, there have been dramatic breakdowns in the health of wild deer in parts of England and a steadily growing incidence in cattle.

27 A WALK OUTSIDE

By the time the Queen's Award ceremony had come round, several months after the award itself had been announced, I could see the future was not going to be easy. The notification of the award had come during the same week that we had abandoned our investment at the Deer Centre. The tuberculosis had still been running at the farm in Sussex with no end in sight except more and more meetings with intransigent ministers and civil servants. The combination of the Deer Centre debacle with the loss of two herds of deer brought our Reediehill business to its knees. The compensation eventually received had all gone into restocking Reediehill. And to make matters worse there came a collapse in the confidence of UK deer farmers.

Most had started to farm deer in anticipation of disappearing subsidies: they had been encouraged by successive governments to think that 'diversification' was the right thing to do. But European agricultural policy still showed no sign of dramatic subsidy cuts. Deer farmers became doubtful; some returned to the cushioned world of support, and hind prices fell.

Then came the introduction of sheep quota. This meant that any farmer with a given number of ewes was awarded an equivalent amount of quota, free. Quota is a tradeable commodity worth a great deal of money. A deer farmer who had given up his sheep perhaps a year or two previously missed out on this golden handshake and found his farm dramatically reduced in value as a consequence. And if that misguided deer farmer now decided he wanted to resume his sheep enterprise he could not, because the quota was all allocated. Instead he would have to *buy* quota from sheep farmers who had been *given* it. Well, nobody ever told us that life was fair!

Then Britain entered the European Exchange Rate Mechanism at an artificially high rate, and the strength of the pound suddenly made exporting very difficult. Interest rates soared. Our income was in free fall and our overdraft was growing at a fearsome speed. I felt it was only a matter of time before the bank would foreclose. All that we had worked for was at risk. The farm and the house would have to go. Our overdraft was more than the value of the deer, the house and farm and everything else we had. And all the time interest rates were rising.

Although very few deer farmers were like us in having no other enterprise to fall back on, others were feeling the pinch: by 1996 about 30 per cent of British farmed hinds had disappeared, mostly to the game dealers, and the stage was set for a big shortage of farmed venison.

I made it clear to Nickie that, while I would do the best I could on my side of the business as a vet and consultant, with occasional live sales, venison marketing must now be the absolute priority for Reediehill. We had to effect all the cost cuts we could and yet work together to build our meat sales.

We had come to Reediehill in 1973 determined to pioneer the production of a new, delicious and much healthier meat in a humane, environmentally sound way. At that time we were the only commercial deer farmers in existence and it was obvious that it was up to us to make shift to sell our production in the best way we could. We had exploited the only avenue open to us and had constructed our own venison-processing plant and farm shop and continued to kill the deer in the field with a rifle. These facts were to stand us in good stead.

The farm shop and mail-order venison sales had been growing steadily but slowly and from a very low base, and we had not worked too much to try and develop them. When a breeding hind at eighteen months can find a ready sale at £450 there is much less incentive to develop sales of the male counterpart who, as meat, is worth perhaps only £150. But soon we found that we might also have to start killing potential breeding hinds for meat. Nickie was obliged to work even longer hours and together we manned venison stands at shows like the BBC Good Food Show and the Country Living Show, as well as the usual agricultural shows. There was little time for jewellery and no time to write more cookery books, even though *Game for All* had gone into a third printing.

We settled down to several years of hard graft with Nickie working on the venison sales, talking endlessly on the phone or in the shop. It wasn't unknown for people to phone her for advice as they put the joint in the oven. And sales did grow.

Meanwhile I cut my prices to the bone and continued to search for new markets. That spring Nickie came with me to Verona where we exhibited at a trade fair. As we arrived at the show there seemed rather a lot of excitement with an even larger number of police than usual. In the evening there was a banquet at which the British Minister of Agriculture, John Gummer, was to have toasted his Italian counter-part – but we soon found out that the reason for the police presence had actually been the arrest of the guest of honour, who was imprisoned and so unable to respond to our minister! We certainly welcomed the banquet where we drank some of the finest wine I have ever tasted.

However, when we had driven back from this show we were sum-moned to the bank. It was the year end and the results would, I knew, be dreadful. The manager was polite but the figures were plain to be seen. If there was no improvement in the next six months we would have to sell; the level of borrowing was far too high. As we left he said, 'Do you really think that you will ever be able to trade your way out of this?'

Nickie went through the accounts with me and it was manifest that the venison side of the business was sustaining the farm. It seemed as though the obvious thing was to sell most if not all of the breeding deer and merely buy in enough to satisfy the venison sales.

I went for a walk in the forest. Clambering over the deer fence and into the trees I soon found myself in an area I did not recognise. I was above the farm and I could see it all in the sun (illustration 4): the garden, the drystone wall I had built around the garden, the road we had struggled to improve, the fences that had been the root of political argument over grant aid; the house itself, now more than doubled in size since we had arrived, the huge deer shed to protect the animals from the wind, rain and snow, and finally the deer, some of them wallowing exultantly in pools, some spreadeagled on the ground basking, and a group of calves playing. And I wept.

28 THE POUND FALLS BUT VENISON TAKES OFF

Although the prospects for our recovery seemed very slim, I did have a number of sales to France organised for the next winter. I had quoted for these in French francs, since I believed that Mrs Thatcher had entered the European Exchange Rate Mechanism with the pound fixed at an unreasonably high level. It seemed to encapsulate her delusions of British superiority, and somehow, driving around Europe, I just didn't believe it. I had taken a risk which I could not really afford to take, but I believed that small French farmers would not work so happily in pounds, and above all I had to secure the sales.

We were driving to a friend's house that Wednesday to dart some stags and remove their antlers. The news was riveting. Speculators were attacking the pound. Nickie came with me in the car because it was just too tense to do anything else. We were then paying the bank around a hundred pounds per day in interest. As the Chancellor increased interest rates almost hourly it became clear that we would not be able to survive financially. Somehow it was all quite surreal and

I no longer felt dejected. The sun was shining and it was all outside my control. I had done my best to start a new industry and it had been absurd from the start. Perhaps we would be able to rent a small cottage and settle down to a less gruelling lifestyle. Maybe I should try to return to routine veterinary practice if anyone would still employ me.

We had tea with our friends, I darted the stags and we returned home. And then we heard that Britain had decided to come out of the ERM. There was hope. Surely the pound would fall to more reasonable levels? The interest rates came down again that evening. It was looking very much better. Over the next few weeks the pound fell by around 15 per cent. All my French sales consequently yielded 15 per cent more and this effect was maintained for the next two years. We hung on.

Less lucky was a friend who chose that Wednesday afternoon to shoot himself.

There is no doubt that, like those fevers in Victorian novels, this one had reached its crisis. With the sudden deliverance from the absurdly high price at which the pound had been pegged in the ERM we had room to manoeuvre again. The bank manager granted us a stay of execution.

It was then, of course, that Mad Cow Disease chose to rear its sick head. Suddenly everything agricultural was in chaos, including the meat trade; there were no winners in the BSE drama but we came near it. In the weeks after the March declaration by Stephen Dorrell that there might be a connexion between bovine spongiform encephalopathy and Creutzfeldt-Jakob disease, our sales rose fivefold and we have maintained increased sales to this day. Our winter 1998 sales were up 30 per cent on the same period in 1997, and we managed to keep prices stable despite colossal fluctuations in the price of wild venison.

Gradually it emerged that my consultancy business had not died. A series of fascinating and highly satisfying jobs arose in Spain, Thailand and Vietnam. My exports also began to look up. I have a great customer and friend in Belgium, and he asked me for 150 breeding hinds for yet another new deer farm.

The pressure was off now, and Nickie was able to find time to write regular newsletters to those on her venison mailing list as well as to accept more jewellery and silversmithing commissions. Among these was a request for a facsimile of the exquisite and complex fifteenth-century reliquary constructed to hold the tenth-century crosier of St Fillans. Work on this sacred relic seemed especially fulfilling and relevant.

Slowly, almost imperceptibly, we began to feel a little more light-hearted.

For the deer-farming industry as a whole there has also been encouragement: the large retailers are beginning to look with renewed enthusiasm at alternative and healthier meats produced in less intensive ways. They can see for their own reasons, I imagine, the strength in being diversified. At the moment of writing, one of the biggest supermarkets has just told me that its venison Grillsteak (rather like a Veniburger, I should imagine) has outsold any other red meat products in its stores. This single fact has inspired me like no other. Could it really be that we are witnessing a change to a healthier meat? It is sad that the Grillsteak has to be made from New Zealand farmed venison, but at the moment there just isn't enough British.

Also as I write, Nickie is in London selling venison from an outdoor street market and has phoned me up to say that she has sold out the whole three days' allocation in only two days. How very satisfying that so many people now want to eat the venison that I learnt in my days on Rum was the best possible of all meats.

Many cancers are becoming more common, particularly in the developed world, and diet is often implicated. The World Cancer Research Fund and the American Institute for Cancer Research published *Food, Nutrition and the Prevention of Cancer: a global perspective* in 1997, and pointed out that 'increasing consumption of meat and fatty foods will lead to a massive increase in incidence of a large number of diseases that are expensive to treat' and that 'obesity is an increasing major public health problem not only in developed countries but also now in urban areas of developing countries. As well as increasing the risk of a number of cancers, obesity increases the risk of cardio-vascular disease, adult onset diabetes and other major chronic diseases and reduces life expectancy.' They conclude that 'if eaten at all, red meat to provide less than 10 per cent of total energy ... but consumption of meat from non-domesticated animals is preferable'. They also highlight the stupidity of a system in which 'for many years subsidies have been given ... to the most fatty foods of animal origin'.

The agricultural grant scene has not materially changed from what it was when we started our deer farm twenty-seven years ago, and indeed I have more or less given up hoping. There is talk of reducing agricultural subsidies and of 'decoupling' them, that is to say paying money regardless of the nature of the production system. Were that really to happen we should be in with a chance, but these things have been talked about for so long that I have come not to build hope. The government is not at all interested in helping anything other than the large power bases such as the cattle and sheep trade represented by the NFUs. Thus the hard-won 50 per cent compensation package for tuberculosis which we squeezed out of the Tory government as they ran scared after Edwina Currie's faux pas about eggs remains at just 50 per cent, whilst the present administration has raised the compensation payable to cattle farmers from 75 to 100 per cent. It seems a rather cynical gesture. If there were to be any increase in deer farming it would save the Exchequer large sums of money because of the displacement of the heavily subsidised cattle and sheep – not to mention savings in the Health Service.

But wait a moment; there is change in the air. Conventional farmers are beginning to squeak whilst for deer farmers the future is suddenly looking good. The supermarkets are beginning to buy British farmed venison despite its much higher price.

Nickie and I have for several years supported an enterprise called Schools Challenge. Each year we dream up a few projects for school students to carry out. One year we suggested that they examine country-of-origin labelling. We knew that one supermarket was selling New Zealand venison and labelling it 'Produce of the UK'. They imported the venison in large primal cuts and then sliced and repacked it. They could have argued that it had been 'substantially changed' in Britain, in which case the labelling would have been legal, but no court of law would sustain the case that simple cutting and packing represented 'substantial change'. We covertly directed the students to that product in the supermarket as well as to the packing plant. Of course they managed to show that it was indeed of New Zealand origin. The trading standards officer was contacted, press releases issued, the children were interviewed on local radio and a great supermarket chain had to change its labels. 'Out of the mouths of babes and sucklings ...' The school won its challenge and its project came top in the judging. The supermarket now sells British Quality Assured Farm Venison despite the fact that it could buy from New Zealand much cheaper.

There is a welcome revival of deer parks for large country houses. These parks provide the perfect setting for impressive mansions; they are beautiful, they give pleasure to many – and they produce venison of very good quality. This development thrills me.

The British Deer Farmers' Association has been working hard over the last few years to create a stringent quality assurance scheme. Each farm is examined minutely to ensure that the deer are well looked after and that standards are met. This quality assurance scheme has transformed the approach of British supermarkets, who are now seeking British farmed venison, only to find that there isn't enough for their Grillsteaks. And conventional farmers seem at last to be waking up. The British Deer Farmers' Association has increased its membership for the first time in years. Once again I have been elected Chairman. I look forward to a campaigning two-year stint just eighteen years after my last term.

What has been achieved worldwide in those thirty years since I first went to work with deer on Rum? In New Zealand there was no deer farming then, but now there is a thriving industry with nearly two million deer and export earnings of about £100 million sterling per annum. Most of those exports come to Europe where consumption of venison is steadily rising. In the United States there are now some 250,000 farmed deer valued at about £35 million, and Australia has a similar-sized industry.

In Britain and the rest of Europe, with an agriculture ossified by subsidies, deer farming has developed much less rapidly. Yet there is a realisation that we can produce more of this meat in a green and humane way to allow grassland farmers another form of livelihood.

Eventually, maybe when we're dead and gone, those subsidies will be redistributed; then deer farming can compete with other enterprises on an equal footing. We have unquestionably and by all measures achieved a new domesticant and its meat is one which mankind is supremely well adapted to eating. The public health advantages are enormous and real if we can build on this start. Even gourmets rejoice.

And what about Reediehill? After all these years, I have located a generous grant for planting hedges, and even wild flowers under the hedges. How strange a cycle ... twenty years ago, and even until much more recently, farmers were paid to uproot their hedges. Reediehill didn't have any then but it will soon. We have planted three-quarters of a mile of hedges this year. I have always wanted to do that. The deer benefit from the shelter and will trim the hedges as they grow through the fences. And now we are getting grants for ponds, so I have dug three of those too.

Stella and Martha have grown up and Nickie and I know now that we have been and still are very lucky. We may never be rich but it looks as though we and the deer should be able to afford to stay here. As the trees and the hedges grow around the deer, the view from our windows becomes more and more beautiful. Jewellery commissions trickle in, Nickie is writing another book, and we can continue to sell venison through our farm shop and the mail-order business. And as deer farming grows and the demand for healthier red meats from consumers overwhelms the inertia of bureaucrats and governments, well, we can sit back and say we were a part of that radical change in eating habits. Maybe one or two people will have lived longer. And maybe that reverie before I was stolen away in my little old lorry on the road to Jura was not rubbish after all ...

BIBLIOGRAPHY AND SOURCES

Anon., *Food, Nutrition and the Prevention of Cancer: a global perspective*, World
  Cancer Research Fund and American Institute for Cancer Research Washington,
  1997.

Babbage, Charles, *The Works of Charles Babbage*, edited by Martin Campbell-Kelly,
  London and Pickering, 1989.

Bannerman, M. M., and Baxter, K. L., *The Husbanding of Red Deer* (Proceedings
  of a conference held at the Rowett Institute, Aberdeen in January 1969), The
  University Press, Aberdeen, 1969.

Bath, Michael, *The Image of the Stag* (Iconographic Themes in Western Art), Verlag
  Valentin Koerner, Baden-Baden, 1992.

Baxter Brown, Michael, *Richmond Park – the history of a royal deer park*, Robert
  Hale, London, 1985.

Blaxter, K. L., Kay, R. N. B., Sharman, G A. M., Cunningham, J. M. M., and
  Hamilton, W. J., *Farming the Red Deer – the first report of an investigation by
  the Rowett Research Institute and the Hill Farming Research Organisation*, Her
  Majesty's Stationery Office, Edinburgh, 1974.

Blaxter, Sir Kenneth, Kay, R. N. B, Sharman, G. A. M., Cunningham,
  J. M. M., Eadie, J., and Hamilton, W. J., *Farming the Red Deer – the final
  report of an investigation by the Rowett Research Institute and the Hill Farming
  Research Organisation*, Her Majesty's Stationery Office, Edinburgh,
  1988.

Cameron, Allan Gordon, *The Wild Red Deer of Scotland – notes from an island
  forest on deer, deer stalking, and deer forests in the Scottish Highlands*, Blackwood,
  London, 1923.

Cameron, Archie, *Bare Feet and Tackety Boots – a boyhood on the island of Rhum*,
  Luath Press, Edinburgh, 1988.

Cantor, Leonard, *The Mediaeval Parks of England: a gazetteer*, Loughborough
  University, Loughborough, 1983.

Carew, Richard, *Survey of Cornwall 1602*, edited by F. E. Halliday, Andrew Melrose,
  London, 1953.

Chan, W., Brown, J., Lee, S. M., and Buss, D. H., *Meat, Poultry and Game*, fifth
  supplement to the fifth edition of McCance and Widdowson's *The Composition
  of Foods*, published by the Royal Society of Chemistry and the Ministry of
  Agriculture, Fisheries and Food, 1995.

Clutton-Brock, Juliet, *Domesticated Animals from Early Times*, William
  Heinemann and British Museum of Natural History, 1981.

Clutton-Brock, Juliet (ed.), *The Walking Larder – patterns of domestication, pastoralism and predation*, Unwin Hyman, London, 1989.

Clutton-Brock, T. H., Guinness, F. E., and Albon, S. D., *Red Deer – behavior and ecology of two sexes*, University of Chicago Press, Chicago, 1982.

Clutton-Brock, T. H., and Albon, S. D., 'Trial and Error in the Highlands', *Nature*, vol. 358 (1992), pp. 11–12.

Columella, L. Junius Moderatus, *Of Husbandry, in Twelve Books*, London, 1745.

Crawford, Michael, and Marsh, David, *The Driving Force – food in evolution and the future*, William Heinemann, London, 1989.

Cummins, John, *The Hound and the Hawk – the art of medieval hunting*, Weidenfeld and Nicolson, London, 1988.

Darling, Fraser, *A Herd of Red Deer*, Oxford University Press, 1937.

Dasmann, Raymond F., *African Game Ranching*, Pergamon, London, 1964.

Diamond, Jared, *Guns, Germs and Steel – the fates of human societies*, Jonathan Cape, London, 1997.

Evans, Henry, *Some Account of Jura Red Deer*, printed privately by Francis Carter, Derby, *c.*1890.

Farm Animal Welfare Council, *Report on the animal welfare implications of the harvesting of deer antlers in velvet*, FAWC Secretariat, Government Buildings, Hook Rise South, Tolworth, Surbiton, Surrey, KT6 7NF, 1980.

—*Report on the welfare of farmed deer*, FAWC Secretariat, Surbiton, 1985.

Fiennes, Celia, *The Journeys of Celia Fiennes* (1696), edited by Christopher Morris, The Cresset Press, London, 1947.

Fletcher, Nichola R., *Game for All – with a flavour of Scotland*, Victor Gollancz in association with Peter Crawley, London, 1987.

Fletcher, T. J., in *Management and Diseases of Deer – a handbook for the veterinary surgeon*, edited by T. L. Alexander and D. Buxton, second edition, Veterinary Deer Society, 1994.

—in *Evolution of Domesticated Animals*, edited by I. L. Mason, Longman, London, 1984.

—in *Wildlife Production Systems*, edited by R. J. Hudson, K. R. Drew and L. M. Baskin, Cambridge University Press, 1989.

Forrester, Rex, *The Chopper Boys – New Zealand's helicopter hunters*, Whitcoulls, Christchurch, 1983.

Galton, Francis, 'The first steps towards the domestication of animals', *Transactions of the Ethnological Society*, London, n.s., 3 (1865), pp. 122–38; reprinted in *Inquiries into Human Faculty*, J. M. Dent, London, 1907.

Gasset: *see* Ortega y Gasset.

Gilbert, John, *Hunting and Hunting Reserves in Medieval Scotland*, John Donald, Edinburgh, 1979.

Hackett, Frances, *Henry the Eighth*, Jonathan Cape, London, 1929.

Haigh, Jerry C., and Hudson, Robert J., *Farming Wapiti and Red Deer*, Mosby-Year Book Inc., Missouri, 1993.

Haldane, A. R. B., *The Drove Roads of Scotland*, Edinburgh University Press, 1952.

Hart-Davis, Duff, *Monarchs of the Glen – a history of deer stalking in the Scottish Highlands*, Jonathan Cape, London, 1978.

Hughes, Ted, *The Guardian Saturday Review*, 9 January 1999: interview with Thomas Pero of *Wild Steelhead and Salmon Magazine*, Seattle, USA.

Jarman, M. R., 'European deer economies and the advent of the Neolithic', in *Papers in Economic Prehistory*, edited by E. S. Higgs, Cambridge University Press, 1972.

Johnson, Samuel, and Boswell, James, *Johnson's Journey to the Western Islands of Scotland (1775) and Boswell's Journal of a Tour to the Hebrides with Samuel Johnson, LL.D. (1786)*, edited by R. W. Chapman, Oxford University Press, 1924.

Kip, Johannes, *Britannia Illustrata or Views of several of the Queen's Palaces as also of Principal Seats of the Nobility and Gentry of Great Britain*, London, 1709.

Kyle, Russell, *A Feast in the Wild*, Kudu Publishing, Kidlington, Oxford, 1987.

Legge, Anthony J., and Rowley-Conwy, Peter A., 'Gazelle killing in Stone Age Syria', *Scientific American*, vol. 257 (1987), pp. 76–83.

Love, John, *Rhum, the Natural History of an Island*, Edinburgh University Press, 1987.

MacCulloch, John, *The Highlands and Western Islands of Scotland*, 1824.

McCance and Widdowson: *see* Chan, W. et al.

McNally, Lea, *Wild Highlands*, J. M. Dent and Sons, London, 1972.

Magnus Magnusson, *Rum: Nature's Island*, Luath Press, Edinburgh, 1998.

Martin, Martin, *A Description of the Western Isles of Scotland*, London, 1703.

Miller, Hugh, *The Cruise of the* Betsey, William P. Nimmo, London and Edinburgh, eleventh edition, 1874.

Monro, Donald, in *Account of the Western Isles of Scotland* (1549), edited by D. Munro, Morrison, Glasgow, 1884.

New Zealand Deer Farming Journal, various issues from 1979, WHAM Deer Ltd., P.O. Box 11 092, Wellington, NZ.

Ortega y Gasset, José, *Meditations on Hunting* (1942), translated by Howard Wescott, Charles Scribner's Sons, New York, 1972.

Payne-Gallwey, Sir Ralph, *The Crossbow* (new edition), Bramhall House, USA, 1958.

Pennant, Thomas, *A Tour in Scotland and Voyage to the Hebrides*, Chester, 1774.

Potts, Malcolm, and Short, Roger, *Ever since Adam and Eve – the evolution of human sexuality*, Cambridge University Press, 1999.

Red Deer Commission Annual Reports, HMSO (*now* The Stationery Office), Norwich.

Shirley, Evelyn Philip, *Some Account of English Deer Parks*, John Murray, London, 1867.

Simmons, I. G., and Dimbleby, G. W., 'The possible role of ivy (Hedera helix L.) in the mesolithic economy of Western Europe', *Journal of Archaeological Science*, vol. 1 (1974), pp. 291–6.

Soyer, Alexis, *The Gastronomic Regenerator*, London, 1846.

Stanley Price, Mark R., *Animal Re-introductions: the Arabian Oryx in Oman*, Cambridge University Press, 1989.

Thiebaux, Marcelle, *The Stag of Love – the chase in medieval literature*, Cornell University Press, London, 1974.

Turbervile, George, *The Noble Arte of Venerie or Hunting* (1576), Tudor and Stuart Library reprint, Oxford, 1908.

Walker, John, *Report on the Hebrides of 1764 and 1771*, edited by M. M. Mackay, Edinburgh, 1980.

Whitehead, Kenneth, *Deer and Their Management in the Deer Parks of Great Britain and Ireland*, Country Life, London, 1950.

Whitehead, G. Kenneth, *The Deer of Great Britain and Ireland*, Routledge and Kegan Paul, London, 1964.

Yerex, David, and Speirs, Ian, *Modern Deer Farm Management*, Ampersand Publishing, Carterton, New Zealand, 1987.

Zeuner, Frederick E., *A History of Domesticated Animals*, Hutchinson, London, 1963.

INDEX

* NB There is always confusion about the nomenclature of elk, wapiti and moose. When Europeans reached North America they saw for the first time the large relatives of red deer, *Cervus elaphus cenadensis*, called by the natives, wapiti. The Europeans familiar with elk, *Alces alces*, therefore called the wapiti elk, whilst Europeans continue to call *Alces alces* elk, rather than use the North American native name of moose.